WRESTLERS WITH CHRIST

KARL PFLEGER

WRESTLERS WITH CHRIST

TRANSLATED BY
E. I. WATKIN

Essay Index Reprint Series

BOOKS FOR LIBRARIES PRESS
FREEPORT, NEW YORK

First Published 1936
Reprinted 1968

LIBRARY OF CONGRESS CATALOG CARD NUMBER:
68-16968

PRINTED IN THE UNITED STATES OF AMERICA

CONTENTS

The Living Christ — Page 7

Bloy, the Pilgrim of the Absolute — 29

Péguy, the Good Sinner — 73

Gide, the Prodigal Son — 121

Chesterton, the Adventurer of Orthodoxy — 157

Dostoievsky, the Man from the Underworld — 183

Soloviev, the Prophet of Divine Humanity — 221

Berdaiev, the Orthodox Gnostic — 267

THE LIVING CHRIST

> Apart from Christ we know neither what our life nor our death is; we do not know what God is nor what we ourselves are.
>
> Pascal, *Pensées*.

I HAVE here conjured up spirits that were for many years my companions. I gave them my time and they repaid me with the gift of timeless values. I have forgotten my own life and absorbed it in theirs. Their thoughts and aspirations, their sorrows and sufferings, their passions and temptations have become my own; but also their ascents and escapes into light and life. My own life and the life of us all I have found in them deepened, fulfilled, shaken by tragic storms and lit by the dawn of eternity; the sorrowful and sublime mystery of human life. Human life! At all times and in all places the same! In their profoundest destiny all the children of men are alike, however they may differ externally. In this book three Frenchmen, one Englishman and three Russians utter the secret of their lives. Were a German, a Norwegian and an Italian added to their company, that secret would be still the same, simply presented from a different individual standpoint and experienced by a different personality. The individual can snatch only isolated phrases and fragments of the mighty symphony played by life itself through the instrumentality of its spiritual executants. He does not sit in the cosmic theatre as a purely objective hearer and spectator, remote from the life at whose drama he assists; he shares himself in that life and its conflicts. Attracted to particular personalities by disposition, and by a spiritual and intellectual affinity, he is drawn into the orbit of their lives which in turn revolve in ardent motion around a mysterious and invisible, yet well-nigh omnipotent centre ; or at least traverse its atmosphere. If any of my readers thinks this choir of seven spirits turning around Christ too small and too arbitrary a selection, I would point out to him that their wrestling with Christ has proved sufficiently powerful to hold the practically exclusive attention of one who has found himself after his own fashion drawn into it.

For these men the whole of life, no less, is at stake. As artists, men of letters and philosophers, they are aware that life is infinitely various. They marvel at its manifold riches, and seek in their halting speech to describe it. Then of a sudden they take alarm. For they are not mechanical and unfeeling spectators and delineators of life. They are themselves the conscious possessors of a living substance that is the core of their personality which may or may not mingle with this untroubled sea and lose its independent existence. This is the alternative which fills them with terror. They are living men and as such they are afraid. In this false infinity there is no fixed locality, no firm foundation for man. It has no meaning and man by his very nature seeks a meaning. Does existence then possess no other meaning, no higher purpose than simply itself ? One of our seven acts as though he believes it. But he can believe it only when he has betrayed his inmost spiritual self to the outer world, that is always passing on and passing away. The more interior a man is, the more inward, profound and spiritual his self-possession, the less can he pass away, the more powerfully does he will to endure. Only those who are or have become unreal love nothingness ; those who are real, spiritually real, hate it as their mortal foe. For they live for what is great and beautiful. For what else could they live ? And in nothingness there is nothing great or beautiful. The longer they live, the stronger becomes their conviction that mortal life was given them to win immortal. For a real man the life that is truly alive first receives its adequate form in immortal life. That is the true infinity in which the spirit is at home, the sphere of its life and activity. For spirit is essentially an unending penetration of reality. For it the infinity of space-time is an inadequate and false infinity. It is literally too restricted for it. "The close prison-house of the world," groaned the same Pascal who was terrified by the "silence of the infinite spaces." Whenever great souls wrestle with Christ they are seeking to escape from the prison of their immediate existence.

We must however be careful not to suppose that spirits whose orientation is religious and Christian are therefore pessimistic and world-renouncing in their outlook. Such a belief would be as false as its contrary is true. Let us hear the witness of men who are not Christians but just honest and honourable observers of life and who have no wish to be taken for anything more.

Tolstoy writes in a letter, "It is laughable. People tell you to make yourself useful and be virtuous and happy as long as you live ; but you yourself, happiness, virtue and utility depend on truth. And the truth which the thirty-two years of my life has taught me tells me that our situation is desperate. When man has climbed to the highest level of his development he sees at once clearly that everything is falsehood and deception. . . " And André Suarès, lonely and hungering after a great and full life, finds that in the second quarter of the twentieth century it is no different. "All men lie and those who boast that they do not lie are the worst liars. They are deaf men who do not hear themselves shout and would make us believe that they are silent or at most whisper. All men lie. Life will have it so. The lie of life is a form and condition of its endurance. Nature herself gives birth to the universal lie of life. For she imposes on every one the belief in himself, in his unity and in his personal immortality."

What under these conditions life must mean for man is clearly expressed in the following words of Montherlant, a convinced adherent of the immanentist view of life : " To seek an answer knowing that the problem is insoluble, to serve whilst smiling at it the cause we serve, to overcome oneself without purpose or profit, to write in the profound conviction that the work has no significance, to perceive, to comprehend, to endure while keeping before one's eyes the painful certainty that to be right serves no purpose whatever ! Nevertheless I must accustom myself to secure a fixed position from which to raise myself aloft and reach above myself. How and by what means ? By means of the soul and that is as much as to say by folly. I fling myself into the arms of the absurd. — O soul."

Pessimism ? That is easily said, especially by men who have not yet lived. Pessimism. Yes, but it was not discovered by Schopenhauer or even by the Preacher with his cry "All is vanity." It was discovered by life. It is the dark primeval melody of earth-bound life. Melancholy is the primitive, pervasive and dominant chord of earth's music. What these melancholy men say is the truth, the truth and reality of *this* world. No proclamations of the "new men" modify the adamantine structure of the world as it is. In whatever latitude, under whatever political and social conditions man may live, the depth of his soul soon discovers that the world "is a narrow prison." Within its unsurmountable walls the triumphant shout of fashionable slogans has soon worn itself out—for those who know. The most ardent hopes have soon cooled to a numb despair. And the idols fashioned by himself, in whom man trusted to redeem him and lead to a new life, for all the renown of their power lie helpless on the ground. They were but creatures of his imagination. But the prison walls rise sheer and mock his hopes, unsurmountable as of old.

"The science to which I pinned my faith is bankrupt. Its tales were more foolish than all the miracles of the priests. . . What it spread was not enlightenment but a malignant disease. Its counsels which should have established the millennium have led directly to the suicide of Europe. I believed them once more whole-heartedly than any religious fanatic believed his superstitions. For in their name I helped to destroy the faith of millions of worshippers in the temples of a thousand creeds. And now they look at me and witness the great tragedy of an atheist who has lost his faith."

It is Bernard Shaw who, in his last play, *Too True to be Good*, so frankly announces the loss of an atheistic faith, and this through the mouth of the moralizing and philosophic swindler Aubrey. There is, in truth, an atheistic faith. It is faith in science, technical invention, a law of progress immanent in nature, an unlimited progress guaranteed, so to speak, by nature herself, and in diverse forces credited with absolute power—class, blood or race. Atheists are many, unbelievers few. The subintellectual brute lives because it is absorbed by its immediate existence. Without faith man cannot deal with the world because as a result of his nature he must take an intellectual view of it. Whether he wants it or no, he *must* form some conception of the world and life. The history of the last century is an appalling object lesson which proves the astounding fact that man, as soon as he departs from revealed truth and thinks on his own account and at his own risk, raves like a lunatic throughout the entire domain of ideas, ethics and society ; and is capable into the bargain of concocting out of his mad hallucinations and foolhardy experiments a species of diabolic mysticism, a mysticism of earthly happiness. The Bolshevik dream has been Bernard Shaw's latest dream. On awakening from it he sees the world as follows : " So I clearly perceive that we seem indeed to separate peaceably to accomplish very different tasks. . . Nevertheless they fall hopelessly and for ever into a bottomless void in which there is no firm ground. All these men have about them something fantastic, something unreal and perverse, something profoundly disturbing. . . What raconteur, were he ever so shameless a liar, would dare to invent such improbable figures, men and women whose souls are stripped completely nude ? Nude bodies no longer shock us. . . but the disgust aroused by a naked soul is intolerable. . . You may even shed the outer coverings of your soul, the forms of social intercourse, morality, shame. . . But how shall we endure this fearful new nakedness, the nudity of souls that hitherto have always clothed themselves with a fine if impracticable idealism ? The fatal word ' not ' has crept into all our confessions of faith. . . But is 'not' sufficient? For a boy, perhaps; for a man, never. No, to preach I need affirmation. Without affirmation youth will not listen to me, for even youth is weary of denial. . . The preacher must preach the way of life. Oh, that I could but find it. I am ignorant and frightened. I have lost my nerve. I know only this, that I must find the way of life for myself and for us all. Otherwise we shall be irretrievably ruined."

It is no sentimental romanticism that raises this cry of anguish. This is not the lamentation of souls into whom Christianity has introduced the poison of world renunciation. For these souls have long since rejected this so-called poison of Christianity. They belong to a world dominated by the fundamental rejection of the supernatural in any shape or form, by a rationalism or irrationalism carried to the extreme (the latter is not much more enlightening than the former) and a temper of robust realism. But this very realism proves to be bewitched and bedevilled in a most uncanny fashion. When life is accepted thus realistically, given an immanental interpretation, purged of all supernatural and metaphysical 'parasitism,' it becomes in part servile and evil and chaotic. And the greatest chaos produces not the widest world but the narrowest, "*the narrow prison of the world.*"

The deeper spirits among the non-Christians have realized this. The nobler of them are seeking, as Shaw, with heavy hearts "the way of life." It is time to ask how it can be found.

It is gradually becoming clear that the way which leads from the prison-house of the world to the freedom, beauty and greatness of life can be found, if it can be found at all, only in the ultimate depth, in the abysses of our mysterious humanity.

It is this conviction that has given birth to the demand for a "new mythology." And this is no mere demand but a stormy clamour : a new mythology as the Gospel of the twentieth century. It comes forth red-hot, pregnant with passions that ascend from the depth, swollen by longings that strive to reach the depths. An ecstatic sense of deliverance takes possession of the captives in the narrow bondage of their cosmic prison. A light dawns upon the vast masses who have never before reflected upon the hidden causes which determine the incurable disease with which culture is smitten. If men are insolent and base, unjust to one another, lacking in mutual understanding, and unhappy in their relationships, may not the reason perhaps be that they have remained too much on the surface of life, and have lost contact too long with its elemental deeps? How indeed could they have failed to clash with abuse and clamour, since they have all been packed together on the two-dimensional surface, the surface of purely material interests? How could they get out of each other's way, since there were no depths into which they could plunge, depths in which the symbols of the eternal and the divine appear, in which they can contemplate their own nature and man's true vocation in the universe? On the surface of life the whole of culture shrivels into a system of nicely calculated and secured pleasure or, if that breaks down, degenerates into a selfish and brutal struggle for existence. True culture, a lofty type of human life, comes only from the elemental deeps. Vitality is fed from a mystical source. This is the real secret of human history that whenever the fountains of the deep dry up, a period of vital drought sets in, man's creative forces fail, and intellectual diseases of every description, moral and social epidemics break out. Human culture experiences a crisis only because man has experienced it first. The fruits are bad because the tree is diseased, because its roots lack a fertile soil or have been gnawed by rats.

As I said just now, this truth is to-day dawning even upon the man in the street and is being shouted at him by all the loud-speakers of fashionable public opinion. But it is most certainly not a revelation which first descended to earth from the stormy heaven of the post-war epoch, as so many of our brave young contemporaries seem to believe. In the ardour of their revolutionary zeal, they have mistaken the date of their birth for the year one. The modern world did not begin to-day, nor yet the crisis of culture and modern humanism. The entire life history of the subjects of this book as it is here presented is nothing else than a settlement, not merely in theory but in actual life, with this humanism which, as one possessed, is rushing into a suicidal anarchy. Even to-day there are no writers to depict the crisis of modern humanism with Dostoievsky's razor-like keenness and explosion of creative power. That no culture can be produced by economic systems and budgets, that no culture nor even policy can exist without "mysticism" was the central conviction of that passionate dreamer of the true human community whose name was Péguy. He was the man who understood that the genuine revolution, the revolution which establishes on earth truth, justice and love can be made only by the " pure of heart " ; he said that the fundamental presupposition of all co-operation towards a common end of the vast energies stored in man—and this is what culture means—is the mystical accord of minds and hearts. The *mystical* accord :

B

for the power which enables man as a social being, universal man, as Dostoievsky put it, to become the miniature God and secondary creator of a new and higher living reality is a mystical nature, a gift of grace implanted in man's fundamental being, a supernatural capacity. Mystical also is the touch of puritanic austerity, the almost priestly aristocratic ethos with which every genuine community commits its members to aims without any immediate bearing upon the welfare of the individual or even of society as a whole. Péguy was well aware of all this. By a laborious process of " deepening the heart " he achieved the perception that man is completely human, and creates a complete human culture only when his goal is eternity. In virtue of this insight he has become, more especially since his death, the patron of those young contemporaries who are bent upon establishing at any cost a new order of human life. This however they propose to establish by a " pure and spiritual revolution." They also display in their speech and writings that "dynamism" of which we hear so much—and possess it in their hearts. But they know what those who expect a complete solution from the unfettered action of human forces have failed to grasp, that there is a dynamism from below and a dynamism from above. Periods, in particular the period of contemporary history, in which life has been almost literally converted into a prison and a mad-house, are apocalyptic. With the fervour of despair, millions are invoking the spirits of the abyss. And who can tell whether the assault of their dark, confused and unpurified incantations may not unlock the abyss sooner and more readily than heaven? He that hath ears to hear hears the sweep of diabolic pinions. Dostoievsky heard its distant approach. What he perceived present in embryonic theory in the hearts and brains of men who lived more than half a century ago as possibilities or first beginnings is to-day full-fledged reality. The " man of the underworld " has given birth to " humanity in the underworld." A poetic symbol of human tragedy has expanded into an all-embracing tragic reality. When man and modern man in particular has thought out his position with absolute sincerity, when his glance has penetrated his own being to its inmost nucleus, to the ultimate realities and possibilities of his life, nothing remains for him but to ask himself that question on whose answer everything depends, the question which through bitter birth-pangs first took shape in that dark prophetic prototype, Dostoievsky's *Sketches from the Underworld*. Is there or is there not an escape from an existence imprisoned in the pure immanence of natural life? Does man, like Dostoievsky's " Man from the Underworld," possess a sincere aspiration, a longing " that exceeds all measure " "for something wholly other," for a being that is wholly other than man, yet at the same time essentially man—human in such perfection of humanity that all human suffering and tragedy are in the strictest sense his own—for the new Adam, the Son of Man and the Son of God.

" Everything therefore depends on whether Christ is accepted as the final ideal for man on earth, that is upon the Christian faith." Dark fateful hours led the great Russian to answer in this way a problem which is to-day the problem of mankind. And he bowed before Christ as before Him in whose name and faith alone salvation can be attained. It is more than astonishing that the fatal anguish that encompasses the globe to-day has not yet convinced mankind as a whole of this truth.

For what are we still waiting? Are not the naked realities of life preaching in terrific accents the Gospel of Christ? Or rather we must say with Shaw, the realities of naked life, of life stripped nude. Even if men turn away with a shrug of the shoulders from those who preach the Christian faith, should they not at least take to heart the tragedy of the non-Christians and atheists, "who have lost *their* faith"? Will they not heed the tragedy of those who cry aloud to the entire world the bankruptcy of every ideal of a purely immanent life, the failure of a self-sufficient humanism with no outlook beyond this world, of life without God and Christ? Of those who in a voice quivering with scorn, hot with indignation, and in language tenfold more fanatical than the most fanatical Christian could employ, curse the exasperating lunacy of the world. For what is it but lunacy to pursue for centuries all those great things, called unprejudiced science, redemption by art, technical inventions which vanquish time and space and unite the nations, programmes of reconstruction and new foundations of human life, only to find ourselves at the end of it all in a universal chaos still imprisoned in the dingy and narrow prison of the world, stripped to such a pitiful nudity of soul that we are ashamed of being men? Truly the Christian, Dostoievsky, was not inflamed by such wrath when he observed that "without Christ everything is filthy and servile." And that other Christian, Pascal, who was inclined to speak contemptuously of the world, must be regarded by comparison a calm judge when he remarked, "We might say as an *obiter dictum*, that apart from Christ we understand nothing whatever of our own life and death, of man and God."

Pascal was a calm and for that very reason a more

objective judge. That is to say he *is not indignant* that this is so. He knows that it cannot be otherwise. It is so obvious that Christ is indispensable. It requires all the fearful blindness and folly of sin to hide from man's view a fact so evident. God, in short, has a right in the world He made. If men do as they please in it as though He were the air, He permits it on principle because He is unconditionally on the side of freedom. It is *our* affair if our free will bedevils the world. When the bedevilment has proceeded far enough we shall recover our reason. For the possibilities of rescue contained in the freedom of the human spirit are almost unlimited. But on account of our follies God does not make His creation other than He has made it. For it was made good. It was made and designed from eternity in His Word in whom everything is contained that has been made. "And the Word was made flesh and dwelt amongst us."

And this is the second prodigious fact which God does not annul because it does not fit into the world of "unprejudiced" scholars. But the understanding of what man really is is lost by all those who are led astray by a false science. And that understanding was first bestowed in its fullness by the Incarnation. In one of his sermons, St Augustine speaks of the school of Christ. What does man learn in that school? He puts the answer into the mouth of the Master. "When in the beginning I was God in God, I created you. That is not what I propose to teach you [to create a world that, as St Augustine puts it, has been created once for all by God]. But I have made myself what I have made to save man whom I have made." Christ is the Saviour of our humanity. It is God-made-man who first teaches man to be truly man. To save the core of our being, which came from God and was assumed by God Himself into His theandric personality, to save it through and in Himself, is what Christ wishes to teach us. A humanity that believes in Christ, believes also in itself, in its future, indeed in its eternal future ; and can do so because human nature has been established through Christ from eternity to eternity and for all eternity in the bosom of the Triune God. Not one of the non-Christian religions nor yet the noblest of non-Christian philosophies has achieved such a clear and sublime view of human nature, or has raised it to the same secure dignity as faith in Christ. Apart from Christ, man is simply what nature and (after a certain stage of development) a technique which continues and replaces nature (and has become magic) make of him. And the law of his development, if there is any such thing, will perhaps carry him forward from the beast through the human stage to the fantastic existence of an indefinitely simplified, and, in its simplicity, perfectly rational living machine—unless indeed, before this moment is at length reached in the remote distance of a future millions of years ahead, the cosmic mathematics and chemistry have wearied of this idle play, this cruel experimenting with a living object, and have reduced their poor toy to the dust from which it was taken, and which is its sole beatitude. For if this is his true situation, the most meaningless destiny is as probable as the most purposeful. To look for a meaning has no longer any meaning. And Dostoievsky's " Man from the Underworld " displayed a truly admirable grasp of the situation when he declared that under these conditions there is nothing to be done but " in silence and impotently gnashing the teeth to linger out a living death in voluptuous sloth, bearing in mind that no one has any reason to be indignant with any one else, that no cause can be discovered anywhere and perhaps never will be discovered. Instead there is a hidden deceit, an artificial arrangement of facts, cheating, in short a hotch-potch ; but what or who is behind it all is unknown. . . "

It is indeed a most remarkable fact which demands our closest attention that man lives in an impenetrable mist, wanders to and fro in a no man's land that remains for ever a *terra incognita,* never thoroughly explored and without hope of future discovery, knows nothing and nobody and least of all himself, so long as he does not know Christ as " the Son of the living God." The saying of Goethe that reverence for one's self is the supreme commandment penetrates very deeply into the real secret of man. He can achieve nothing great, if he has no reverence for himself. Goethe saw what the evangelists of class, race and blood always forget, that man's true and essential greatness is individual, not social. If man is only an ant, his work even if it is the product of a hundred million brains and hands is nothing more than an ant-heap, though of gigantic size. Man must reverence himself, if he and his work are to face successfully the tribunal of the spirit. Then just ask a Pascal, a Suarès, a Montherlant, a Shaw, a Gide, Bloy, or Dostoievsky, or any one you choose—provided he has a profound knowledge of men—how man is to arrive at this reverence for himself. Some who do not simply laugh at the question will reply with Montherlant: " Throw yourself into the arms of the absurd, yield yourself without criticism to the megalomania of your foolish soul;" or with Gide: " What is the sense of reverence? Reverence for yourself is impossible. The only thing possible for you is sincerity towards yourself. To live morally is self-deception or hypocrisy. Live in accordance with your own nature. That is sufficient." Those who, though involved themselves in the appalling enigma of human nature, never lose sight of the human countenance throughout the long dark Passion of human history, alone behold in the countenance of man the countenance of Christ, the eternal Brother. It is anything but a pious phrase when we Christians speak of the living Christ. Nor do we merely mean by it that He is living for us. That is a question which, so far as we have the courage to know ourselves, we can answer only with a beating heart. But He is living in the objective sense that He and He alone is for us the possessor and mediator of that supreme and absolute life without which our human existence must be incomplete. Be it granted that the perfect fullness and power of the Christ-like life is a rare occurrence : the outer and inner chaos of life without Him is a constant occurrence, a fact which darkens the earth. Of Christ it may be said in grim jest that He is conspicuous by His absence. The place in human life which His absence leaves empty is a void so vast and so impossible to fill that its destined occupant must necessarily be a manifestation of a superhuman living power at once infinitely subtle and gigantic.

We have seen that without Christ man cannot deal satisfactorily with his environment or with himself. For those thinkers whose intellectual passion is centred primarily upon the mystery of human nature the perception of this truth is a literal revelation, the sudden opening of a door hitherto locked which leads to a new life. Through this door the spiritual combatants of whom this book tells came to Christ. Through Him they have learned to know not only man and the universe, but God Himself, so far as He is knowable by man. And in truth it is a difficult task, a great and perhaps a rare attainment to discover the *Living* God. Goethe is too superficial when in *Faust* he maintains that God may be attained by the mere ecstasy of cosmic and sexual love :

> " Who can name Him
> And profess
> I believe in Him?
> Who can feel
> And venture to say
> I do not believe in Him?
> The all-encompasser
> And all-sustainer,
> Doth He not embrace and uphold
> Thyself, myself and Himself?
> Feeling is everything
> The name is noise and smoke
> Dazzling fire of heaven."

No, God is not the great Something, a nameless vital force, not an absolute idea, nor an ideal, nor a fate. He is a Person, He is, as Pascal experienced Him in his hour of burning supernatural fire, " the God of Abraham, the God of Isaac, the God of Jacob. Not of philosophers and savants. Certainty, certainty, feeling, joy, peace. The God of Jesus Christ."

What God is, is made known through Christ; and when He is not known through Him, He is the absolute Idea, or the blind primordial Will, or the world soul bound up with the body of the universe and flowing forth with demonic force in the everlasting rotation of cosmic history. He is something which at best man can apprehend only in the form of a myth. Or as Albrecht Schaeffer puts it: "Yes, every one knows God; and though with the determination of fury he nail down over Him the lid of his consciousness and though it is only suffering or the fear of death that gives many a man the strength to open it—and many never find the strength to do so—God is inside." That indeed is precisely the fashion in which God is present in the life and thought of a great number: entombed. That is how God lives in the consciousness or subconsciousness of the contemporary world. And even when He is honoured with the venerable name of God, He must pay for it by sacrificing His absolute position, His transcendence of the world. God is transformed into the god, the God who created man into the god created by man. Before He found Himself in the human mind and thereby obtained a name and Divinity in the strict sense He was nothing more than a natural force, the soul of a human tribe, the vital impetus of a race. Nor will the measure of Godhead conceded to Him ever raise Him above the rôle, not excessively sublime, to be sure, of an accumulator from which self-conscious peoples derive the necessary power for great national achievement. And as is only fair, the God who gives so little pledges His servants to nothing more than loyalty, industry and conscientiousness in the service of the nation.

Christ is so indispensable to any genuinely religious thought that where He is denied, religion is degraded to national sentiment and the conception of God to the level of biology. So irreplaceable is the power of Christ that, where it is deliberately rejected, all the most important departments of human activity are thrown out of gear; and reforms attempted, being purely external, cannot put once more in order the dislocated fabric of human life. The living organism reacts to a wound, poison, or improper nourishment by pain and disease. The mystical body of Christ, which, according to St Paul's profound teaching is the Church, and should be the whole of mankind, is reminding us with unmistakable evidence by a world-wide tempest of catastrophes that human life is a Christocentric mystery.

This and nothing else is the stupendous experience which the heroes of this book have undergone in the truly and everlastingly human unrest, which was their individual lot as it is the general lot of mankind. They are wholly products of the crisis of modern humanism, were born in it, are its spiritual children. They were quick to detect how profoundly obscure and unhappy it is, to perceive that it has lost the secret of humanity. They set out therefore in search of the new Bethlehem where the new man could be born. The new man: the name is indifferent to them. Each calls him by a different name. For one he is the pure heroic man, for another the absolute man, for a third the universal man, for a fourth the free intelligence. The important matter is that he is fearfully difficult to find in a world which Péguy termed in his growl " this modern pigsty of a world." Moreover it became clear that not only the modern world but the entire world in every age, *this* world, is a pigsty; or, to use less savage but more biblical language, " lieth in evil." A dark and painful mystery broods over the whole of mankind. Is there then no human mystery that is happy, bright and redemptive? Therefore they go in search of it. Venturesome journeys follow: the start is a venture, the experiences on the journey are adventurous, and the arrival at the journey's end is often an adventure. These seekers and adventurers discover that the birthplace of the new man is the old Bethlehem. One of their number in whom the poison of modern humanism has transformed the sacred unrest of human nature into an everlasting vagrancy, the curse of spiritual homelessness, turns back from Bethlehem to Babylon. Another remains indeed in Bethlehem but even here can scarcely find peace on earth because the glimpse of heaven which he has been permitted fills him with a devouring hunger for the Absolute.

But why anticipate? Here we simply wish to point out that these pages do not depict the life-history of exemplary Christians who pursue a straight course, calm and restful, and carefully avoiding the stormy problems of life, but of men, poor, and in peril, unsupported, and unenlightened by the faith of the Church, and obliged to force their own way through the spiritual wreckage left by modern culture in order to come home to Christ. They are bold, original spirits, often heroic and gifted with genius, who on the battlefield of their swarming thoughts and passions and amid the contemporary muddle of conflicting philosophies literally struggle with Christ. But—and this is the important point about them for the sake of which they are of value to us also, who perhaps in virtue of a faith never questioned " know in whom we have believed " —their agonizing struggle for and with Christ is precisely the positive overwhelming proof—that stirs every man gifted with the least modicum of spiritual and religious sensibility to the depths—of Christ's living presence in every age. The assertion is frequently made that in comparison with the movements now taking violent possession of the historic stage, Christianity has grown weary. And it would certainly be better for the Christian cause if its adherents, particularly the most convinced, instead of displaying indignation, would weigh most earnestly the words in which the poet and doctor Doeblin has stated what was more than a merely personal impression. " I behold Churches, and Christians devout and undevout. But whenever I talked with them—I am speaking of Protestants—I found nothing that distinguished them from other earnest deep men. That is to say : their faith has no distinctive psychological power productive of a unique type of character. . . It seems to me that modern Christianity does not make sufficient use of the stupendous fact of Jesus of Nazareth, and that the enormous power and rapturous bliss contained in this historic phenomenon have not been made sufficiently the subject of living experience. By rights this Figure should be the storm-centre of a tempest of emotion and energy. I am compelled to say this since so much has been lost sight of, has lapsed into oblivion, or has been worn down into platitude."

We do not forget that such criticisms are of necessity one-sided when they are made by those who have no inside knowledge of the infinitely tender yet supertemporally powerful sacrament of Christ living on in the Church. But the Church cannot be identified, without qualification, with the Christian world. The latter—the world which professes Christianity—is deeply enamoured of rest, habit and sleep. This was already plain on the Mount of Olives. But yesterday, to-day and for ever, while the world endures, Christ is living even to the sweat of mortal agony.

What might not Christian civilization become if a mighty revival stirred the Christian world to its depths, if throughout a Christendom embracing all Christian denominations there came in men's minds and hearts a struggle in the literal sense of the term, heroic and passionate, for the Spirit of Christ that gives life and light to the world, and created order. It is to convey some notion of what a humane Christian culture, created by the intensive co-operation of Christians, might be, that I have here conjured up spirits from the entire orbit of Christianity, western and eastern. What a mighty revelation it is of Christ's reality and undying vitality untouched by the hand of time, and of the store of truth contained in His mysterious epiphany; a revelation whose world-enlightening power is an inspiration to us, when we behold this fulness of glory reflected in the many-tinted mirrors of minds and hearts differing both individually and racially. But however many the mirrors, the image they reflect is always the same. From these many experiences and their intellectual interpretations, there emerges with the unbroken force of perfect unity the conviction and the acknowledgement that Christ is not only our best, our most delightful, our highest and our deepest, but, rightly understood, our sole possession here on earth.

BLOY
THE PILGRIM OF THE ABSOLUTE

I have spent my life asking for one of two things : God's glory or death. It is death that is coming. My blessing be upon it. It may be that the glory is following it and that my alternative was meaningless.

Léon Bloy, *Le Désespéré.*

THERE is no modern writer of whom I have had so curious an experience as of Léon Bloy. It was in a strange fashion that I became acquainted with his writings. It was shortly after the end of the war. An extremely cultivated man and very exacting in his intellectual and even his spiritual preferences told me bluntly that after Léon Bloy all other French books had become intolerable. I naturally smiled at his enthusiasm as ardent as a young girl's. But my curiosity had been aroused all the same. I began to hunt for Bloy's books. When an author has written more than thirty books, it is impossible to read them all. But I read about half, in succession, with admiration at first, then with deep sympathy and emotion. As I proceeded my entire soul was stirred and shaken and I felt like a blind man who suddenly receives his sight after long years of darkness, sees the world for the first time as it really is and prepares to begin a new life. But finally when I had been dominated, almost tyrannized over, by him for a year, I bade him what I intended to be a final farewell with the cold and hostile conviction that his "absolute Catholicism" was in any case not suited to myself and those like me. What had happened? Simply what always happens and will always happen to the majority of Bloy's readers : the hour had come when an unbearable disappointment breaks the spell by which the wild mystic had bound them. What caused the disappointment? When Bloy admits that he has left no stone unturned to ensure the failure of his books, he has principally in mind his position in the Absolute. "The Absolute is a journey without return, and that is the reason why those who undertake it have so few companions. Just think! They always pursue the same object, always go in the same direction. They march on day and night without turning to right or left, be it only on a single occasion and for a single moment. They know that the whole of life, every thought, every feeling, every act, yes, even the slightest impulse is simply part of one constant emanation from the primordial decree of the almighty Will. Imagine a man of action, an explorer who embarks on his travels. His stirring appeal has induced a few ardent spirits to accompany him. They did not foresee the suffering that awaited them. . . They are led into a desert, a land of desolation. There awaits them cold, darkness, hunger, thirst, boundless fatigue, appalling misery, agony, a bloody sweat. And the foolhardy leader looks around him in vain for his comrades. Then he understands that it is God's will he should bear his sufferings alone and he plunges into the unfathomable darkness, bearing his heart like a torch before him." (*L'Invendable*)

Did Bloy in this passage foretell correctly the reason why I deserted his banner? No; I parted company with the "pilgrim of the Absolute" not because I could no longer endure the Absolute, but because I could no longer endure him. I was disgusted by the constant storm of uncharitable denunciations, glaring injustices, and coarse abuse poured out in the name of this Absolute on three quarters—nine-tenths would be nearer the mark—

of the human race. The whole of contemporary Catholicism, French in particular, he regarded as the prey of an incurable "mediocrity." Mediocre, lamentable and disgraceful was his verdict upon the *Bonne Presse,* an enterprise conceived on a large scale to make provision for the average Christian intelligence and foster Catholic literature in a country poisoned with secularism. Mediocre and beneath contempt was the work of a Bourget, a Brunetière, a Huysmans which nevertheless was inaugurating a religious revival in France. Mediocre, indeed actually irreligious, was the movement for Catholic social reform initiated by Bishops and priests " devoted to Satan."

It is not surprising that I asked myself whether this anger were a holy anger and whether this wrath proceeded from the Absolute, or from the fact that the ecclesiastical authorities adopted an extremely reserved attitude towards the apparitions of Our Lady of La Salette, which Bloy defended as the greatest revelation in Christian history. Is it surprising that I came to wonder whether writers approved by the verdict of the public but sentenced to death by Bloy were successful simpletons, or knaves, or both, merely because his own books published in editions of three thousand required ten years to be sold out? The bitterness of disappointed love knows no mercy. And the doubt corroded like a foul rust the gigantic monument which " the ungrateful Beggar," " the Old Man of the Mountain," " the Pilgrim of the Absolute " had erected to himself, not only in these books, but in all his writings. Was he just like—certainly not *all* others—but like those other *great* men, those unhappy half-diseased men of genius? And I thought of Nietzsche whose speech became with advancing years a monologue of increasing bitterness, alienation from the world and hatred of mankind. Of Strindberg also, the sick genius and poet of hell, who lived in visions which for every one else were hallucinations and persistent prophetic expectations which were never fulfilled. It was exactly the same with Bloy. Was it possible after all that this visionary who, on the third of November 1917, died quietly in his bed, and to the very end refused to believe *such a death* possible because he confidently expected the grace of martyrdom, was a pathetic fool, the victim of delusions, mocked by the destiny that presided over his life?

These were difficult questions which at the time I felt no desire to solve because I had lost all interest in Bloy. As I said above, I bade him goodbye and for ever. But it appears that Bloy would not bid me goodbye. Twelve years later he knocked so loudly at the door of a soul, now more mature, that it was impossible to postpone any longer a thorough examination of his claims. When Bloy has once taken hold of a man he never lets him go. Indeed no student of contemporary French literature could possibly ignore Bloy, because he was always coming across his name. Nor was this all. A literary battle rages to-day about a man surrounded in his lifetime by a conspiracy of silence.

In a New Year's letter, Bloy wished a friend two centuries of life that he might witness how the writer's books struck like a mighty lightning flash minds emancipated from the gospel of sport and machinery. These words express not the resentment of a wounded vanity, but a calm knowledge of spiritual laws. Spiritual meteors with a core of flame such as Bloy possessed, do not penetrate the atmosphere of our planet without setting it on fire sooner or later. Nor are they extinguished so quickly as corporeal meteors. For they come from the depths not of space but of the Spirit, of the Absolute. Twelve years before I had failed to perceive that in the case of such spirits as Bloy only one thing is material. When he crossed my path twelve years before, the pilgrim of the Absolute, straight from the metaphysical abysses, my eyes were fettered by his dusty and lacerated feet, his ragged beggar's cloak, in short by his entire array of human wretchedness and poverty. I should have remembered that never for an instant here below in the whole of man's history have appearance and reality corresponded, and moreover that their essential discrepancy is a mark of created and fallen being which can never be obliterated. I forgot that from this point of view even Christ is a stumbling-block; and that Catholic dogma presents a corresponding scandal in the fact that as the Church teaches, it expresses Absolute Truth; but the relativity of human thought clings to its formulation, and it can never exhaust the complete supernatural Reality.

Bloy himself had always known this and never lost faith in what he termed his mission. " Be sure, I am a poor and humble Christian, just this and nothing more. It has pleased God to conceal me in a garment of art and literature, so that it was not until I was almost an old man that I caught sight of my miserable soul under the disguise." This was one aspect of the truth. But the other aspect was the fact that Bloy lived in the Absolute, and that his heart and mind were filled every hour of the day with the Absolute. Though a man be but a poor specimen of a Christian, if he lives in the Absolute he lives indeed. There is no killing him, and if he is a writer and a prophet of the Absolute, "a wretched mortal whom the Lord has chosen pretty forcibly to bring down upon our dunghill, this fatal and fading beam from the seventh heaven," there is no silencing him. Who knows, yes, who knows? The depths often produce strange surprises. . . Who can tell whether this poor man may not one day reappear on the upper verge of the darkness with a superb mystical blossom in his hand, the flower of silence, the flower of the abyss? Yes, one day. And not a day a century or two hence. But already, to-day. Even in Bloy's lifetime there were a number of people—they were not and will never be those far too numerous folk who have never had the least inkling of the numinous depths of life—who saw and reverenced in the hand of the pilgrim battling his way out of the chaos of a fallen world, and emerging from the "groaning and travail of Creation," the mystical flower of the abyss, with its petals aflame with the eternal light. What a priest wrote to Bloy in 1909 was anything but an exception. "I cannot but believe that God blesses the readers of your books. I often return to them with devotion, as a man visits a famous shrine because God reveals himself more there than elsewhere."

"On the twenty-fifth of June 1905 two young people of twenty climbed the endless steps leading up to the Church of the Sacred Heart. They bore with them that profound suffering which is the one important product of modern civilization and a kind of active despair which —they knew not why—was lightened by an interior confidence, a confidence that the truth for which they hungered and without which life seemed scarce worth having would one day be revealed to them. . . Meanwhile they cleansed their minds with Bergson's aid from the superstition of that pseudo-science with which the Sorbonne had fed them. But they did not fail to perceive that Bergson's intuition was a poor refuge from the scepticism which was the logical consequence of all modern philosophies. . . They visited a strange beggar who, scorning all philosophies, shouted the Divine Truth from the house-tops, and who, though an orthodox Catholic, judged his age and all who put their trust in this world with a greater freedom than all the revolutionaries in the world. What he disclosed to his visitors cannot be related; the tenderness of Christian charity and the thrill blent of fear and a sense of infinite mercy that stirs the soul to her depths when she encounters a spirit stamped with the love of God. . . To cross his threshold was to expose ourselves to an invisible force which transposed all our values. We understood, or at least felt that there is only one genuine sorrow, not to be a Saint. Everything besides became unsubstantial."

The two visitors were a man with whom the reader is already acquainted as Péguy's friend, Maritain who enjoys to-day international repute as a Catholic philosopher, but at that time was not even baptized, and a Russian Jewess who is to-day his wife. The account comes from himself. Some years later Bloy received a similar visit. His visitors were a Dutchman, Peter van der Meer, a writer, a disciple of Nietzsche and a revolutionary of the extreme left, and his wife who prided herself on being "an active fighter in the Marxian ranks." But in spite of all their loud professions of infidelity, they were conscious of a spiritual unrest. They had read Bloy and must speak with him personally. They found themselves struck dumb. How this deeply humble man spoke of God! His soul was simply an echo of God. "As he spoke every event, every person, every circumstance assumed, so to speak, a divine significance, became a mystery in which God reveals Himself. I cannot recover from my joy and my astonishment that such a man, such a Christian, such an absolute Catholic can be living in this city. What will be the result of this meeting for myself?" This will be the result, that in 1911 he will be baptized with his son—his wife had been born of a Catholic family—and, further, that in October 1933 he himself (the literary director of a large Parisian publishing house) and his wife will enter the Benedictine Order, to which they had first given two children.

Fifteen years have passed since Bloy's death and his spiritual family far from dying out is growing—and in many lands. At the end of 1927 the French geologist Pierre Termier attended a scientific congress at Bucharest. There a man presented himself to him who wished to make his acquaintance because he had been a friend of Bloy's. When Termier asked him what was the general impression he had received from Bloy's work, his visitor answered: "He made me weep a great deal." Where among modern writers, comments Termier, can we find another who could be spoken of in this way? And this savant whose professional interests were as remote as the poles from Bloy makes this personal confession: "I divide my life into two sharply and deeply divided halves, that which preceded my meeting with Bloy, and that which followed it."

These are a few encounters with Bloy which we have recalled to prepare the reader's mind for *his own encounter with him* and to preserve him to a certain extent from misconceptions. This man who called himself the pilgrim of the Absolute was anything but a figure to be placed upon the altar of an uncritical veneration. He was not a soul whose faculties were harmoniously balanced, but a soul so rent by the tension of conflicting passions that he could save the unity of his personality only by forging for its wear the armour of the Absolute. Men of this type must be accepted as they are. They themselves bear their life as a destiny. " The destiny of every one of us is irrevocable. . . The man who is not the greatest artist in the world before he has drawn a line will never become it. We *become* nothing, not even a blockhead, not even a swine. A man is born a great artist as a man is born a Saint or anything else, and education does no more than distinguish spirits. Nothing more. Caesar is not permitted to suck the breast like other babies." (*Le Mendiant Ingrat*)

Bloy was not permitted to live like other men. The reason he reveals in his *Letters to his Fiancée* written at the age of forty-three, such letters as few women have had the good fortune to receive: " I was born unhappy, unhappy in a profound and terrible fashion and if I am possessed by a most fierce craving for joy, it is the effect of the mysterious law by which opposites attract each other. I remember how as a child, a tiny lad, I often refused with annoyance and anger to take part in games and amusements, the mere thought of which had thrilled me with delight. But I thought it nobler to suffer and inflict suffering upon myself by renouncing them. . . The mere word 'unhappiness' enraptured me. This, I believe, I inherited from my mother whose Spanish soul was at once extremely ardent and extremely melancholy, and the chief attraction of Christianity for me has been the infinity of Christ's sufferings, the sublime and transcendent horror of His Passion. . . When I grew up I cruelly fulfilled the promise of my wretched childhood and the majority of the fearful sufferings that I have experienced have been undoubtedly of my own making decreed with a wild frenzy by myself against myself."

A mysterious frenzy, unhallowed at first, then holy, scourged him through life. An unhappy childhood—he was born in 1846 at Périgueux in the south of France—was followed by a wild, confused and aimless youth. His studies at the Lycée were not continued beyond the fourth form. His thorough knowledge of Latin—for he later showed a passionate attachment to that language—was self-taught. He attempted painting for which he had very considerable talent. Then he tried to become an architect, but, making the acquaintance of the writer Barbey d'Aurevilly, became his secretary. D'Aurevilly, though not himself a practising Catholic, brought back this enemy of God at the age of twenty-three to an intellectual acceptance of the faith. After the war of 1870 in which he served he was unable for years to obtain a firm footing in any profession.

From 1877 to 1888 he was a railway official, "one of the most atrocious" conceivable, he confesses himself. It is not difficult to believe him—his head was full of such very different things.

It was at this period that he passed through the most tragic, and most decisive, experiences of his life; he was tossed by tempests diabolic at first, later Divine. Some of these experiences were incorporated by Bloy himself into his largely autobiographical novel *The Desperate,* and he spoke at length about them in his *Letters to his Fiancée.* But for a really clear view of the episode we had to wait until the publication of a book by a Belgian writer Hubert Colleys who had access to the numerous documents placed at his disposal by Mme Bloy, and to Bloy's *Letters to Veronica,* edited with an introduction by Jacques Maritain.

This woman more than any other external factor determined Bloy's destiny and set him once for all—apart from a brief period of distraction after the catastrophe that befell her—on his pilgrimage to the Absolute. She made him conscious of "*his* secret," or rather revealed it to him. "I knew an extremely poor girl, Veronica, as ignorant as it is possible to be, but whose heart burned like all the stars in the heavens. She knew nothing but *her own nothingness and the unreasoning obedience* (*obéissance irraisonée*) which pure love demands. Therefore she was raised to the vision of God's glory and received illuminations so sublime that I cannot think of them without being paralysed by admiration and awe." (*Letters to his Fiancée*) Who was this girl with whom Bloy fell passionately in love "because she was so utterly unlike any one else"?

At this point fate wrote in the book of life a romance which would be regarded as improbable if it had been written by Dostoievsky. It might indeed be a chapter from his *Raskolnikov*. Bloy, it is true, does not correspond to the Russian hero; but Veronica is a second Sonia, and even more than Sonia. Veronica, as she is called in Bloy's novel (her real name was Anne Marie Roule), was a poor seamstress who eked out her insufficient earnings by prostitution. "The place where Anne Marie was then living," wrote Bloy three years later, "was sensibly haunted by the devil, so that I almost died of fear. It was perhaps a perverted taste for the supernatural that compelled me to return to it again and again. To-day I can scarcely comprehend this episode now remote even in time and moreover do my utmost to efface the hideous memory." If we revive it here, it is for the purpose explained by Maritain, "that the unknown friends for whom Bloy wrote may enter more deeply and more sympathetically into the secret of a life of incomparable suffering in which the abyss of the Divine and the abyss of the human heart ceaselessly called one to the other."

Is there any need to emphasize the fact that Bloy plunged headlong at first into the abyss of the human heart which contains an abyss of sin? She whom he wished to draw out of the mire drew him into it. It was not without a most violent resistance on his part. From the day on which by his tears and entreaties he persuaded his friend to be enrolled in the Archconfraternity of the Immaculate Mother of God the worst was at an end. "That day effected a complete and final change in her way of living." This however meant only "that Anne Marie ceased to be supported by any one who came along and was supported by myself alone not without sin." A heroic struggle of which the *Letters to Veronica* give a terrifying picture enabled him to win the victory over himself and her. We shall not speak of the other despairing struggle which Bloy, once more without a job, had to wage in order to beg maintenance for the two of them. Journalism rejected him after his first attempt on account of his unbending Catholic convictions. Nevertheless he would have married the girl. But the alternative happened; the abyss of the Divine Heart opened and swallowed the erstwhile sinner. Or, as Bloy puts it, "God's love smote her like a lightning flash." This happened in September 1878 in the Church of the Sacred Heart, a few weeks after Bloy's return from a Trappist monastery where for the second time he had made a retreat to obtain the necessary graces to overcome his own interior crisis.

Hitherto he had been his friend's teacher in the spiritual struggle. For it was he who took the lead. Though his fierce nature and seething passions attempted again and again to drag him back from spiritual to fleshly love or rather, because this was the case, he fought with a still fiercer intensity the spiritual combat. It may well be that many a Christian who knows the phrase only from hearsay becomes acquainted for the first time in these *Letters to Veronica* with the terrific and bloody reality of this interior conflict. It was a supernatural campaign which Bloy organized of two suffering hearts against the Heart of God. He organized it in the most literal sense, making use of all the strategic methods employed by Catholic piety, novenas to Our Lady and St Joseph and the Holy Souls, confessions and communions and practices of penance to gain indulgences. It is touching to read with what a profusion of tender pleadings this man of wrath sought to win his friend to God. But, lo and behold, while Bloy is attempting in this way to drive her before him on the road to God, suddenly before his very eyes she sinks into the abyss of God. There is no further talk of marriage. For Anne Marie there is nothing now but God and prayer, ceaseless, consuming prayer accompanied by illuminations and revelations. The two celebrate an orgy of outer poverty and inner light. To save them from starving, Bloy sought a post as clerk in an office, just as later on in 1894 he applied to a builder for a job as a porter, since a disease of the eyes had made his friend unable to continue her sewing. "Humanly speaking we had no prospect of escaping death from want. But observe, we were supported in a *miraculous* fashion. For two years I received help from unexpected quarters and always in answer to prayer, not abundant certainly, but sufficient for the two of us to continue this life, hidden from the world, a life which could not be approved by the ordinary standards of Christian prudence, but was so obviously the will of God."

The will of God! These two, poverty's elect, became God's elect. They flung themselves upon God like two ravenous beasts on the prey for which they have hungered so long. This strange girl, with no other education than the barest rudiments taught at an elementary school, explained the Bible to him. She had second sight and imparted to him revelations which absorbed him in an excess of terror and joy. The times were, she declared, fulfilled, and the apocalyptic days at hand when the power of God would be revealed in glory. And a personal "secret" was communicated to him, which Bloy never revealed, because the seer forbade him in God's name. In indescribable perplexity Bloy implored all the Saints, for the sake of the Crucified Saviour, to make it clear whether he was or was not the victim of illusions. Her confessor commanded the seer under sacramental obedience to ask Our Lord for a visible and absolutely unmistakable sign that her mystical experiences were true. It was not given. Anne Marie was on the point of losing her reason. And Bloy wrote to his friend, the writer Ernest Hello, who shared his apocalyptic expectations: "Those who like ourselves imagine or expect a great manifestation of God's glory are idiots and fools. . . I am without a past, without a future and without hope, and with a terrible wound in my heart. I have been wounded in my faith, in my hope and in my charity. To-day, Monday, for the first time for a very long time past I have not received

Communion, and no prayer has passed my lips. I am conscious of nothing except the most bitter and savage anger against a God so pitiless and so ungrateful. . . I would be ashamed to treat a mangy dog as God treats me."

When he wrote this he little knew that the chalice of suffering was very far from drained. Anne Marie, deeply disillusioned, gradually sunk into madness. In his novel *The Idiot,* Dostoievsky has a scene which burns itself into the imagination like a diabolic nightmare, the scene in which Myschkin and Rogoshin pass the night lying side by side near the corpse of Myschkin's fiancée, whom Rogoshin had murdered. For the rest of his life Bloy will never be able to efface *this* memory. " For four months I lived shut up without any help with a very dear sister who was attacked by raving madness and whose condition I was obliged to conceal." In July 1882 she was taken to an asylum. According to the report of the matron in charge she passed meekly and devoutly and with an impenetrable melancholy through the intellectual night which ended only with her death in 1907.

For Bloy also there began a long and dark night. Eight years after the girl who had awoken the depths of his soul had been put into the asylum, in 1890, he wrote to his fiancée, the daughter of a Danish Protestant writer: " You speak to me of Easter Communion. I will endeavour to prepare myself to receive Communion with you, if you have reached that stage [in her conversion] by then. But this excellent advice which you, my little guardian angel, have given me, is a good opportunity for me to show you the utterly miserable state of my poor soul. I have never ceased to love God and have always felt myself capable of giving my life at need for his Glory.

But ever since Veronica's appalling fate the spirit of prayer has forsaken me. I have a sore place in my heart, an aching wound which has been enlarged and made worse by further misfortunes. Moreover I have been abandoned to the unbridled lusts of my sensuality, and have been unable to recover my former piety which was truly extraordinary. Under these circumstances I have turned against God and reproached him for having left me in the lurch and for proving a cruel and terrible master to those who love him."

What then in this unutterable misery of a life rushing to the brink of madness, a suffering whose intensity can still be felt by a stranger, has become of the Pilgrim of the Absolute? We see a man stumbling through the night of despair and in fact Bloy wrote at this period his first novel, *Le Désespéré*. We must speak of Bloy *the desperate* before we can speak of Bloy the pilgrim, of the pilgrim of the Absolute. For what he terms his position in the Absolute was achieved only by passing through despair.

There is an entire literature of despair. To maintain that despair is simply a topic for literature, a bookish theme, is a cheap irony which proves nothing against its reality. Who can deny that the despair is genuine and really experienced which leads to suicide? And the despair which kills is merely the briefest form of despair, the despair of the weakling who pours out the bowl, because he lacks the courage to drink it to the dregs. The despair which like a silent and grey spectre haunts all the modern glorifications of a deified universe is greater and more terrible. Oswald Spengler's philosophy of the forms determining the development of cultures is from beginning to end a monumental melancholy draped in the rich robes of contemporary science, which logically enough chants its gloomy prophecy of the doom awaiting western civilization. And the conversion to Bolshevism of André Gide, the Gide in whose cultivated individualism only three years before short-sighted optimists saw a pillar and rampart of the western mind, is simply an affecting proclamation of that metaphysical hopelessness, characteristic of so many modern systems of life and thought for all their external professions of self-confidence. This is a genuine and an awful despair. And a despair finally barren. Is there a fruitful despair? Certainly, at least if wc are to credit Kierkegaard, who knew something of the matter. To be sure it must not be a despair content to be resigned, but the keenest, most living and most dynamic, in short the greatest despair possible to man. And Kierkegaard adds: " The supreme despair is despair that one does not despair." For only in the soul that does not wholly despair is the tension of despair greatest. When a soul despairs completely the tension breaks and it crawls wearily into itself like a dying beast into its lair. The keenest hunger, the unendurable pangs of hunger are felt not by the dying man who is utterly exhausted, but by the man who is battling for his life with the last ounce of his strength. The supreme abandonment by God is felt not by the most ungodly, but by the most holy man. The very Man who in strict justice and in virtue of His nature could not be forsaken by God experienced with such tragic intensity the magnitude of the contrast between what things are and what they should be, between their existence and their essence, as philosophers say, their painful reality and the glorious ideal of their nature that He uttered the most direct and the most sincere, if we may say so, the simplest and frankest cry of desolation that was ever heard. There is a holy desolation, a holy despair. It is this despair which breaks open with its explosive force the oppressive and strangling armour with which man is clad by the false humility which asserts that things actually are what ideally they should be, and thus allows him to breathe the air of the transcendent and the Absolute.

" She is silent as empty space. When she does speak it is as though she descended from some blissful star of an unknown universe. This impression is given by the distant tone of her voice which age has made more solemn without destroying its tenderness. And it is even more sensible in her words.

"*Everything that happens is adorable,* she is wont to say. And she says it with the ecstatic look of a creature on whom graces have been heaped a thousandfold, who can find no other formula than this to express the movements of her heart and soul, and could find no other even in face of a pestilence or if she were just about to be devoured by wild beasts.

"You must be very unhappy, my poor woman, said a priest to her, who saw her kneeling dissolved in tears before the Blessed Sacrament exposed and who by a piece of good fortune happened to be a true priest.

" I am perfectly happy, she replied. We have not to wait until to-morrow or the next day or for ten years before going to paradise. *We can go to paradise to-day if we are poor and crucified.*"

This is the holy despair which we have in mind or rather which Bloy had in mind and which he experienced himself, as it has been the lot of very few to experience it, and to which in his novel *The Poor Woman* he erected a monument in its purity and greatness such as it has been given to few artists to erect to a great and holy idea. The novel represents the soul breaking her way through a despair which is not experienced as the more or less accidental psychological condition of an individual, but is seen metaphysically as the essential destiny of the world. Not only is the heroine poor, but all the characters of the book, of which the second part is autobiographical, are poor and moreover poor because they live in a "poor" world. For Bloy "Poverty" symbolizes the fundamental nature of the world as at present constituted and as we experience it, a condition which he cannot conceive as its original or final state. A man who has read *La Femme Pauvre* will understand why out of the whole of French literature Berdaiev seems to be acquainted almost exclusively with Bloy and appeals to his witness as the principal testimony to many of his leading ideas. This Frenchman, who markedly betrays the limitations of national pride and has very little sympathy with foreign thought and in particular with the Teutonic mind, displays in fact an astonishing affinity with the mystical temper and outlook of the Russians, the way in which oriental Christianity regards the world, though he had never read a line of Dostoievsky or Soloviev and probably had never even heard of them. Yet not only such a saying as this: "There is only one excuse for living, to await the resurrection of the dead," but entire scenes and lengthy dissertations of an eschatological and apocalyptic character could take their place in any work of Dostoievsky's.

But let us take a closer look at that first novel which Bloy devoted to the problem of despair. But no, in heaven's name let us beware of that academic expression, which might well provoke Bloy in the next world to one of his old explosions of anger. Problem indeed! He knew despair, naked despair, raging, seething revolt or its extreme opposite, a blissful experience of the Absolute, of God, which moved him to tears. That however came later. The first massive experience nourished, fed and, if we may say so, over-fed by long years of inner and outer suffering, was despair. It was the despair of a man who cannot *wholly* despair because the mystery in the background of his soul, the Absolute, does not permit it, but who for that very reason revolts the more passionately and the more tempestuously. *Le Désespéré* is revolt in the pure state, a flow of glowing lava at the moment of eruption. Though Bloy later on retracted much that he had cast up into the light of day from a heart in revolt, he always liked to be spoken of as the author of *Le Désespéré*, because he was proud of the " frankness " of the book, a frankness which he never equalled and which he believed made his autobiographical novel unique in literature. This may very well be true. And it strikes us in the face when for example we compare with *Le Désespéré* the chief document of Dostoievsky's despair—which however does not belong to exactly the same plane as the attitude described by Bloy—his *Sketches from the Underworld.* Not to speak of the fact that the Russian writer warns us in a footnote not to identify him with his hero from the underworld, there runs through the entire work a remarkable vein of secretiveness and malicious cunning, a reserve which in spite of all the barbaric exhibitionism and brutal self-mockery prevents perfect frankness. It is as though a sulphurous fume of Satanism rose from the fire of this despair, though certainly a Satanism doomed itself to be consumed in its flames. Bloy's book is a daring act of arson proudly admitted, a conflagration blazing to the skies : his vocabulary spouts fire to a degree elsewhere unknown. And into that conflagration he flings practically all the contents of his epoch, persons and conditions, in the Church and in the world, in art, literature and journalism. Has this man escaped from a mad-house? The scandal was immense, and as immense the wreckage of his devastations which all his life blocked every road to success. This disagreeable and unsocial kind of despair thoroughly disgusted the public, whom he had invited to a friendly view.

Nevertheless the despair in this work of genius is something totally different and far greater and more fundamental than scandalized contemporaries perceived. It is something overpowering, something sublime, something which men must experience or at least of which they must acquire knowledge. " Oh, to utter this new word and then so far as I am concerned die, spat upon and scourged by the entire world," cries Cain Marchenoir, the desperate. What is this new word? We should hear it more clearly, if the battle against the contemporary environment (the reader is even treated to long-winded literary manifestos by Marchenoir-Bloy) were relegated more to the background and instead the battle against the essential nature of *this* world which remains the same in every age were placed more prominently in the foreground. But in truth this was part of Bloy's despair that these people were so satisfied and so comfortable in their mediocrity, so contented with *this* world; and the desperate was alone with his despair. They were healthy and cheerful; they babbled about progress and enlightenment and the blessings of democracy, all these folk with the souls of flunkeys and eunuchs, and not once did an inkling of the fact that the old chaos prevailed enter their senile brains. The chaos of a sinful and accursed world where nothing is in its right place, no one knows his real name or his true features, or whether he is worthy of eternal love or eternal hate. This is the subject of the sole philosophy which the desperate will accept. He had also studied Schopenhauer formerly. To the devil with that Teutonic manufacturer of mists! If this kind of philosophy is not exactly an accursed, at least it is an unprofitable occupation. To enquire whether we can think, whether reality is really real and space not a dream, has no interest for the desperate. If the milky way does not exist in the universe, at any rate it exists in the human mind and in that case the mind is our universe. Granted that what we experience is a dream, that dream is then our sole reality. As if names mattered in this connection! " Our life is impossible and like a perpetual miracle," Bloy will say when he has long ago left behind him the stage of despair. And Bloy the desperate is particularly insistent that God Himself does not attach such importance to words and concepts. " Every conceivable violence may be done to what it has been agreed to term the human reason by a God who *suffers*." Words, what are words? Words are blind lions seeking water in the desert. So then we will call life a dream. But "we are dreamers who cry out in their sleep." And it is the cry that matters. We cry out; therefore we exist. We cry out because the dream is so frightful. And this precisely is the great despair, that we never escape from the dream, that we never completely awake. We no longer know reality as it is, or we do not yet know it. We merely divine it obscurely in this dream of life, of which nine-tenths are filled with disorder, confusion, baseness and sin; and this divination of God in the night of His absence makes the dream even more hideous. The reality of *this* world is suffering and misery. And the desperate is poor and wretched in this world, that he may understand and proclaim that the world is nothing but the vast mystical blossom of some vast mystical poverty. "All earthly things are predestined to suffering. This suffering was in his eyes at once the beginning and the end. It was not simply the distant goal, a threat to be fulfilled later, but the strict logic of those mysterious writings in which God's will, he assumed, must nevertheless be read. The dread sentence pronounced at the expulsion from Eden he applied in its full rigour to the birth-pangs of the most insignificant happenings in the ecumenical story of earth."

The world is the blossom of a mystical poverty. *Whose* poverty? What must not we conclude, when the Son of God Himself became the perfect and complete pauper who chose for His dwelling place the misery of utmost abandonment, and who gathered up the million-voiced sorrow of all ages into a single cry of agony? In view of the tragedy of God made man, the desperate considers any violation of thought legitimate. For his thought is a desperate thought. " He was convinced that we are faced with a God who by His own decree is barren, of His own free will bound, nailed and agonizing to death in the unclotheable reality of His essence, a condition symbolized and rendered visible in the bloody venture of His Person. He had the intuition of a species of Divine impotence, provisionally held fast between mercy and justice, whose goal is an inexpressible recovery of the substance which has been squandered by love." Appalling double Dutch, but necessitated by this unique situation! The Triune Mind has for many centuries stopped payment, and it remains for human patience to support it from man's own purse. The master of Eternity, able to pay in full, can need only time, and it is precisely time which constitutes man's despair. That is why the Saints and Doctors of the faith have always insisted upon the necessity of suffering for God.—Here the fiery neophyte, who divined these truths, extracted the thorn from the lame foot of the late arrival in the Church that he was, swooped upon suffering and made of it a sword which he thrust into his own body, having first put out his eyes. "Now more than ever he despaired, but it was with that sublime despair which flings the heart into heaven, as the shipwrecked mariner throws his cargo into the sea that he may not be drowned without having at least seen from afar the shore of safety. Moreover he believed that the end of man's age-long tragi-comedy was at hand." But the hero of the novel did not witness it. He experienced only his own end. With broken ribs, far from his friends and from Veronica who in his absence had been placed in an asylum, he died without the consolation of a priest, kept from him by a brainless and heartless concierge. But not in despair. For his dying words were these: "I have spent my life praying for two things, the glory of God or death. It is death that comes. My blessing upon him. It may be that the glory follows on his heel and my alternative was meaningless." Bloy himself was to have many years before him in which to recognize the absurdity of the alternative. And in the exact measure that he *came to recognize it, he became the pilgrim of the Absolute* and his despair was revealed as the pilgrim's dusty and torn garment which at the end of his earthly pilgrimage in the dark entry to the Absolute he will at last strip off for ever.

When with an unyielding obstinacy Bloy persisted in

speaking of the Absolute, he was not speaking as a philosopher. Still less had he in view any system of so-called absolute philosophy. In his novel, to be sure, he makes the desperate expound his ideas of a "symbolism of world history"—the scheme of a book which was to be a sort of Paralipomena to the Gospels. But however closely this may appear to resemble the religious gnosis of the great modern Russians, Bloy does not and will not concern himself with a philosophic knowledge of the mysteries of religion but solely with the mystical experience of them. He was content to know that all the events of history were grounded in the Absolute Reality that is the object of religion. And this knowledge he obtained from faith, the universal faith of Christendom, and will know nothing outside or beyond that faith. " You must know," he wrote to the lady who was to become his wife, " the sort of man I am. It would be a serious and mischievous mistake—because it would make a perfect spiritual unity between us impossible—to believe that I am a thinker, an intellectual. In reality I know very little and have never understood anything save what God showed me when I came before Him as a little child. First and foremost don't forget this, I am a worshipper. And whenever I have attempted to act otherwise than by love and the inspirations of love I have sunk below the brutes."

No, Bloy was not an intellectual in the sense given to the word by the arrogant snobbery of a caste. Nor was he even in the innocent and laudable acceptation of the term. All the same he knew a great deal that the intellectuals do not know; and therefore many genuine intellectuals, those, namely, for whom man's pilgrimage is not solely a voyage of discovery undertaken by the pure reason, a mere adventure of the brain, feel an instinctive attraction towards him. In the book describing his conversion Leopold Levaux relates how he attended in Berlin a performance of *Parsifal*. He was moved, but not satisfied. Wagner aroused in him a hunger for the ultimate Truth and Beauty of God, but did not appease it. It was not in his power. " For that he must have been a Christian like Bloy," felt Levaux, the non-Christian in search of God. " I have nothing, it seems, to hope from men. What can I hope from God? " So ran the none too hopeful entry in his diary. But he made it in the train which was taking himself and his wife from Russia to France via Berlin direct to Bloy. For Bloy was the one man in the world from whom he still hoped he might hope something. His long journey was richly repaid. How it was accomplished, this vastly difficult business of winning the faith, cannot strictly be told. It came about of itself. The old man who would not allow those he liked to address him as " Monsieur " but insisted on their calling him Léon Bloy led his guests by the hand to his house. Cigars were smoked and coffee drunk, and they had a heart-to-heart talk. The visitors were a little astonished when the entire family said the Angelus as the most natural thing in the world, but felt that this very thing was a gift for which they had unconsciously been looking for a long time past. The visit proved successful. A few days of this patriarchal hospitality, a hospitality such as was practised by the early Christians, and from the souls of Bloy's two guests, opened without reserve, enlarged and enlightened, all their tormenting religious difficulties vanished like a nightmare on awakening from sleep. They had been blown away, had evaporated in the fresh strong atmosphere of the supernatural which filled the house.

Bloy was a man of prayer, of exceptional prayer. During the Veronica period he spent the entire morning in a large church hearing all the Masses in succession. He remarked once to his godson Jacques Maritain that all his later books were nourished by the illuminations received in that ardent prayer. It was then he learned that "prayer is the work of free men, as work is the prayer of slaves." And with the exception of the spiritual catastrophe, of which we have spoken above, he remained true to this perception for the remainder of his life. Every evening he recited the entire Rosary with his family, and he dragged himself from his deathbed to recite the Office of the Dead on his knees. Daily Mass and Communion were taken for granted. No, not taken for granted, but a solemn feast. And he always brought home a brief Latin phrase or sentence which revealed to him exactly what he needed at the moment, what he needed in order to maintain his daily life, which was an unbroken war, intellectual and spiritual, with the contemporary world, on the supernatural plane. When his book on " the soul of Napoleon " refused to fall into shape, the novena made before he began it having obviously failed to obtain sufficient guidance, he even thought that it might be possible to approach the secret of this secular figure by studying the decisive dates of his career in the light of the liturgical feasts which fell upon them. Such was the degree, shocking to the average man, to which Bloy was convinced of the supernatural character of the chain of cause and effect.

If we would enquire what meaning Bloy attached to

his Absolute, it is in this direction that we must look. "Above and before everything I am a Roman Catholic and I have long ago accepted every possible consequence of my religious belief." *That he drew with the utmost rigour all the practical consequences of his faith made him the pilgrim of the Absolute.* And Bloy, in this radically different from the majority, was the man to draw this further consequence.

He was deeply convinced that we become only what we already are. " I am so much at home in the Absolute that the man who does not speak the language of the Absolute tells me nothing." He was a man who in virtue of a destiny more than individual, was at home in the Absolute from his birth and moreover before he became aware of it. Even as a child he experienced suffering with the keenest sensibility. And he felt at home with suffering. Suffering intoxicated him without his knowing the reason, a psychological state shared by Dostoievsky as the almost malicious analysis in his *Sketches from the Underworld* reveals. He knew it later. Later, when experience of the world's suffering " thrust him into the absolute of a vision of injustice which could make the pride of the coolest philosophers howl." Then he understood, or believed that he understood, that he must endure the vision of absolute injustice to be scourged through it into the vision of absolute justice. " It is necessary that I suffer ; it is the will of God." That Bloy's faith might be made absolute! We must repeat, Bloy's Absolute was no literary device, no philosophic abstraction, but an experience, an experience of suffering, a *saltus mortalis* of despair into the ocean of faith that enclosed him securely in its depths. Suffering and faith were secret accomplices. The more he suffered, the more absolute became his faith. For what other reason have we been given the spectacle of a suffering God? It was not without satisfaction that he discovered that his bodily strength admirably fitted him to suffer and found when he reckoned it up and added all the periods together that he had passed an active eight years in a strict and of course involuntary fast on bread and water for the most part without the bread. It must have been rather more unpleasant when he was obliged to write an entire book at a stretch without leaving the room because. . . he actually had no trousers, no hat and no shoes. And it was even worse when in the depth of winter he was obliged to burn the furniture to save his wife and children from perishing with cold. And even that in the end was of little help, since two children died all the same of under-nourishment. There was no danger that his suffering or the constant disappointment of his exaggerated apocalyptic expectations might have made him waver in his absolute faith. The disappointment was part of the suffering, and the suffering of the world, this " poor " world. Above all it was part of himself who from the first hour of his conversion had prayed for suffering, the utmost measure of suffering, for the salvation of those souls that were specially dear to him. This precisely was what he called his ultimate and most intimate secret. He was first and last a member of the Communion of Saints. In it he lived with an awareness whose intensity amounted to vision, lived in it not as an idle beneficiary and parasite but as a most active fellow worker. And how could he, Léon Bloy, make his contribution save in his own fashion, by suffering, hungering, begging, writing wild and unfair books and being silenced completely in consequence? The great Pascal had said: " Jesus will be in agony until the end of the world; we may not sleep during that time." Bloy did not sleep. He assisted at Jesus' agony, not as a sleeper but as a sufferer. Do you imagine he enjoyed writing begging letters, that it was an accident of fortune that he, a writer of importance, was treated as a fool and silenced? Bloy knew better, and because he knew it, he begged and suffered in a grand and moving style peculiar to himself. He did not beg with the humble demeanour of a man ashamed of his poverty, but as one who has power, a hidden power, which one day will make the world cry aloud for astonishment and dismay. He begged as "the ungrateful beggar." And he suffered with the profoundest abandonment to God's will. "Everything that happens is adorable." But he suffered with indignation against men who in the person of the "poor man" crucify God afresh. He suffered with a wrath which he termed a holy wrath and words crossed his lips which sounded like blasphemies and which he himself called blasphemy, but the "blasphemy of love."

Whether his contemporaries or posterity like it or not, this was the authentic portrait of the man who called himself the "pilgrim of the Absolute." Possibly it might have been better, and more pleasing, and he might have done more good had he presented a slightly different, only a very slightly different, aspect; had he been a little more moderate, a little less extreme. This has always been said of him, and his best friends still say it. Maritain writes: "Bloy—we may think—sought the Absolute for whom he lived a little too much in the personal intimations of his heart and the intuitions of his artistic genius, so that he took too slight account of the universal deliverances of the intellect and reason; and often made his sentiments the starting point in his acquisition of practical knowledge and the basis of unqualified assertions." Maritain, the neo-Thomist philosopher, is a wise man and is no doubt right. But Maritain is Maritain, and Bloy is Bloy. " We *become* nothing, not even a blockhead, not even a swine." Every man is what he is and Bloy was the man who hungered for the Absolute. As others require bodily food every day, Bloy by day and even in those dreams experienced a tormenting hunger, an unquenchable greed for the Absolute, and the Infinite, but the living Infinite. A hunger for the living Infinite which is as really within us and around us as the finite, or indeed more real, since unless we are plain fools we are aware that it is not only within but above and before every finite thing. The infinite is present as a deep and precious spring. But how much water do we draw from it? And it was the complaint of our pilgrim of the Absolute that he had insufficient access to this spring, his most beloved and most precious fountain. For he had, he wrote to a friend, other springs in the desert of his life. Springs of suffering, broad and without a brink. His two children had fallen in. And the spring of unrest into which he himself was in danger of falling if ever he attempted to shirk suffering. Yes, and not far off the spring of hope gushed forth with the sound of heavenly waters. It burst forth with a roar like the waters of a sea—in the depths, the inaccessible depths. It was an unplumbed abyss which had been so covered over and boarded off with the old planks and beams of Noah's ark that no one can approach it. And before it stood the exacting pilgrim of the Absolute like a patriarch of old "shaking with sobs because he could not water his camels from it." As Jacob wrestled with the Angel for his blessing, *Bloy all his life wrestled with God for the blessing in a measure sensible of the Absolute, for an anticipation of the beatific vision and the heavenly mode of existence.*

St Augustine spoke of exceeding the measure of one's condition, *supergredi modum conditionis suae*, as the essence of disorder. It is a disorder when man seeks to overstep the limitations and measures assigned him. In so far as this spirit of immoderation pervades Bloy's thought, feeling and conduct there is something in him that is not in order. It is possible to treat of so delicate a matter without attempting with an ill-mannered pedantry to force upon another one's own type of humanity and Christianity. It can be done if our purpose is not to judge a life moulded by a stern destiny but to draw from it a lesson for ourselves. Where goodness and right were concerned Bloy knew no measure. Had he been Pascal's contemporary, there can be no doubt that he would have stood with him against the Jesuits, who in the religious interest of the masses compromised with the facts of the world as it was, a compromise indeed which always has been and must be practised by a Church which intends to be a universal Church, not a sect. According to Bloy, "if any one tramples upon the Gospel by maintaining that it is possible to be a disciple of Jesus without forsaking all things, I become an idiot on the spot incapable of understanding anything." When he said this he did not remember the distinction drawn by the Church between commands and counsels; he refused to remember it, because the distinction ran counter to his "absolute" temper. He understood and practised religion as a maximalist. He hoped and passionately desired to close his life on earth by a violent death for Christ, and when he was asked on what lines he was educating his children he gave the monumental answer: " For martyrdom." Had his interlocutor expressed a doubt of Bloy's mental balance, he would have broken out into such contemptuous laughter as only a reader well versed in his books can conceive. Balance? The devil take it! He has indeed taken it long ago. I am a Christian who draws the full consequences from my Christianity. What happened at the fall? The entire world, you understand, with each and every thing in it, lost its balance. Why on earth should I be the one to keep it? The world and mankind were balanced so long as they were still held fast in the Absolute. Now the world is in the domain of the relative, in the phantasm of time and space which is governed by the principle of the struggle for existence, is subject to death and corruption. And what the average man means by balance is the worst and most dangerous one-sidedness into which he can fall, the renunciation of his heavenly birthright for the pottage of this sinful world. And it is precisely this sinful balance that the Christian must upset, as St Paul also will have it upset, when he beholds the groaning of man conspiring with the groaning of every creature to hasten by the force of this universal conjuration the " day of Christ," when the world will be transfigured by the glory of God's adoption. We have already enough and to spare of those accursed artists of balance who here on earth presume to dream of the identity of all life. How right he was there, though he never even heard the name of the most celebrated advocate of balance among his countrymen, André Gide, who from sheer balance has lost Christ, his soul and his entire faith in God. For this reason he, Léon Bloy, had determined to shatter this balance and in face of the world to dream out his dream of the Absolute with a clamorous relentlessness. Moreover it is the only dream which is not a dream but the beginning of the eternal reality. " I am a poor man who with tears and loud cries runs along all roads calling upon my God and seeking Him."

" For more than a quarter of a century," wrote Bloy in his diary, *The Pilgrim of the Absolute,* " I have endured every hardship to obtain one day by my literary value sufficient prestige to occupy a chair of the supernatural from which I can address souls. For in truth I have something to tell them, something which has been entrusted to me for them and which no one else can tell them." This message is that new word of which he had already spoken in his first novel and whose utterance he regarded with a conviction increasingly intense, as *his mission.* We have no need to puzzle our heads with the enquiry what, in his belief, has been given to him and moreover to him alone for the benefit of souls. We have spoken enough about him to know that it was the "absolute" view of life and religion. To preach this to men and give them an example of it in his own life: this was Bloy's mission.

Was his mission genuine or merely imaginary and usurped? That Bloy's temperament and fashion of speech might well grate even upon religious men and that his air of a grand inquisitor—he himself gives the title to his hero Marchenoir—must antagonize the sensibilities of ecclesiastical circles is obvious. That is a matter by itself, and the question of his mission another matter altogether. With his intensely vital Catholic sentiment, it was impossible for Bloy to doubt that the universal priesthood of Christians left a place in the Church beside the official priesthood for the layman who preaches religious truth and ministers to souls. It is a view which has been officially sanctioned by the summons to Catholic Action. Every man in the Catholic camp, Bloy replied to his opponents, has his mission. Why should I alone have none? It is true. In real life every genuinely intelligent and spiritual person is marked by a distinctive vocation, a mission. That mission is simply the recognition that he occupies in the universe a place appointed and predestined for him. The more spiritually a man lives—which he does when he aims at union with the Divine Spirit in a permanent state of religious contemplation—the more is he filled by an idea which is in him, though he is not the source of it. This idea is in him before he has conceptual knowledge of it; and the development of his personal life is nothing but its progressive self-revelation. If the career of a Péguy or a Bloy arouses such profound human interest it is undoubtedly due to its extremely clear and distinct expression of this mysterious process. We behold at work in such lives an exceptional fidelity towards self, to the profoundest self which cancels and overcomes all petty caprices and mistakes, conscious or unconscious, in the higher and final truth. To be sure it is only after the subject's death that a mission is revealed in the original splendour and purity of its idea; because death alone frees it from all the stains with which the process of its earthly embodiment had inevitably defiled and overlaid it.

More than many other chosen souls, " the pilgrim of the Absolute " suffered the tragedy of what Péguy profoundly styled the "pitiful actuality." Nor was it only in the objective sense. With all respect be it said, in face of the Absolute Bloy felt his own shortcoming and unworthiness as a stigma and brand of infamy, a searing pain. " Everything that I write here must appear exaggerated, because no one but myself could know all the affliction of my soul, it would break your heart. But just consider this: I live with a single thought, a single emotion and that so intense that finally my will, my memory, and the nerve centre of my mental faculties have been consumed by it." (*Letters to his Fiancée*) Gide has an easier time with *his* severe harmony. When a man throws away his soul it is not difficult to worship with what little of him yet survives the "identity of all life" as the ultimate law. But when a man would far sooner throw away his body, thereby the more nimbly to follow his soul and the better to realize the heavenly identity of this soul and the whole of life, his life is a hard one. It is no light matter to be a pilgrim of the Absolute and to be compelled to drag along with one the heavy burden of the flesh and rebellious nature. Bloy was no Manichee. But in the painful days of his last illness he dismissed expressions of sympathy with a remark in which we can catch a note of sarcastic satisfaction: "I am suffering for the baseness of my nature." At the crisis of a life too tightly strained, it comes naturally to such a man to offer God the ultimatum of death or glory. And it is as natural to him later to be ashamed of it and to recognize that this is sheer nonsense and that he has far more important things to do. What are they? He replies by the mouth of his "poor woman": "There is only one sorrow, not to be a Saint."

Is this the language of the heroine in a novel, the artificial desire of an artificial human being? Most certainly not. Bloy the novelist was no objective creator. His characters are always himself or people like himself. They never go beyond the sphere of his most personal problems, an area which can never be enlarged but at most deepened. When he wrote *The Poor Woman,* the process of deepening had already begun, and it was a descent in the dimension of holiness. He felt with increasing intensity that he had no alternative, that in no other way could he fulfil his vocation to be the missionary of the Absolute. For what does it avail to assume prophetic attitudes—though Bloy does not say this in so many words, we take the liberty of secretly tracking the processes of his tragic thought—and fill your mouth with the Absolute and all the while attempt by importunity and clamour to bend and dispose the Absolute to your personal views and will? With it all you do not bring the Absolute into yourself, you are and you remain essentially not absolute, but relative, and He who is the Absolute in person, though you call Him Father, is to you the wholly other. You do not understand Him in this world. Give up commanding Him, begin to obey Him. Seek Him in the night of the faith which He has given to you as to all others. Seek Him as the Saints seek Him by opening your arms and your heart with a blind trust, whatever happens, knowing that whatever happens comes from Him and leads to Him. Then suddenly in impenetrable night you will sink down upon the breast of a friend who, how no man knows, has found you in the midst of the night and this friend will prove to be Himself.

"The friend of God! When the thought comes into my mind, I begin to weep. I no longer know on what block to lay my head, where I am, or where to go. One's heart burns so in one's breast that one would fain tear it out; and it is impossible to look at any creature without being overpowered by love. One would like to drag oneself on one's knees from one church to another with rotten fish hung round one's neck, as the great Angela says. And when one leaves these churches after hours in which one has talked to God, as a lover to his beloved, one pictures oneself as one of those poor ill-drawn and ill-painted figures in the Stations of the Cross who move across gold backgrounds with devout and simple gesture. Then all the thoughts hitherto unknown because they were imprisoned in the recesses of the heart come running up together like tormented and blinded maidens, like hungry and naked maidens bathed in tears. Yes, there is no doubt, at such moments of all possible forms of martyrdom you would choose the most frightful—and with what enthusiasm."

We repeat, this utterance is not the fleeting suggestion of a pious mood, but the bitter fruit of an unremitting process of self-discovery. In 1890, that is to say before he wrote *The Poor Woman,* he wrote to his fiancée: " For a long time I have been very clearly conscious at the bottom of my heart, an impression arising from a profound and mysterious reality, that I am not what I should be, do not possess what I should possess, have in some way lost an inheritance which is mine by right and has now come into the possession of others who are not entitled to it. I know that the notion seems foolish. But I have never been able to get rid of it, not even in prayer."

On the contrary it grew as time went on into the tragic conviction that his life was a failure. In one of his last diaries written between 1913 and 1915 (*On the Threshold of the Apocalypse*) there is a touching letter to a sorely tried friend. Is he, Bloy, the man to comfort him? As though he were a pillar on which a man could lean. A broken and ruined pillar perhaps but nothing more. " The little I possess God has given me without my co-operation and what have I made of it? The worst is not the wrong that I have done, but the good that I could have done and have not done. This is the sin of omission which again is nothing but the sin of not loving, a sin of which no one accuses himself. Any one who watched me at the first Mass every morning would see me often weep. They might be holy tears; they are in fact only very bitter tears. I am not thinking of my sins, some of which are fearful. I am thinking of what I might have done and have failed to do, and that I assure you is heinous, very heinous. Do not reply that the entire world is in the same case. God has given me the sense, the need—I don't know how to put it—the instinct for the Absolute as he gave the hedgehog its prickles and the elephant its trunk. It is an extremely rare gift of which I have been aware from my childhood, a more dangerous faculty and more pregnant with suffering than genius even. For it involves an insatiable and ravenous hunger for what the earth does not contain and its effect upon its possessor is an unbounded loneliness. I might have become a Saint, a miracle worker. I have become an author. I have written sentences and pages which are admired. If my admirers but knew that these are simply the relics, the dregs of a supernatural endowment, which I have shamefully spoiled and for which an account will be demanded which fills me with terror! I have not done what God wanted for me; that is certain. On the contrary, I have done nothing but *dream I wanted God. And therefore now at the age of sixty-eight I stand before him with nothing but paper* in my hands. I know quite well you won't believe me but will put down what I say to some trick of humility. No, when one is alone, alone in God's presence at the entrance of a very dark road, one knows how one really stands and has no desire to pose. One knows perfectly well that one has not got true goodness, the completely pure and good will, the simplicity of little children, everything that merited a kiss from Jesus' lips, and that one has truly nothing to give to poor and suffering hearts in need of help."

We however know that Bloy has in fact given—and still has to give—gifts of extraordinary value. Apart from the narrow judgements and the outbursts of petulance due to his fanatical temper, all his books are full to overflowing with the spirit of a Catholic and Christian action so passionate and so powerful that we men of to-day with our clever talk of vital Catholicism are reduced to an awestruck silence. Seldom has a layman with hands anointed by the bitterest suffering to the service of God held up before the world with such a loftiness and sublimity the flaming monstrance of the Faith. If the Catholics of his age and country had but shown him half the sympathy and understanding which they kept for minds of incomparably lower literary and religious worth, Bloy would have been the pioneer of a powerful religious movement. He knew this himself. And it was not his weakest motive in becoming a pamphleteer. He knew it. But at the last when he stood at the entrance of the "very dark road" that leads once for all and without return to the Absolute, authentic and manifest, he humbly smote his breast and uttered his *mea culpa*. And this final humility is perhaps the highest and the best which this mystic of holy passion has to give us. He recognized and trampled into dust whatever remained of his self-will, that he had merely dreamed what he wanted from God instead of dreaming what God wanted from him. And that even his holy dream of martyrdom was but the titanic gesture of a holy man who in his very sacrifice of self still sought himself. Such a superhuman renunciation to which, when death approached him, the tempestuous pilgrim of the Absolute stooped like a little child, may well have merited in spite of everything that " kiss from Jesus' lips."

For Bloy passed over like a child happily excited by an approaching journey. To be sure his death occurred under somewhat different circumstances from those he had imagined. But what difference does it make by what route one arrives, provided one arrives? In any case, astounding surprises await us in the native land of the Absolute. As he lay on his deathbed Termier asked him: " What are you feeling, Bloy, in prospect of the last things? " To which Bloy replied: "An enormous curiosity."

PÉGUY

THE GOOD SINNER

It takes creatures of every kind to make a creation, parishioners of every kind to make a parish, and Christians of every kind to make a Christendom.

Charles Péguy

PÉGUY'S name stands for a man and an achievement not easy to estimate. The reader who, unacquainted with the contemporary history of France, takes up one of his numerous books, will be asking himself before a quarter of an hour has passed whether the writer or himself is not perfectly normal, or perhaps, by a heroic exercise of courtesy, to what category of literature the book in question belongs. Suppose for example it is his *Victor Marie, Comte Hugo*. The title naturally makes him expect a literary study of Victor Hugo the poet. This indeed is not excluded in Péguy's intention. But first of all: *solvuntur objecta*. Therefore the first word or rather the first theme which meets the reader on the first page is this " Objections are answered." Criticisms and difficulties are discussed, those, namely, which almost cost him the friendship of Halévy, a collaborator in his *Cahiers de la Quinzaine*. Then it all bursts out like a tempest: recollections of their common experiences, of work, suffering, anxiety, anger and indignation, success and failure, but above all and as a constantly recurring note of war, the fiery combat of ideas, which totally bereft him of rest and peace from the day when he plunged into it. Then suddenly when for a hundred and fifty pages he has stormed, rejoiced and wept—plumb in the middle of these confessions, with nothing to lead up to them, the most valuable, most acute, most professional, yet most unacademic study of Victor Hugo. But it is interwoven with the writer's most personal confessions. Péguy could not have done otherwise. For he is convinced that reality is impossible without personal confessions and that, when we have once had a taste of their reality, any other kind of realism seems very artificial. All his books are passionate autobiography. Or rather they are subject to the constant explosions of a personality in effervescence—literary criticism, politics, poetry, history, philosophy and the philosophy of history. Most certainly Péguy is not always pleasant reading. Even the typography of his books is grotesque and his style so wildly original that it defeated the efforts of Maurice Barrès to secure his protégé a seat in the academy. One writes as one can and must, observed Péguy. "*Opus cuique suum*" (every man has his own work). There are many who are better and purer than we. Many who are more fortunate. Hosts who are braver and holier. But we are real beings, real men, assaulted by cares, scourged by tempests, smitten with afflictions, driven with blows into this pigsty of modern society.

One writes as one can and must. Whether the result is or is not agreeable is for the reader to decide. Péguy wrote as it was dictated to him. Dictated? Certainly, that is his exact expression. When he considered one of his literary works successful he did not say, "I think it is good." He said, "*C'est dicté.*" It was dictated. Dictated by his entire temperament, his character and the heritage of his blood. By the rhythm of the life led by his forefathers as peasants and handicraftsmen. There is good reason for the ennui, and even the positive distaste which in the long run Péguy's fashion of speech provokes in his reader. For he talks and talks, and never stops talking. He talks as a peasant talks, with an assertiveness and a verbosity which do not avoid repetition, but actually delight in repeating the same words. He talks like a peasant on whom God has bestowed the gift of the great orator. His style is stamped with his forbears' life, which is in his blood, by memories of the monotonous strokes of the smith's hammer, of jolting along in the farm waggon, of the tramp of horses' hoofs for hours at a stretch on a lonely country road. The passages in his writing that bear quotation are very few. There are no pregnant condensations, no brilliant phrases which stand out from their context and claim our special attention. On the contrary there is a rank jungle of thoughts, images and words, springing up interlaced and at random, without beginning or end. But in compensation what originality, what natural force, what a vigorous sap of sound human reason, of intelligence, incredibly real and in close touch with life, of simple and profound heroism is there to be found in this primeval forest of Péguy's! Even those who dislike his writings must admit that they could not be different. In them there speaks not only a strong and self-willed personality, but the people of France; there speaks that typically French genius which incarnates the traditional wisdom and the social, religious and mystical aspirations of his race. This is one of the reasons why to-day, twenty years after his death, Charles Péguy is a force in his country as living as he was during his life, indeed more living. Twenty years are a long time; and we might have expected that Péguy would have become by now a figure of the past; the more so since his work was so intimately bound up with his life, and his life in turn with his age. His friends, his collaborators in the

Cahiers de la Quinzaine are now in their sixties. In their memory his voice, his intellectual figure and the heroic music of his life live on with an indestructible magic. When they die, will he not die with them a second and a final death? There seems no prospect of this. In 1933, the name of Charles Péguy is mentioned as frequently in the French press as it was in 1913. Those young Catholics who are destined to share in the intellectual leadership of France display a keener and more passionate interest in him than the Catholic contemporaries of the war. For their programme, a spiritual revolution, understood in a sacred and profoundly religious sense, they can find no symbol more arresting and more inspiring than the name of Péguy. What he himself foresaw and foretold to his friend Lotte has been fulfilled: " The Catholics do not trust me. They will begin to trust me when I am dead."

We are not here primarily concerned with Péguy's contribution to the intellectual life of France, nor even with the values he can contribute to the life of religion in general, though obviously the Catholic intelligentsia of which we have just spoken find them in him. We are concerned with " the case of Péguy " as an extraordinary but nevertheless *typical chapter in the history of the Christian soul*. This man, genuinely a man of the people, represents with an unexampled impressiveness the France robbed by her recent history of her Christian faith, yet cherishing in her subconsciousness an unextinguishable longing for Catholicism, a vocation to the Catholic religion matured by nineteen centuries of Christian and Latin tradition. What moves us so profoundly is the religious adventure of this spirit. When Péguy, in pamphlets which he alone could have written, was fighting for the pure ideals of Socialism, he was fighting without knowing it for Christianity. When he was seeking to sanctify Socialism, he was sanctifying himself. In the attempt to make of Socialism a mysticism and a religion of this world, he found the mysticism and religion of the world above; he found Christ, the Mother of God and the Saints of Heaven; and with tears of joy, for God gave him the gift of tears, he wrote, in his *Cahiers* for Freethinkers, Jews and Protestants, mystery plays about the theological virtues of hope and charity, the Maid of Orleans, the Holy Innocents, Eve and God the Father Himself. He took his place among the great Christian poets. But he did not go to Mass, the Mass for which his heart was hungering. For years he fought his way to Christ and when he had reached Him he fought for Him on the intellectual battlefields of the world and on the far more tempestuous battlefields of his own heart. But he did not receive the Sacraments, and remained outside the Church in which he so ardently believed. *He fought for Christ in his own way as a free lance.* This is the tragic aspect of his great religious adventure. It is for God to judge; for us, to understand.

Charles Péguy was a born fighter. The son of a poor woman of Orleans who earned her living by plaiting cane chairs, even at the Lycée to which he was sent on the recommendation of his elementary school, he made no secret of his Socialist sympathies. If a strike broke out anywhere, you would have seen the small, squat and square-built youth tramping in his nailed shoes from comrade to comrade collecting for the strikers. He never hated, far less despised the bourgeois and gentlefolk whose sons were his school-companions. But they were people to whom he did not and could not belong, people who do not know what poverty is, and cannot even contemplate the possibility of being poor themselves. And he resolved in later life to work—not for the abolition of poverty, a task neither possible nor desirable, for he regarded poverty as something very precious—but for the abolition of the injustice, and the lack of understanding and love, of which poverty is the victim. Social classes and grades there must always be. But Péguy dreamt of a community in which the peasant and the workman occupied the highest rank, because they alone by their labour in poverty and frugality constitute the aristocratic foundation of human society. He dreamt of an approaching revolution, but a revolution which must be made with "a pure heart," and inspired by a passion for justice and truth. Here he saw the task, the great and sole task of his life. He was already levying contributions from his friends and acquaintance. For he must collect a hundred thousand francs to found the paper, " the truthful paper " which would pave the way for the good and genuine revolution. And with his friends' help he had already founded the nucleus of a new revolutionary party which, under the name of " the group of seekers for truth," he sought to affiliate to the official party. No sooner was the name uttered than the congress burst into laughter : " Seekers for truth? What utter nonsense! We have found the truth long ago."

This was the voice of orthodox, practical and official Socialism, the voice of Karl Marx. And Péguy's heart and head were deaf to Marx, though he could quote him from memory, with the page from which his quotation was taken. For what did Marx, or the great French Socialist leader Jaurès know of poverty? They had never really belonged to the poor. Therefore they knew nothing of genuine Socialism. They went to the people; he came from the people. He knew what poverty and toil are, how splendid and holy. This was in fact one of the fundamental experiences of his early life. He derived his real knowledge of Socialism from the handicraftsmen of Orleans and his mother, the maker of chairs. "A tradition which sprang from the depths of our race, its history, demanded as an unqualified obligation, a point of honour, that the leg of a chair should be well made. Every part of the chair which was not visible was as perfect as those portions which were in view. That was the principle on which the cathedrals were built." What did the current Socialism know and what did it care for these natural virtues of the people? It was destroying them. Péguy saw this ever more clearly. He was a Socialist and he remained a Socialist all his life, but not as the proletariate, or the politicians, or even the intelligentsia were Socialists—but as a St Francis or a St Joan were Socialists. *Péguy's* Joan. She was the second great experience of his youth. And the abiding experience which determined the character of his spiritual, mystical and religious life. "Every path which leads to the centre of the French nature must start from Joan," wrote Friedrich Sieburg in his *Gott in Frankreich*. And to understand Péguy we must begin with this marvellous peasant girl. What then has he in common with the Maid of Orleans? Orleans itself. To mention Orleans is to mention Joan of Arc. And Joan of Arc had been Péguy's childhood and the soul of his parish, St Aignan's. Péguy, the scion of peasants and craftsmen, did not forget his childhood. He forgot his parish, became a bitter anti-clerical, denied his Christianity. And not Christianity alone but all faith in God. Among his revolutionary fellow-students none rejected the faith in such uncompromising terms as he. Even the anti-Christian Renan was too religious for him, because he still toyed with metaphysics. He regarded belief in immortality as "a commonplace Paradise of the catechism class," an "ideal for celibates," and any sort of prospect for man transcending this life as "meaningless trifling." "We are concerned with only *one* kind of survival, only one species of immortality, and that is the immortality of the Socialist groups of which we are members."

Yes, Péguy was an atheist, a convinced atheist. But this did not prevent him taking with him in his small trunk, when still a student during his years at the University, a mysterious manuscript at which he worked in secret and which he jealously hid from his friends' eyes. It lay at the bottom of his trunk, neatly packed up and bearing on its wrapper the words, "Please do not touch." He had good cause to conceal it. For it contained the secret of his inner life and that secret was called Joan of Arc. This was actually the title of the manuscript. The Saint and the revolutionary; and the revolutionary under the spell of the Saint! How will this end? The revolutionary of course has no conception. Reason is a short-sighted fellow. Pascal said so. Not, of course, in such crude language, but as a Pascal would put it: "*Le cœur a ses raisons que la raison ne connaît pas.*" Plays on words, especially when they are so pregnant with meaning as this, are not easy to translate. But what he would point out is that the heart perceives truths invisible to reason. Péguy's heart was Joan of Arc. And his heart will save him. The important matter is not that he shall perceive straight away the ultimate goal at which his heart is aiming, but that he obeys his heart. The two brothers, friends of his youth, Jean and Jérôme Tharaud, in the moving biography which they have conjointly dedicated to his memory (*Notre cher Péguy*), have aptly described this mystical relationship: "This girl who with a reckless and unquestioning courage paid no heed to external obstacles or her lawful superiors, and submitted herself neither to the experience of the soldiers, nor the counsel of politicians, nor the admonitions of churchmen; who in a word obeyed only the inspiration of her own soul represented for him the attitude of mind and heart with which a man must enter the social conflict, if he intended to be victorious. The difference of period was immaterial. Joan was in fact the type of the Socialist hero, indeed of the hero in general."

In the person of Joan, Péguy intended to glorify the Socialist heroine, and to sanctify Socialism by giving it for patron Saint the Maid of Orleans. It was a task which left no room for anything besides. He left the University at Paris and fled to Orleans, where alone he could complete the work. Finally there issued from a Socialist press a drama of eight hundred pages, in three parts—"In Domrémy," "The Battlefields," "In Rouen"—with a quaint dedication to all those who "live and die, have lived and died for the Establishment of the world-wide Socialist Republic." It was obviously impossible to produce, and entirely failed to reach the public, which owing to the complete lack of advertisement knew nothing about it. So much the worse for Socialism and the public. Péguy continued to believe in Joan because she was the embodiment of the best, the deepest and the most intimate in his own nature. But in what exactly this better part consisted he has as yet no clear idea. For the moment he called it Socialism, understanding by the term the ideals of brotherhood and justice. Later he borrowed a term from the Christian vocabulary and called it mysticism. Finally he perceived that its true name was just Christianity. A great man is always more than what he knows of himself; his nature is deeper than his understanding of it. When Péguy's conscious reason had to a certain extent caught up with his heart, he would write: "I would be a fool, if I were to let all that go—my peasant ancestry—the faith of my forefathers and Joan of Arc. . . It has been granted me to make a beginning—to state whatever a man can express of his own being in these fourteen or fifteen mysteries, in the single mystery of the life, vocation, sanctity and martyrdom of the greatest Saint that in my opinion has ever existed."

So Péguy will write in 1910, when at last his great tempestuous heart has been caught up by the reason that limps behind it; when the camp-followers of the class war have convinced him, by simply being what they are, that Socialism must inevitably prove a dangerous delusion when it is not a product of the Christian spirit; when he has wholly become a "real man, assaulted by cares, scourged by tempests, smitten with afflictions, driven with blows into this pigsty of modern society." Then he will have lost interest in anything but the mystery of holiness, Joan's or his own. "There is only one way to be holy, only one way to be a Christian, and the drama is always the same—we have simply to look into ourselves." For the moment he still lacked the time to look into himself. For the moment he looked before him and around him, intent on finding the road through the contemporary wilderness, on discovering the Promised Land. He must provide himself with provisions, weapons and comrades. Above all he must fight. Joan was his leader; he will and must conquer. He has only to follow the star of his inner life. If the star, the saintly heroine, refused to shine out upon the world through his drama, she shone in his heart. He has nothing to do but to follow the star. And moreover without delay. A friend died during his service with the army, a victim, Péguy believed, of militarism. His mother and sister were left alone in the world. In a spirit of genuinely Socialistic fellowship with his deceased friend, Péguy considered it his duty to marry the sister. Man is not here for his pleasure. For he felt, as already he could not but feel, that he did not fit into this family of freethinkers of Puritanic austerity and Protestant descent. But it was in accordance with his serious view of life to assume responsibility as early as possible. To found a family seemed to him a more hazardous adventure than to become a monk. The disposition always to choose the more difficult of two alternatives remained characteristic of him throughout his life. The consciousness that in his heroic purpose he had always been the same made him later on show resentment whenever he was called a convert. It was his ambition to be true to himself, not to become a different man. " I don't like those who are called converts. I am not a convert, I have always been Catholic. I've always been an honest man; I have indeed. I've never had a mistress, never. And I've always worked hard, always led a hard and severe life."

Therefore he married. *But* as he had left the University once: to finish his Joan of Arc; he now left it a second time, and for good. To found a family is more important than study. Even more necessary was the regeneration of the Socialist party. That the Socialist movement had become choked by the pettiness of party routine and petrified by party formulas shocked him profoundly. He set his hopes on the Dreyfus case. The deliverance of an innocent Jewish officer condemned to the Devil's Island on a charge of spying, assumed in his powerful imagination the character of a tragedy destined to arouse men's dormant desire for truth and justice and all the noble sentiments without which no revolution is possible. The dawn of the social revolution had broken, the dawn of the great mystical and moral renewal, in which the world should be converted to justice, benevolence and freedom. For *him* it had broken. The hour had come when he, the Socialist heretic, must save Socialism as a spiritual movement. In 1900 he founded the *Cahiers de la Quinzaine* (Fortnightly Sheets) which became celebrated, and which he continued until his death in the first year of the War. And at the same time he purchased the printing works and premises for a bookshop. Here, in his intention, a cell "of genuinely Socialist work" should come into existence, a model in its combination of intellectual and manual labour. And it was actually realized, at least so far as Péguy himself was concerned, who wrote, commissioned others to write, read authors' manuscripts, set them up in type himself, made corrections and, in addition to all this, managed the finances of the undertaking. With his collaborators—many of whom, for example the brothers Tharaud, André Suarès, and Romain Rolland, possess to-day a great reputation in France and abroad—and his fifteen hundred subscribers he intended to constitute the élite of the pure spiritual Socialism. Everything that might assist its construction was to be collected in the *Cahiers*. But the greatest stress was to be laid on the Socialist mysticism.

This somewhat enigmatic conception must not be dismissed as a mere crotchet of Péguy's. It stood for something fundamental in his intellectual outlook, which was inspired in its essential features by the philosophy of Bergson. But more than that it expressed for him the mainspring of the spiritual life, his own life above all. If Bergson's philosophy of the *élan vital* meant so much to him, it was because it was the generalization by a metaphysical genius of an essential law of his personal experience. This vital urge, this intrinsic dynamism which moved him without intermittence and drove him from the surface into the depths, from isolation to the whole, from the individual to the social and from the social to the universal, to the eternal and the divine, to sanctity and salvation—was precisely mysticism. There was no other term for it. Idealism? The word was too colourless, insipid and stale, and above all misleading, because it suggested that the spirit could achieve its salvation apart from the temporal. " Mysticism " exists where the spiritual, " the eternal, enters into the temporal " in virtue of an uninterrupted creative process in man. When Péguy becomes a Christian he will be amazed and delighted to recognize in the central mystery of the Christian faith, the Incarnation, the absolute justification of this mysticism whose vital operation had indeed brought him back to Christianity. His spiritual history, so sincere because it pulsated with a life bleeding at every pore, is a unique proof of the fact that it is the most powerful intellectual motion that leads to Christ, whereas mental inertia has no inkling of the graces hidden in the depths of Christ.

For the moment "mysticism" meant for Péguy the spiritual tension present in every original, living and heroic idea and in every original and heroic human being. Such a human being was Joan of Arc—a real human being. " We are real beings. We are poor, exceedingly poor. But our humanity, our essential humanity must not be confused with the unfortunate parts we play." Joan was a real human being because she had mysticism in her soul and body, was possessed by mysticism. And Péguy considered himself a real man because he was posssesed by the mystical ideal of uniting men under Joan's banner in a new social friendship, not hitherto realized even by Christianity. But if the only real human beings are the heroic mystics, real human beings are few and far between —and Péguy's position was not an easy one. He became ever more aware of it. With growing indignation he discovered how completely "modern society" had become a society of swine. "All these people think 'ready-made' thoughts, feel 'ready-made' emotions, utter 'ready-made' catchwords, pursue 'ready-made' party aims, and cherish a 'ready-made' party truth. How can anything new come into existence under these conditions, that genuine and original novelty which is the product solely of an inspired spirit, of mysticism, and not of politics."

So Péguy began a bitter struggle against what he termed politics. Had he been aware of the noble meaning which Aristotle gave to the term, he would have chosen some other name to denote the opposite of mysticism. He called it politics; but he meant the caricature of genuine politics, that system of universal degradation, into which in practice politics always degenerates as soon as it has lost the "mystical" afflatus. What became of that generous spiritual movement inaugurated by the Dreyfus case? Better that France, our native land, should be ruined, than saved by wronging an innocent man. That was the mysticism of Dreyfusism as Péguy understood it.

And it was in precisely the same way that his Joan of

Arc, the Socialist Saint, understood the mysticism of patriotism. To her it was a moral problem, a conflict between the absolute and the relative, between the end and the means. She entered the war but only " to kill the war." When she learnt from the adventurer Gille de Rais that for the soldiers the war had only one object and that was not to save Christendom by bringing to an end a century of slaughter, but the gratification of the lust for adventure, robbery and pillage, her heart broke. " If the deliverance of France requires such words as Sir Knight has spoken in my presence then... I had rather... France were not delivered."

The revolution of which Péguy dreamed was a spiritual and moral renewal. That was the dream. What was the reality? The reality broke his heart, as in his drama it broke the heart of his heroine. The victory over militarism and clericalism was followed not by the conversion of France to justice and freedom but by its base exploitation for the material interests of the successful party, a senseless anti-clericalism which robbed churches and expelled religious orders, a persistent attack on personal liberty, and the maddening attempt made by the state to rule, enslave and violate the mind and spirit of man by education and a new species of philosophy, justifying its claim on metaphysical grounds. Disappointment upon disappointment. Of what use was it to outpour the vials of his wrath in the *Cahiers* which became increasingly a court of justice to whose bar he summoned the great offenders against the human spirit and against liberty, the professional politicians and the intellectuals who, perverted into politicians, murdered the "mysticism" of the new movement? What did it avail to state an unanswerable case against them? The politicians triumphed; the mystic was defeated. It could not go on like this. Neither with the *Cahiers* nor with himself. Many subscribers found the attitude of the periodical far too mystical for their taste. They scented already a religious inspiration behind it. So they ceased to subscribe. Deprived of the financial assistance of the powerful political friends he had been compelled to surrender, Péguy could no longer surmount the growing difficulties. Overwork made him ill. And his ill-health was increased by anxieties of a wholly private nature of which even his closest associates had no suspicion. In the September of 1908 a man who had been his friend from youth and shared his outlook, Joseph Lotte, an author and professor of philosophy, found Péguy in a state of complete exhaustion on the brink of physical and mental breakdown. Péguy complained that he was weary of life and told Lotte that he was longing for rest, for an appointment in some provincial Lycée where he could be free from his worries and would be able to give out what was in his heart. Then suddenly with tears in his eyes, "I have not told you everything. . . I have regained my faith. . . I am a Catholic." What followed is memorable and enables us to understand the power over souls which Péguy still exercises to-day so long after his death. From the very first moment in which he professed himself a servant of Christ he won souls for Him. Lotte, who relates the episode, continues: "Suddenly, something in the nature of a powerful emotion of love took hold of me. My heart melted and weeping hot tears, my head in my hands, I said to him almost against my will, 'My poor old friend, we have all reached that point.' 'We have all reached that point'—how did those words come to my lips who at the moment was still an unbeliever? Of what interior travail, of what slow, obscure and profound spiritual process were they the outer revelation? At that moment I felt that I had become a Christian." And Lotte had been a tough unbeliever. Neither the deaths following in rapid succession of his little daughter and his young wife had softened him, nor the touching deathbed of the fifteen-year-old son of the novelist Emil Baumann, a boy whom he loved as a younger brother. A quarter of an hour before his death the boy had made a last appeal to him. "Lotte, kneel down, make the sign of the Cross and promise me you will be converted." It was to no purpose. Péguy obtained his conversion without asking for it. An immediate complete and formal conversion. In the *Bulletin des professeurs catholiques de l'Université* which he founded in 1910 he came forward as the untiring Apostle of a strictly Catholic and Eucharistic life. What then did Péguy do, the first begotten of grace in this holy quest?

Hic incipit tragœdia — here the tragedy begins. Or rather let us say, since tragedy is perhaps too gloomy a term: here begins *the real drama of Péguy's battle with Christ.* Hitherto he had struggled *for* Christ and most of the time without being aware of it. At last the truth began to dawn upon him and finally the day came when he saw clearly that when he sought the pure and complete Socialism he was at bottom seeking Christianity. For a man who had once declared with a careless shrug of the shoulders that the millennium and a half of ancestral Christianity had vanished from him without leaving a trace it was a shattering discovery. All his life he sought a home for his profound and earnest soul and its heroic aspirations. It must be a *home,* not one of those fusty caves and jerry-built slums of a stolid positivism and superficial individualism in which the great mystical community of mankind cannot possibly live. Péguy had this essential trait in common with Soloviev, a writer completely unknown to him and not otherwise intellectually akin, that he could think only in terms of human solidarity. A deeper study of his spiritual history has established beyond doubt that the rock on which his faith split was not levity of mind or laxity of conduct but the Catholic dogma of hell. "We are one with the eternally damned. We cannot admit that there are human beings who must be thrust away from the entrance of any community."

We must never lose sight of the fact that this fierce fighter in the war of ideas was at the same time a man of profound contemplation, for whom ideas were no mere intellectual play without binding force, but represented the essence of reality. We make it more difficult to understand Péguy if, by applying a superficial standard of classification, we attempt to place him among the anti-intellectualists. What then of his trumpetings against the "party of the intellectuals"? They were never directed against those "who pursue philosophy in the accurate, that is in the honourable and morally noble sense of the term." They were directed against those modern scientists who detest the eternal philosophy of mankind, suck and bore out the spirit until it has shrivelled into that disgusting and pitiful thing which arrogantly entitles itself "modern freedom from prejudices." "The battle is not being fought between the heroes and the Saints; it is being fought against the intellectuals who scorn equally the heroes and the Saints. . . Everything whose mission it is, a mission officially bestowed, to safeguard culture, everything whose appointed task it is to protect culture and the humanities is betraying culture and the humanities. Culture and the humanities are now defended only by us who have received no commission to defend them. . Once again the Sorbonne has capitulated to scholasticism. And it is to the scholasticism of materialism, the worst of all scholasticisms." This then is Péguy's anti-intellectualism. It is simply an anti-rationalism, an attitude of mind which submits objects to the criteria, not of the intelligence alone, but of the heart also. Only an anti-rationalist, not a man who depreciates the intellect could write the following words. " When we behold and verify the loss of a metaphysic, of a religion and a philosophy we must not be content with saying that it has been lost. We must understand that together with it we ourselves have been lost in the same measure. . . When a metaphysic and a religion, when a philosophy vanishes from mankind, it is equally true, if not truer, to say that mankind has vanished from that metaphysic and that religion, from that philosophy. An intellect which is beginning to outgrow a philosophy is simply a soul which is ceasing to be in harmony with its tone and rhythm, its speech and its echoes. When we have lost this harmony we say that we are beginning to feel emancipated."

What a profound insight and intuitive vision Péguy shows here of the laws that determine human nature. Only a man who has himself experienced it could express himself like this—a man who has experienced in his own life that he himself has vanished, is no longer a real being, when philosophy, metaphysics and religion vanish from him. But Péguy was too deep, too essentially real to continue permanently under the illusion that he was "emancipated," when he had merely ceased to be " in harmony " with his Christian heritage. But had he ever ceased to be in harmony with it? Intellectually yes, but not in his heart. What then was his "mysticism"—which God knows was anything rather than a vague romanticism—but the undying echo of this abidingly human harmony? What was this affection for Joan of Arc, so strange in a Socialist, but a bridge never broken between himself and the Communion of Saints? What is more—throughout the entire period of his incredulity, which began about his twentieth year, he never descended from this bridge which offered him a passage into that vast community. For we must again insist, no idea in the world, in time or in eternity was dearer to him than this. Life had no object, had not the least significance, if there were no community.

But if he experienced so profoundly the mystery of communion, why did he not remain in the communion in which his birth of Catholic parents and his baptism had placed him? This question confronts us with the central secret in the drama of Péguy's life. If we can answer the question *why Péguy left the Church,* we shall have some prospect of answering *the second question, why in spite of his prodigious exertion and even his Christian heroism in the literal sense of the term he never returned to the external communion of the Church.*

Péguy's conduct after this September of 1908, after his conversion, to employ for brevity this not wholly suitable term, remains absolutely unintelligible so long as it is judged in the light of his outward activities. "I am a Catholic," he said. And no profession of Catholicism, wherever and however made, could be more sincere and inspired by a more whole-hearted conviction than this cry from his sick-bed which burst from a soul matured by bitter suffering and burning insights. But what action did Péguy take, what followed? In any case it was most certainly not what his Catholic friends expected of him. He had Catholic friends. There was the friend of his youth, Baillet, who had made the atheist Péguy, during his time at the University, president of the Conference of St Vincent de Paul—he was dispensed from the opening prayer—and who, on his return from a long journey abroad, instead of going back to his father's home went straight into a Benedictine monastery. Every day until his death Dom Baillet had offered his Mass for Péguy because he was unshakeably convinced that a man of such nobility of heart and mind could not finally be lost to God. And there was Jacques Maritain, well known, even in German-speaking countries, as a neo-thomist philosopher. He was not always a neo-thomist. He had stood at the opposite philosophic pole. Spiritually France is a land of limitless possibilities. Maritain was a Protestant; and that only on his baptismal certificate. He was a rabid free-thinker who from a nook in Péguy's printing house published a children's paper designed to inspire French children with a loathing for the clergy and the army. But in secularized France the expectations of free thought are very often disappointed. Who would have dreamt that Bergson, the mild Jewish mage of philosophic speculation, would have provoked such powerful spiritual explosions by lectures delivered to a fashionable audience at midday on Fridays? This Jew who only to-day has come to believe in a personal God helped Péguy and Maritain among many others towards Catholicism, by clearing the road of the spirit from materialist, positivist and intellectualist barriers. But Maritain in conformity with his temperament at one bold leap jumped over the intermediate stage straight into a life of Catholic practice and replaced

Bergson as his teacher by St Thomas, whereas Péguy. . . Yes, what did Péguy do? Maritain could no longer understand him. After this profession of faith bestowed upon him by an extraordinary grace it only remained for him, thought Maritain, to make his confession and communion, complete his civil by a religious marriage and have his children baptized. There can be no doubt that *he* would have cut the Gordian knot of these domestic difficulties at a stroke. For Péguy they were insuperable. How could he, who never bowed to the bare command of any authority, do violence to his wife's free-will, by compelling her to submit to the baptism of her children and be remarried in church? If it would give Maritain any satisfaction, he might try to persuade her to change her mind. He was sufficiently ardent or at least sufficiently brave to make the attempt. But he had no success. Then Péguy must at any rate make public profession of his altered convictions by having the children over whom he had sole authority baptized and thus obtain the right to receive the Sacraments. He was shaken but a few days later he wrote to Maritain: "I have thoroughly thought over what you said to me the last time we met. I have prayed much over it. The course you advise seems to me not only unseasonable at the present juncture but no way of escape from the actual difficulty. . . Please do not add to my troubles which are boundless. I have examined my conscience and can see in those things only trials which are indeed terrible but which with the help of God I shall overcome. . ."

But the most terrible feature of the situation was the fact that the way of escape decided upon by Péguy himself was anything but a way of escape. It merely rendered the torment perpetual.

Maritain's sister, a recent convert and very anxious about their common friend, paid him a visit. "How are you," she enquired. "In a thoroughly bad way. It's all over with me. My liver-disease is devouring me. I have not much longer to live." "Is there no other disease which is eating up your strength?" "Ah, you know it then; everything comes back to that; I am suffering terribly; I'd like to die." "Before you have lived as Our Lord asks of you?" "I am tired, at the end of my tether, worn out. I've made a hash of my life in this world." "You can change your life if you will change your heart. But you can do nothing without Jesus." "I pray constantly. But I am fearfully unhappy all the same." The girl replied that she was not surprised, since he took no steps to carry his Christian life any further. "I receive graces of which you have no conception," he burst out passionately. "For that very reason you should be unboundedly thankful to God and prove your gratitude." "My life is hard. I am broken up. Strife at home. I am suffering terribly." "It's your fault, my dear Péguy. You can put it right. How can you expect your wife to change her attitude if you are gloomy, distracted and no doubt also nervy and unjust in your daily life with her." To which he answered with tears in his eyes: "*Oh if only I could receive communion.*" This was Péguy's struggle with Jesus in whom not only did he believe but for whom he was consumed till the end of his life by an inextinguishable longing but whom he could not find where He is most certainly to be found, according to the teaching of the creed which Péguy so ardently professed. As the girl saw him standing before her pale and livid, veritably torn in pieces by his inner conflict, and with heart-felt compassion commended him to the Mother of

God, words of profound insight fell from her lips: "My friend, I am afraid you take pleasure in your suffering... You do not love God as one should. You live in a state of depression and perplexity. But God created us to live in joy." The tears burst out afresh. "That is true; *lack of trust is my sin...* Oh to find peace, peace with Jesus!"

It is absolutely necessary to keep this scene before our eyes, if we would not judge Péguy's illogical conduct more severely than He judges it whose heart hungers for love and to whom therefore earth can perhaps afford nothing more wonderful than a human heart on fire with a supreme love, though perplexed and tragically torn asunder. And Péguy's longing for peace with Jesus was not, as it is for so many believers, a fashion of speech borrowed from books of devotion and never personally realized, but to his life's end a genuine and concrete suffering felt night and day. It was an open wound always bleeding, as an utterance preserved by the critic Henri Massis too plainly suggests. "I never go to Mass. I can never hear Mass, never assist at the Holy Sacrifice. It would be too painful for me. I could not get through it. It would do me harm. I go to Church, to any church, to pray, but always before Mass, before the Mass begins." Why did he, who would go to Jesus at any cost, keep away from the Sacraments which Jesus has instituted as the way to a living communion with Himself? It is difficult to believe that the sole reason was the opposition which he feared from his wife. His wife who was still living, after Péguy's death, entirely of her own accord and without any external pressure, entered the Church with her children. Something more profound must have underlain this terrible mystery. A soul of Péguy's stamp is not made the victim of tragedy by purely external circumstances.

The sole reason was the difficulties of his inner life which prevented his finding peace. He was faced with a problem of an entirely personal character which he was spiritually and intellectually incapable of solving. That girl had an inkling of it when in a sudden flash of illumination she replied to his obstinacy with the rejoinder " I am afraid you take pleasure in your suffering." It was the truth. Péguy *would* not be relieved of his interior sufferings. But he would not, because he *could* not. He could not as yet. Maritain's sister did not understand this, and Maritain the logician even less. Therefore Péguy broke with him. Maritain, he concluded, cannot wait. God is not impatient. God has time for the poor perplexed soul, and a better method of employing time than the syllogistic. The sole result of his conversation with Maritain's sister was the conviction that his sin, his particular and essential sin, was lack of trust in God. And his nature happened to be such that it became increasingly plain to him that no one could help him but God alone. Only God knew and understood the obstacle that he could not surmount and why he could not surmount it. " The clergy cannot help in this matter," he maintained. And this was not pride but at worst a mistake. In the same way it was no fundamental hostility to reason when he refused the advice to read St Thomas given him by Maritain (who regarded his Christianity without the Sacraments as Bergsonism transposed into the language of Christian mysticism) and refused in the following terms: " Don't bother me with your St Thomas. . . I would give the entire Summa for the Ave Maria and the Salve Regina. The certainty of faith is not attained by arguments. . . Your Thomas is an algebra in which I find nothing for my soul. . . "

If this is not hostility to reason, not a verdict against

St Thomas delivered as the considered judgment of the mind, what pray is it? The cry of a soul in anguish, a soul that has no need to begin by convincing itself of its faith by philosophic and theological considerations. What purpose would that serve? "We believe the entire contents of the catechism, and its contents have become and remain our flesh and blood." It is the cry of a soul that possesses the faith and because it possesses it not simply as theoretical conviction but as a living experience, has been gripped to the marrow by a particular dogma of this faith, and plunged by it into hopeless anguish. It was for this reason that Péguy felt that he personally, "who had no desire to be a father of the Church but simply her son," could not be helped by any argument, but only by faith, hope and charity. The last was what he lacked; herein lay *his* sin. He must fling himself into the abyss of God's love, with the last effort of his faith and hope. He must just let himself fall into it, abandoning every created support and stay, upheld by nothing save faith and hope. Yes, he must risk his own salvation, perhaps even sacrifice his own eternal bliss. But this precisely was the stake of the fearful venture, that became the obsession of his last years: to vanquish the abyss of hell ever yawning before his eyes and unendurable to his heart, by throwing open an abyss even deeper, more eternal and of mightier reality, the Divine Love.

Péguy wrestled with Christ about hell. It was an enterprise the reverse of commonplace, rarely to be found among Christians. The French writer Bernanos, in his novels which have become famous, *Sous le Soleil de Satan* and *L'Apostat,* has depicted characters who have believed it to be their vocation to snatch a particular soul from hell by a sacrifice of their lives offered in the inmost depths of the soul. Such people are not confined to novels but exist also in real life. History knows of mystics who took damnation upon themselves to save one soul already lost. The logician can but shake his head at this. But what at the bar of logic is nonsense may at the bar of the heart be approved as profound wisdom and a sign of deep and genuine humanity. Péguy desired to rescue from hell not a single soul but all the lost souls. It was a prodigious error which reveals at the same time his inadequate theology and his noble heart.

For we must make a distinction. The protest against hell may conceal the turpitude of a soul that would indulge its lusts without restraint and escape the sanctions of Divine justice. But it can also express the magnanimity of a soul that feels the eternal exclusion from the organic community of mankind of any who were once its living members as an unutterable personal torment. This was the case with Péguy. Any one who would have approached him with the cold and clear deliverances of theological logic would merely have bolted more firmly upon him the prison house of his suffering. For him it was not a theological problem, but a personal anguish. The consciousness of such suffering isolates the sufferer. Hence his distrust of the clergy and his breach with Maritain. Only a theologian who combined with his science experience of the same anguish and a profound and understanding charity might conceivably have helped him. He found no such man, probably because he did not search for him. Pain, every profound experience of the suffering of the world, makes its victim lonely. We frankly admit that we are seeking to enlist the reader's sympathy for a man whose spirit was seared by the problem of suffering in its most acute form, the eternity of suffering in hell. Hell is a mystery from which only the Saint has the right not to shrink.

The best way to see Péguy's case in the right light is to apply to it the profound and understanding observations upon the problem of suffering made by Alois Wurm (*Seele,* June 1933): " It must be possible to view all the dark and dreadful things in the world and in our lives on earth, for example the spectacle of children killed by the victim of a sudden access of suicidal mania, in a different light *with an inward vision which essentially alters our estimate of them.* The tragic emotion, whose deepest core contains an acceptance, is a symptom spread throughout the human race of this perception. There is an ultimate significance and context in which we can accept even the most atrocious evils of human life and history, an inner aspect of those very evils in which their sensible frightfulness has lost its terrors. God sees things in this light. He views them from every aspect and *therefore in His eyes what from the only standpoint accessible to us impresses us most powerfully is relegated to a subordinate position.* Were things only what they appear to us, *if God saw them in that light, His bliss would be impossible.* But He sees them in their integrity. The man whose soul is filled by God shares to some extent, as a dim apprehension, which however is more positive than the intuition lurking in our sense of the tragic, God's inner vision of things which in heaven we may hope to share in perfect clearness. . . And if we are among the number of those who will never on earth be wholly possessed by God, we are indeed exposed far more helplessly to the dark torrent of the world's pain, but on the other hand, are more closely linked in heart, blood and nerves with our human brothers than are those chosen few."

This expresses the case exactly. It was given to Péguy to experience profoundly the mystery of hell, but not as a man filled with God, but from the human point of view, from the standpoint of human solidarity, the kinship of the human family of common blood and jealous for its members, which in a sense he emphasized as against God. This can be clearly seen in the first version of his *Joan of Arc.* The Saint chosen by Péguy as patroness of the new Socialist community of mankind cannot refrain from remonstrating with God against hell. "When I consider," thus she addresses God, "that at this very moment that I am speaking with Thee, all my words find Thee occupied in damning souls. . ." She will suffer anything, take any suffering upon herself, if only the nightmare of hell may vanish from existence.

"If to save from the eternal flames the bodies of the damned that despair in their torment, I must yield my own body to the everlasting fires, then, O God, thrust me into the everlasting fires."

"If to save lost souls from the torment of eternal banishment from Thee souls that despair in their banishment I must devote my own soul to everlasting banishment then, O God, let everlasting banishment be my lot. . ."

It is most significant that Péguy incorporated these verses exactly as they stood into his later poem on Joan, *Le Mystère de la Charité de Jeanne d'Arc.* In all those years the problem of eternal damnation had never been absent. On the contrary his return to the faith had made it once more acute. If the original *Joan of Arc* was essentially a struggle with the evil that afflicts mankind in all its forms, the second was from beginning to end a struggle with the metaphysical and eternal embodiment of evil, damnation.

We must not forget that in all his books Péguy wrote his autobiography. His writings are a direct response to the problems of his personal life. When he cut himself loose from the official system of education, when his patriotism awoke to full consciousness, when he recognized in the magnates of finance the poison of the modern world—in every instance his spiritual discovery discharged itself explosively in a book. In 1908, not by conversion but, as he put it, by a simple organic "deepening of the heart," he became once more a Catholic. From henceforward the only true human community is the communion of Saints. The discovery gave him enormous joy. He shed tears of happiness, revelled in his new knowledge. But then the old metaphysical terror took hold of him once more. Hell remained an ever-present reality, that incomprehensible and awful restriction of the beloved community of God and mankind.

Should he deny it? Most certainly not. Either a man has the faith or he has not. It is impossible to find any middle position between faith and infidelity. He believed the entire content of the catechism, and since he believed it, he must also believe in hell. But what then would be the lot of his dear ones, of his wife, his children, his friends? What noble characters were to be found among these Protestants, Jews and free-thinkers! "I know Jews," he remarked, "who possess extraordinary graces and Catholics who possess none." To a lady who was a free-thinker he wrote: "My dear friend, your little finger is more Christian than the entire person of all these imbeciles." What then was to become of all these good people? Was he to enter the boat of the Sacraments and reach safety and abandon the others to sink or swim? If the teaching of the Church bade him save his own soul, his conscience and the dictates of his heart forbade him to leave them to their fate. That was how he looked at the matter. Obviously he was mistaken. He would not have been in the very least obliged to abandon the others to their fate, had he obeyed the logic of his faith, received the Sacraments and made an external profession of his Catholicism. But being the man he was, he could not bring himself to take the step. As Maritain's sister had intuitively perceived, he took pleasure in his suffering. And the necessity that he felt of living in a tragic situation sprang from his innate heroism, which bade him choose the hardest course and at the risk of his own salvation cleave to those whose salvation was in the greatest peril. It was a sublime and moving example of a perplexed or what theologians term an invincibly erroneous conscience.

In any case we have no doubt that this was the root of the illogical attitude adopted by Péguy after his return to the faith. He made it difficult for his contemporaries and successors to find the key to his conduct, because he never mentioned his secret directly. This pamphleteer observed the strictest reticence in regard to his inner life. He hid his heaviest sorrows in his mystery poems and there he placed them in the heart and on the lips of his characters. For example in *Le Mystère de la Charité de Jeanne d'Arc,* the future Saint, when still a child, fights out Péguy's personal struggle with hell. The book, which we can scarcely term a drama, since it has only three characters, no action, and consists in the main of a meditation performed in a state of trance, remains obscure, chaotic and shapeless until we have realized that the *leit motiv* of the entire work is this problem of damnation, which moreover explains the enigmatic title of the book. It may perhaps be possible, for Péguy will not affirm it positively, to abolish hell by the mystery of love.

For the little Joan all the misery, outer and inner, of the Hundred Years' war between France and England is focussed in the problem of eternal damnation. The victims injured or slain by the war do not merely lose possessions and life; they lose their faith in God and eternal life. "And so to whichever side you turn, on both sides you witness the same play, a play in which whatever the fashion and motive with which it is played, it is always salvation that loses, always perdition that wins; and there is nothing but the loss of grace, nothing but perdition and damnation. When Joan obtains a meeting with Gervaise the mystical nun, her chief object is to receive some consolation, the hope that a candle may be lit in the lonely darkness of her melancholy, the pain of her abandonment by God. " I can bear no more; I can go on like this no longer. Oh that death would come to me quickly, quickly. My God, have compassion upon our poor human lives, in which those we love are eternally separated from us." Like a wild beast confined in a cage, she turns round and round, runs backwards and forwards within the charmed circle of this thought of damnation. Willingly would she be damned by God, if her voluntary damnation might redeem the others from the damnation imposed upon them. For there would then be only one sufferer, herself, and her suffering would at least not be barren. But in God's world there is wasted suffering,

suffering everlastingly barren. It avails nothing that Sister Gervaise shares with Joan her sublime visions of the communion of Saints, founded by the suffering and dying Christ. As an incurable wound wakes a sick man from the sleep he has obtained with such difficulty, the question that she cannot lay to rest always intrudes itself into these consoling visions. "Is it possible that there is so much wasted suffering?"

To this question there is only one answer. It is possible, because it is a fact. There is a suffering from which not even Jesus, the Redeemer, can redeem us. Was not His cry of anguish on the Cross, "that unnatural sound of a blasphemy on the lips of God," extorted by His knowledge of that suffering from which there is no redemption? And even Gervaise, her comforter, is obliged to admit: "Hell is a mystery, the greatest mystery of creation. It is a greater mystery than the Incarnation and Redemption, than the mystery of the Incarnation and the mystery of the Redemption. For the suffering of Christ—at least we see its purpose. . . " If she does not know what purpose is served by the suffering of the damned, she knows at any rate that the suffering of Christ is an everlasting and inexhaustible treasury of graces. And we are in God's hand. It is not for us to demand an account from God, we must trust Him. Madame Gervaise sings the canticle of trust in almighty Love. She sings it throughout the book in every tone and key. Little Joan, on the other hand, does nothing else from the first page to the last but repeat the brief words which utter the vast despair by which she is possessed. "We see, you see, that even Christendom, the whole of Christendom, is slipping down gradually and deliberately into damnation, is slipping down into damnation. What if that were the universal rule?" To which Sister Gervaise replies for the tenth time: "We shall see, we shall see, my child. What can you see? What can you know? What do we know? We shall see this later. Let God's will de done, let Him come. The world is going to ruin; the world is sinking into damnation. That you see, that you have observed. How long? Let us say eight years. You have heard your elders say it. How long have they been saying it? Forty, fifty years. Let us suppose that it has been said from father to son for a hundred and fifty years. What does that amount to? What are a hundred and fifty years in comparison with what was promised to the Church? And even if it were thirteen hundred years. What are centuries of days, centuries of years? What are centuries of minutes? There will be centuries of centuries. We belong to the eternal Church. We live in the eternal Christendom. In the eternal Christendom. This age has come, other ages will come. What do centuries of centuries weigh in the scale of eternity? The true, the real eternity. In view of the eternal promises, the promises made to the Church. In view of the promises. In prospect of the promises what imports the event, the poor pitiful event and everything that happens? What then do we know? What can we see? But whatever may be the truth, it is the concern of God. Christendom is His, the Church is His. If I have made my prayer well and borne my suffering well, He hears me according to His will. It is not for us or for any man to call Him to account. We are in His hands. The ways of God are unsearchable." And she dismisses Joan with the words: "God be with you my child. May Jesus our Saviour save thy soul for ever."

On this problem, nothing further can be said. On the subject of everlasting bliss and damnation the believer has no other light than an unconditional trust in the Divine Love. This is the lesson which the girl Joan, and with her Péguy, learned from Gervaise the mystic. "The mystery of love" is the power, the only power, which conquers hell. To a reader who has never worried over the problem of hell, the statement means little. To Péguy it was the quintessence of the continuous meditation of two years, a meditation that questioned and complained, to conclude with a jubilation of exultant hope, and found concrete embodiment in this book of Joan of Arc. The reader will ask to what extent did this meditation Péguy help to deal with the problem of damnation that tormented him so sorely. The indications at our disposal go to show that inwardly he approached the solution as closely as is possible. And the only solution is a faith in the universality of redemption that takes possession of the entire soul. But outwardly in his relation to the visible Church this powerful and intense struggle with the problem did not advance him a step. Indeed we have reason to suppose that it was when the mystery of Joan's love, that obstinate love which refuses to surrender even the lost, had become fully alive in him, that he finally decided to take the path of trust rather than the road of the Sacraments. Sister Gervaise's parting words to Joan: "May Jesus our Saviour save your soul for ever" was his ardent desire for his own soul. But he could not separate this desire from a second which as an axiom of his most personal thought and feeling stands on the opening page of his *Mystère de la Charité de Jeanne d'Arc*: "*We must be saved together*. We must come to God together. Together we must be presented before Him. Together we must all return to our Father's house. We must also think a little of others, and one must work for another. What would God say to us, if some of us came to Him without the others?" This was and remained the conception of human solidarity from which Péguy throughout his life never moved an inch. If this conception originally divided him from the Church which teaches hell as a dogma of faith, it compelled him now that he was a Christian to interpret the communion of Saints in accordance with his view of solidarity. Whoever belongs to the communion of Saints by prayer, grace and good works is saved even without the Sacraments. This no doubt is true, even according to the official teaching of the Church, for the man who through no fault of his own is ignorant of the Sacraments. Péguy knew the Sacraments, longed for them, wept when they were mentioned, but refused to receive them until grace had also brought his family to receive them. "We must be saved together." He was one with them and he left his and their salvation wholly to the grace of God.

George Fonsegrive, the theologian and philosopher, wrote of Péguy's attitude as a Catholic: "It is said of him, that he returned to the Church with the temper of a heresiarch. This is a strange misconception." Péguy had himself suffered keenly from this charge, made both privately and publicly. When Lotte informed him of Dom Baillet's serious illness he observed: "I love him as I love no one else. And he in turn loves me. But he distrusts me, is afraid I may turn out a heretic. This is utterly absurd. Monks do not know what life is. . . They cannot understand my life. Nor can you. You are too innocent. I am a sinner. But I pray a very great deal and receive very many graces." Yes, he received many graces. This is easy to believe. We can feel it, or rather see it clearly. But why then did he stick halfway on the road by which this evident miracle of grace was leading him, like a stubborn ass who halts just short of the goal? The best of his Catholic friends became angry. Renan's grandson, Ernest Psichari, whom Péguy's writings had brought back to the faith, wrote to him: " You are a coward, Péguy. I prefer the most miserable wretch who is converted on his deathbed to a man like you." So Péguy's life became a lonely one. His last poem on Joan of Arc had indeed aroused considerable attention. André Gide was charmed by it, and Maurice Barrès tried to obtain for it the honour of being crowned by the Academy. But members of that fraternity of intellectuals with whom Péguy had waged war for years had no taste for " a Suisse who mixed vitriol with his holy water." Péguy's Catholicism, proclaimed in the *Cahiers de la Quinzaine* with an unquestioning faith exasperating to the unbeliever, estranged the non-Catholic subscribers, and the Catholics, with the exception of the faithful Lotte who was his doughty champion, turned with a frown from this new and all too original comrade and defender of their faith.

Life became solitary and sad. It was as though he had found the faith only to multiply all his difficulties inner and outer. Is this life made for despair? Péguy did not ask himself this question which had long ago lost all meaning for him. He knew that life is made for absolute trust. A trust that originates in " that enormous adventure." He alone trusts or has the right to trust who knows " of the greatest event in the world's history. And also the greatest event in the history of heaven. The greatest event in the world. The greatest event of all time. The sole great event of all time. The greatest event in the whole world. The sole important event that ever happened." Just think: God in His own Person became man, and dies for us on the Cross. "Ye cities, ye cathedrals, this you have not seen. Your cathedrals enclose centuries of prayers, centuries of Sacraments, centuries of holiness, the holiness of an entire people that arises from an entire people. But this you have not seen." The Incarnation of God, the Redemption accomplished by God on the Cross. It is something stupendous that happened then. At this point everything must cease, the progress of evil in the world must come to a stop and in the other world even the eternal fire must be quenched. Something new has begun " boundless and eternal pardon " and the confidence that no boundary set by finite sin limits the omnipotence of the Divine Redemption. Confidence, trust. And Péguy lives a lonely life. As a man fallen into a dark gulley without an issue, he sat in the deep and gloomy vale of his sufferings and took counsel with himself. No, not with himself, with God. Nor did he sit still, he acted; he defended himself, fought and bored a tunnel for himself through the heavy and oppressive mass of his troubles leading out to the light, to the great all-conquering trust. For he felt that he still lacked trust, that a want of trust was still his besetting sin. And from his deepest personal experience, and inspired by his most intimate longing he wrote two new mysteries: *Le Porche de la Deuxième Vertu* (The Porch of the Second Virtue) and *Le Mystère des Saints Innocents* (The Mystery of the Holy Innocents). For Péguy they represented a mystical training in the academy of hope. And it was not unsuccessful. In 1912, he could write, "I have reached the point of resignation. I am no longer attached to anything. I care not a straw for fame which only two years ago meant much to me. I resign myself. I am following the counsels that God gives me in 'the Holy Innocents.' *The Holy Innocents* is an anticipation. What I expressed there I have never practised. But now, now at last I have abandoned myself wholly to God."

In fact the day came when as though in execution of a programme he did himself what the woodcutter of Lorraine does in his mystery play. The woodsman has three sick children. What can he, poor devil, do for them? He cannot help them. But the Mother of God can help them. Therefore he must take them to her. So Péguy, when one of his children fell ill, set out for Our Lady's shrine at Chartres. Like his peasant ancestors in the days before railways, like a medieval pilgrim he walked the fifty-five miles between his publisher's office in Paris and the shrine of his pilgrimage, with a rosary in his hand and halting at every wayside cross for a brief rest, filled with the devout recitation of Hail Mary's—halts far more precious than even those rests in Mary's company which he had as he recited the Rosary walking the city streets. After a three days' journey at a slow and meditative pace, inspired by an inexpressible trust he reached his goal. A strange pilgrim, holy and unholy. Then he prays the prayer of his woodcutter, makes his final assault upon the heart of the Mother of God. The brothers Tharaud, who know their Péguy, describe it as follows: "Mother of God, I can bear no more. I understand nothing more. It is beyond my strength. I have enough, more than enough. I cannot cope with it all. Thou knowest I have a work to do, to produce the *Cahiers,* an enormously difficult business. I lead no ordinary life. My life is a risk. No man is a prophet in his own country. My little ones are unbaptized. It is for Thee to see to the matter. I have not the time. I do not know what to do about it. Take the children. I hand them over to you."

This is the complete Péguy—his perfect likeness as he lived and prayed. We see a man of genius, a genius not of the intellect but of the heart, though at the same time something of a fool. A lovable and mystical fool, who for love of his neighbour risks his eternal salvation. A man who always puts the troubles of others before his own. His jesting definition of epic poetry is, in the Tharauds' opinion, perfectly applicable to himself: " to throw yourself frantically into everything that does not concern you." But it would seem that the Mother of God has a tenderness for fools of this kind. The sick child was quickly cured and his two children and a third born after his death were—later—baptized and his wife with them.

And Péguy himself, did she for whom he had such an inexpressible veneration, heal him? His external restoration to the bosom of the Church was never realized. But that he was permanently excluded from interior and spiritual membership of the Communion of Saints is simply incredible. A man who lives, thinks, feels and writes as Péguy did and does not belong to the mystical body of Christ would be a contradiction, a sheer impossibility. How many Christians, indeed how many priests even, are capable of such a passionate and charismatic experience of the Community which is the fulness of Christ, with which his Mystery of Joan overflows? Even if the book were placed in their hands they would be baffled by the idiosyncrasy of the style, perhaps not even able to recognize in it the authentic expression of an intuition, the gift of grace, which had penetrated the fundamental depths of the Christian mystery. Yet there is no doubt of the fact. An illusion conjured up by literary art is out of the question. It is one thing to depict revealed truths with theological accuracy or poetic imagination, another thing altogether to spread around one the atmosphere of a supernatural spirituality, the product of struggle and prayer. How many days and nights of spiritual wrestling between the soul and God must it not have required to fill the heart so full with the mystical flood; until the lips overflow, and there is no end of speech, of the stammering attempt to utter the sacred mystery? No, the irregularity of his position in regard to the visible Church cannot invalidate the fact that Péguy was to the core of his being a Christian, and, in essentials, an exceptionally profound Christian. And no one will be able to refute Lotte's judgment: "Péguy's vision is so penetrating that it plunges us into the very centre of spiritual reality. Certainly we can never get to the bottom of his work by breaking up its content into excerpts. Its inner movement will always escape our grasp, if we approach his writings in this way; and this precisely is everything because it expresses the spiritual current *that unites the poet with God*." No one was better acquainted with Péguy's religion than Lotte in whom the lonely fighter, Christ's free lance, confided most frankly during the last years of his life. Lotte knew the heroism with which his friend pursued his task of deepening his heart, how he made it the sole and entire purpose of his life to penetrate deeper into Christianity. Péguy was not content to remain at that point of his spiritual development where he stood when in that autumn of 1908 grace enabled him for the first time to recover a firm contact with religion. His mystery poems are records of the uninterrupted religious training to which he subjected himself. In 1912 he wrote to Lotte: " My old friend, I have been a different man the past two years. I've suffered and prayed so much. I am an entirely new man. . . Yes, I live without the Sacraments. That is a venture, a risk. But I have stores of graces, an abundance of incomprehensible graces."

There is no exaggeration in these words of a man who, as the result of most profound experience, had come to divide mankind into two and only two fundamentally different groups, those who did and those who did not possess grace; and for whom the operation of grace in the world constituted its sole important and essential history. Intellect and faith, culture and faith are in his eyes inseparable wholes; and that not in a general but in the most strictly Christian sense. "All spiritual and bodily, all eternal and temporal questions," he observed during his last years to the writer Stanislas Fumet, " turn around a centre about which I never cease to meditate and which is the pillar that upholds my religion. This pillar is the Immaculate Conception." The remark is another proof that in his view the supreme problem of history is redemption from sin. A philosophy of history from the standpoint of faith which he had planned and which was to be entitled *Veronica*, as a contrast to his *Clio* which was concerned with profane history, would have handled this problem. Death prevented him from carrying out his design. It would have prevented many other works, had not a strong presentiment that his end was near stirred Péguy to a feverish activity. " One must produce," he told the Tharauds. " To this consideration I subordinate every other. The older I become, the more clearly do I see that I am nothing and my work everything. At my age there is no time for postponement. You have no notion how much I still have to write. *I intend to cover the same ground from the Christian that Goethe covered from the pagan standpoint.*" It is always the same theme: Christianity. His final and supreme, indeed his sole concern in this world is to grasp and make known "the stupendous adventure" of Christianity, the sole adventure of importance to his own soul and to all other souls. His head and heart were now full of an idea or rather figure in which he saw embodied the entire supernatural drama of humanity, namely *Eve*. This drama is literally enacted in every human soul—in the soul of man which is related to all the metaphysical forces of the universe. What sordid dealers in trifles novelists are! How ridiculous to make a marriage or an adultery an issue of the first importance when the only question of importance is whether man, with his infinitely complex character, will accept or reject the Kingdom of God. Here, Péguy reflected, was the subject matter for a new *Divina Commedia*. But not as Dante wrote it. "Dante," he told Tharaud, "is a tourist, a tourist of genius, but a tourist all the same. He abandons himself to the picturesque, tells stories and is looking the whole time at what is going on around him. I do not raise my head, I do not walk about in heaven and hell. I tell no stories, nor do I converse with sinners whose names are in the biographical dictionary. Eve is yourself, myself, the most commonplace sinner. And the whole time for some ten to twelve thousand verses the sole topic handled is whether the poor devil is saved or damned." But where shall we find people to-day who are passionately concerned whether a soul is damned or saved? Péguy was so intensely concerned about it that with his heart's blood he wrote his *Eva* which interested nobody. Its failure was due to his style of composition of which we spoke above, but above all because he must almost inevitably bore any one without a pronounced understanding and an innate receptivity for holiness and purity. " I am a sinner. But in my work there is not a single sin. I do not work in sin." It is a bad recipe for an author who is looking for large sales. Péguy looked for the Kingdom of God. And he felt that the Kingdom of God was near to him, felt it with an inner joy. If he lacked the approbation of the earthly, he possessed the approbation of the heavenly public. " People have no idea what St Geneviève, St Aignan, St Louis and Joan of Arc are doing and obtaining for me."

There can be no doubt that these Saints who understood him, for " the Saints are not the idle folk " most Catholics believe, obtained for him the one thing for which he hungered, admission into the heavenly Communion of Saints.

On the fourth of August, 1914, he went to the front " to fight for a universal disarmament and in the last of all wars." And since he had a presentiment that it would also be *his* last war, his final bodily combat after so many spiritual conflicts, he hastily mobilized yet another shock brigade of prayer to come to his assistance at this critical moment. Its composition was strange; such that of a hundred thousand in the same position only a Péguy could have brought it together. It consisted of four women, a Catholic, a Protestant, a Jewess and a Freethinker. And they all promised him to make a pilgrimage every year to Our Lady of Chartres, if he never returned. From a letter written to Maritain's sister, we learn that on the Feast of the Assumption he went to Mass. It was his first and his last Mass since his return to the faith. On the fourth of September he was quartered in an abandoned religious house. He employed the night decking with flowers the altar of that Virgin for whose *Salve Regina* he would have given the whole of St Thomas. The next day he fell in an attack.

Was he not right when he said, "I am no Saint. I am a sinner, a good sinner"?

GIDE
THE PRODIGAL SON

I was like the prodigal son who went into a far country and wasted his goods.

André Gide

WHEN in November 1929 André Gide entered with his sixtieth birthday upon the somewhat melancholy period of public apotheosis, he was acclaimed by his admirers in terms of almost extravagant homage. And he was acclaimed by men of the right as well as by men of the left, by Christians as well as Freethinkers. The German publishing house Stuttgart-Leipzig-Berlin, drawing the conclusion that the hour had arrived to introduce Gide to the German public, translated his complete works. The review *Latinité, Revue des Pays d'Occident* proposed to address a threefold questionnaire to the writers of every nation. What was their opinion of Gide's personality, his influence and the "Catholicity," meaning by the term the universal character of his work? Whether the plan was actually carried out we do not know. But we do know that Catholic critics in Germany—most certainly not in France—unanimously agreed with the Liberals in praising Gide as a prominent representative of a spirit which, while universally human, is typically European. Were they justified in regarding with Klaus Mann as "a fitting object of our love and admiration the phenomenon presented by André Gide or a brilliant diversity of facets, amounting even to contradiction yet held together by a strict unity, a phenomenon which for all its reserves and artificial variety of colours has already begun to take its place as an accepted and indispensable contribution to man's intellectual store"? And what is it that they prize at so high a rate in this dazzling, contradictory and many coloured magician? Is it the quality to which Mann calls our attention, "this preference for the evil, the absurd and the dubious which recks nothing of moral bonds and obligations, the psychological audacity, and the devouring hunger with which he flings himself upon the utmost possible complication"?

If there is any contemporary writer crowned by official recognition whom the Christian should approach with the most critical caution, it is Gide. His name stands for one of the most complex and—from the Christian standpoint—the most tragic stories in the history of literature. This can no longer be questioned after the appearance of the most important contribution to the literature dealing with Gide, Charles du Bos' *Le Dialogue avec André Gide* (Sans Pareil, Paris, 1929). It is an altogether remarkable work. Weighty, profound and solid as only a rigidly scientific discipline could make it, clear-sighted, intimate as a diary, pulsating with life, a dialogue of poignant stress and tragic emotion, it is the last appeal of a man who wrestles for the soul of his best friend. In literal truth for his soul and his eternal salvation. This is the note on which the dialogue concludes. It begins as pure literature, ends as religion. Gide will certainly not have laughed at it, far less even than when Claudel tried to arouse his conscience and Gide replied (he tells the story himself in his *Journal des Faux-Monnayeurs*): "I have ceased to worry about my soul and its salvation." For if he has already forgotten his soul, he has forgotten it not light-heartedly but with a heavy heart. For it could not have been otherwise. And has he really forgotten it? He says so too often and therefore we cannot altogether believe him. His writing, after the cold reserve which marked his earliest work, has increasingly become a personal confession, often brutally frank, which even after the collapse of his faith still displays a kind of mysterious fear combined with a craving to give an account of himself at any cost.

If there were nothing in Gide beyond purely literary qualities, so much importance would scarcely have been attached to him. He observed once of the hero of Barrès' *Les Déracinés* that he would not have been interesting, had he not been an uprooted man and had he not committed murder. What makes Gide what he is to-day, an original and unique phenomenon of the contemporary intellectual world, is the fact that the atmosphere of destruction and self-destruction which surrounds the typical man of our day is focussed in him with an exceptional visibility. I do not propose to undertake the absurd task of estimating Gide's importance as a literary artist. If Gide did not say what he has to say with the charm of an exquisite artistry, did he not say it as a writer whose greatness is acknowledged alike by friend and foe, it might as well not have been said and his peronal and essential message would have perished unheard. His incontestable and genuine artistry is simply the technique and the instrument of a communication, a revelation which far, far exceeds the domain of literature and art and has nothing to do with them.

We are already confronted with what may be termed the problem of André Gide. It is a problem which perplexes, indeed torments, his reader even in his purely literary and artistic appreciation. Even from the external standpoint no writing is more disconnected and disjointed than Gide's. Anybody who begins to read him without having first read any study of his work will soon find himself with the uncomfortable conviction that he is to some extent being made a fool of. Let us suppose that he begins his reading with *La Porte Étroite*. If it were a volume of critical essays he would naturally be prepared for surprises. It is a canticle of heavenly love, pervaded by a melancholy charm, and heart-felt, indeed springing from the very depths of the heart. It is a poem which has blossomed, a flower of infinite chastity in the mystic garden of the Imitation of Christ. So this is Gide, Gide the Protestant! Under the spell of this profound spiritual experience he proceeds with the highest hopes to other books bearing the name of this man who has portrayed with a master's hand the most delicate emotions of the soul. Here is a small and thin volume, *Prometheus Ill-bound*. It is of a totally different character. It is a fantasia breathing from the first line to the last an atmosphere of grim and biting satire. What, one asks, can this mean? What is the subject of this satire? Roughly speaking, everything that filled *The Narrow Gate* with a holy awe: God, the soul united with God, and conscience. God is here depicted as an enormously wealthy banker, who displays His transcendence of everything earthly and the absolutely gratuitous character of graces by giving a present to any chance passer whom His momentary whim may choose and boxing his ears the next moment. And Prometheus is man who merely from a sense of gratitude and guilt in regard to the Divine giver allows himself to be devoured by the eagle, that is by his conscience, until finally he hits upon the simple idea of eating the eagle. From that moment he becomes healthy and cheerful and lives happily on earth. Gide calls the book "*Soti*" (farce), and farce it is: a huge blasphemous farce.

Involuntarily the reader looks at the date of publication. It is 1899. *The Narrow Gate* was published in 1909. Has Gide then undergone a profound conversion in the interval? The reader takes up with curiosity *Les Caves du Vatican,* dated 1914, which also calls itself a farce. In compass a bulky novel, it is nothing of the kind. It is a fantasia of improbable adventure which with a dazzling and sparkling shower of fireworks, an *allegro con spirito,* pours out ridicule of a brilliant audacity upon a host of things sacred to a large portion of mankind. That spirit of universal ridicule which inspired *Prometheus Ill-bound* has found its incarnation here. We cannot get away from the idea that Lacfadio the sly anarchist and superhomunculus with his hysterical search for "a crime without a motive" was introduced simply as a travesty of some theological doctrine, possibly Calvin's unmotived predestination from eternity. Later when we are better acquainted with Gide we recognize in this creation one of his favourite ideas. Then we are informed, for example, by Gide's personal friend, the critic Paul Souday, that Lacfadio, like many another "immoralist" in Gide's work, is meant as a satire upon the ideas which lead to wrong-doing. But the work itself is very far from suggesting such an interpretation. Quite the reverse. In Dostoievsky too the notion of an unmotived crime, meaningless and without an object, plays an important part. Stavrogin in *The Demons* is a mystic of the *acte gratuit.* But Dostoievsky leaves us in no doubt that Stavrogin is what he is, only because he has fallen a victim to the diabolism of the unsubstantial life-denying nothingness. In the case of Gide, on the other hand, the most impartial critic can reach no other conclusion than that he regards this denial of the significance of life as broadening and deepening the life of its subject.

But after all, who can tell? Who really knows where he is with Gide? He is frankly a mystery-monger. His earliest books were published anonymously. He let the critics guess. He inscribed the first edition of his *Caves du Vatican* "A farce. By the author of *The Swamps*." (*The Swamps* is a satire on everyday life written in his early years of authorship.) Gide never brings out his trumps until it is absolutely necessary. This becomes clear when you read him in chronological order. Or does he perhaps do it in his *Symphonie Pastorale* of 1919? Does this tale signify a return to the intellectual and spiritual world of *The Narrow Gate*? A Protestant pastor relates in the form of a diary the spiritual disaster in which he became involved by taking a blind girl into his family to educate. Obviously a rough summary can give no idea of the restrained and subdued but finely shaded manner, the mysterious half-light which invests the characters and their thoughts, or the atmosphere of distinction and refinement, rural and touched with the spirit of evangelical religion peculiar, one would imagine, to a Protestant parsonage. The book is a masterpiece of craftsmanship in its description of the gradual change in the pastor's feeling for the girl from Christian charity to natural love. And under the spell of his love he made the girl believe in the natural goodness of man and a sinless world. But she had scarcely recovered her sight through an operation on her eyes when she also saw the sin of her illicit love and drowned herself. And the pastor too saw the sin; but we are not sure whether he repented of it or secretly revolted against a religion which made a sin of the sweetest experience of his life. Even less can we tell what Gide thinks of the story which he tells with the coldest reserve. Is the entire book a satire upon the pastor, whose lapse drove his son into the Catholic priesthood, or simply a soft but bitter lament at the antinomies which leave man only the painful choice between the satisfaction of his senses and peace of soul? This at any rate is certain: no heathen devoid of moral scruples could have written such a book, but only a man who is suffering deeply from the Christian conception of sin—or has suffered.

But which then is the true Gide, the author of *The Narrow Gate* and *The Pastoral Symphony* or of *Prometheus Ill-bound* and the *Cellars of the Vatican*? Gide could not permanently evade this question which his readers must and did raise. In a chapter of the critical studies entitled *Letters to Angèle,* he frankly admits his responsibility for the false picture formed of him. How could it be otherwise when after *The Cellars* he wrote *The Pastoral Symphony*? A sharp-sighted critic had in fact correctly guessed that he had not been entirely comfortable when he wrote the latter work. Gide proceeds to give an explanation which throws considerable light upon the riddle of his literary activity. Hitherto he had not written a single book which had not been planned before the age of thirty, so that every book drew him back into the past and in no way represented his present intellectual position. With *The Pastoral Symphony* he had intended to liquidate his last debt to the past and had written it only with an intense reluctance and an enforced misrepresentation of himself—*j'avais dû terriblement me contrefaire*—since his mind was now full of very different ideas.

We must not take too seriously Gide's alleged aversion to the enforced misrepresentation. It is indeed a principle of his art on which he has built his theory of classicism which he claims to represent in its purest form. Classicism holds his allegiance because it makes it easier " to conceal the deeper meaning " of works written in its spirit. The romantic artist is too eloquent; he expresses more than he has to say, whereas the classical artist says more than he expresses. In this sense Gide terms " disguise one of the conditions of art." To write as one who has a secret, and a secret to keep; to speak softly and unemphatically, where possible in a commonplace fashion and steadfastly renouncing all search for originality; to subject an inner romanticism to the discipline of an even and controlled style; to restrain it and render it innocuous by imposing upon it the form of the pure work of art—if this is the genuine classical ideal, we must allow that Gide has been driven by an inner compulsion to make it his own. Not indeed because he had extraordinary passions to control, as he would perhaps have us believe. He does not possess the volcanic temperament of a Montherlant or a Bernanos, not to speak of Dostoievsky by whom he is hypnotized. Strictly speaking he does not restrain his romanticism but exploits it to the remotest veins with the instruments of an insatiable curiosity, an extensive knowledge and a rich and mobile intelligence, charged with a measure of craft and cunning. Only Flaubert in the whole of French literature can compare with him in this deliberate struggle with his own temperament to extract the utmost from it and convert it into art.

If Gide cultivates the controlled classic style, this is primarily due to the instinctive need of his nature to communicate itself only with the utmost possible reserve. He conceives of his art as a means whereby to reveal himself by concealing himself. He conceals himself behind his characters. " I am quite prepared," he remarks in *Un Esprit non Prévenu,* one of his latest works of criticism, " to lack any clearly defined existence provided the beings that I produce out of myself possess one." The remark is one of the keys with which this inaccessible spirit unlocks for us an entrance to himself. There are other keys more important and more direct which must be wrung from him by a stubborn wrestle with his soul. For ourselves, concerned for the moment with Gide as a "wrestler," the confession just quoted has the advantage of throwing light upon his personality through his artistic practice.

In fact Gide's work is a unique attempt, elaborated by literary methods, by varied artistic devices, to escape from himself. Whether he is depicting simple and pious characters, as in *The Narrow Gate* and *The Pastoral Symphony,* or complex characters who break loose from all social, moral and religious bonds as in *Nourritures Terrestres, L'Immoraliste,* or his last great novel *Les Faux-Monnayeurs,* he is always writing his autobiography. The psychologically sensitive reader is unshakeably convinced of this, long before he has read in the book of Gide's reminiscences *Si le Grain ne Meurt* an explicit confirmation. And as the reader feels with a certain discomfort, he portrays his life under a sense of heavy pressure in order to thrust it away from him, to thrust it away piecemeal like a block of floating ice. Over the literary waters fragments of a living personality are floating up and down, have solidified themselves into independent literary forms, bear fictitious names and present a very diverse appearance. But each possesses its distinctive features and a "clearly defined existence" and something can always be made of it. What can we make of Gide himself? Of a man who in the literal sense sacrifices his own "clearly defined existence" to the creations of his art and has fed them with the flesh and blood, the spiritual substance of his own personality?

It is a case—on this let there be no mistake—of a self-sacrifice which is evil because it is made in the service not of God but an idol. The idol is art. Gide does not simply adopt the principle of the autonomy of art, the aesthetes' dogma of art for art's sake. It is not enough for him to place art on an equality with life; he regards it as a higher value. Indeed it is the supreme, the absolute value. "Ethics are an annex of aesthetics." It is not that he has no interest in moral and religious questions. On the contrary he is exclusively interested in them, but only in so far as they furnish material for his art. Gide treats his entire life, his moral and religious experiences, even his most intimate experience of God and the devil, grace and sin, as pure material, in itself indifferent, for his art. The romantics have long since claimed the right to adventures of the heart. Gide claims the right to taste in his life all possible experiences, be they as opposed as fire and water, to obtain from them artistic material for his books. That the latter may exercise a grave and disastrous influence upon the reader he is well aware. But to distort his thoughts on that account would be the great sin against the spirit for which there is no pardon. For "it is the purpose of our life to reveal. The laws of morality and art are identical. Every work which does not reveal is useless and therefore evil. . . All things must be revealed, even the most unwholesome. . . Woe to him through whom scandal cometh but scandals there must be!" He says this at the dawn of his career as a writer in his *Traité de Narcisse*. And at its meridian he repeats it, but in far franker and more unambiguous terms. "For heaven's sake let us get this question straight. Whether a man is licentious or not does not matter; what matters is whether he has the right to be so. And this right art must uphold at all costs." (*Nouveaux Prétextes*)

It was one of the great errors of the last century to invest art with the mission of guiding, healing and sanctifying the soul of man, a mission which of her nature she is incapable of fulfilling, but which was committed to her by those who, having lost faith in the true agent of redemption, Christ and the Church, would not abandon the desire for a higher sanction of human life. In this spirit Gide replaced religion by art, as his religion died. The more relative religion and ethics became for him, the more absolute became the value he assigned to art. As the objects of faith gradually faded into natural phenomena, the work of art assumed greater prominence, until it became the only supernatural miracle granted to man. That the religious parentage of art and an intrinsic bond between artistic creation and religious faith are still accepted jars somewhat upon his nerves, since he has reached the point where he prides himself on his complete emancipation from prejudice, on being an *Esprit non prévenu*. Faith? It is a state of mind like any other, with surcharge of emotion, it is true, from which art often profits, but otherwise a matter of complete indifference. "Whether I believe or do not believe, what does that concern you? What does it matter to myself? It is as impossible for me to believe sincerely what you believe, as to believe that the sun moves round the earth." He therefore consecrates himself to art and binds himself to its service, as another pledges himself to God or the devil. And he pledges himself with a religious devotion, with a final and irrevocable determination. And above his betrayal of the transcendent aims of the Christian soul he inscribes the Gospel text, " He that will save his life shall lose it; he that will lose it shall save it."

Gide has lost his life, has sacrificed it, but not in the service of that Christian and truly classic ideal which by controlling man's destructive, and enlightening his dark, instincts seeks to purify human nature, until man becomes a personality superior to the world. Not in that service has he sacrificed his life, but in the service of an art which under the cloak of classicism advocates the disintegration of personality, pleads for the legitimation of anarchic passions, and regards itself at bottom as a species of laboratory for experiments which by breaking up the classical and Christian type of humanity attempt to liberate forces which will produce a new human type. " The dark elements of the spirit will be the best to-morrow."

Nowhere has Gide revealed so clearly the aims of his artistic creation of which he himself for a long time was but vaguely conscious, as in his *Dostoievsky* (Plon, Paris, 1929, 18th edition). There was no need for him to state in so many words that Dostoievsky was in the main but a pretext for developing his own ideas. The reader is aware of it in any case, and sees in it the chief value of the book. " Without misrepresenting Dostoievsky's ideas," adds Gide by way of a caveat. The assurance is worthless. Any one who really knows Dostoievsky—and he can be known only from his remains published by Piper which include the sketches for several of his great novels, that is to say after a thorough study of the *Unknown Dostoievsky* and the *Original Form of The Brothers Karamazov*—knows without the least shadow of doubt that Gide has, unwillingly of course, misrepresented the great Russian in his deepest and ultimate beliefs. Gide has truly perceived the chaotic elements in his dark and passionate spirit, the anarchic dualism of his nature, " the Evangelical depreciation of the intellect." But he has failed to perceive that Dostoievsky depreciated the intellect, not in order to thrust man back into the monstrous cul-de-sac of the irrational, but to free him from the fantasy and the hallucination, the unreal semblance in which he has been involved by the "pure" reason of infidelity. He has failed to perceive that out of the dark abyss into which a painful but undoubtedly providential destiny had plunged him, Dostoievsky drew the material with which to fashion a new Christian cosmos, that *The Brothers Karamazov* with its moving chapter " Revolt " is a gigantic monument which he erected on the eve of his death to the final victory of the world of Jesus Christ over chaos—the chaos without security, shelter or providence of a wholly irrational conception of reality, where everything is a permanent riddle for which there is no solution, and a Satanic power is the sole arbiter. He cannot see these things, because he will not see them. With such an attitude could Dostoievsky have achieved his creations? Gide is sure that he could not, and in his study of Dostoievsky affirms dogmatically that " good intentions make bad literature." How then is good literature produced? " There is no work of art to which the devil has not contributed." Now, however, when a comparison between the original sketch and the final form of *The Brothers Karamazov* has left us in no doubt as to its meaning and has proved that this meaning is eminently Christian, we are obliged to admit that Dostoievsky's genius has accomplished its greatest work with "good intentions." The "unprejudiced " Gide has never handled any man with greater prejudice than Dostoievsky. He has 'gidised ' him, as he has 'gidised ' the Gospel. Dostoievsky, on the contrary, made the genuine Gospel the secret centre of his work. As no other in the world's literature, this novel depicts a fallen world, the devilry of a world that " lieth in evil." From an experience of unparalleled violence the Russian writer displays this diabolism. But it is not, as Gide would have us believe, in order " to bow " before that throng of characters into which Dostoievsky poured his own soul, bursting with contradictions—with the same brutal frankness with which Gide has mirrored *himself* in the characters of his *Coiners.* The disorder of *The Brothers Karamazov* possesses a powerful inner unity and completeness, whereas the disorder of *The Coiners* possesses none. The former is a chaos in bonds, the latter a chaos let loose without direction or exit. " 'It can be continued,' with these words I would conclude my *Coiners,*" observes Edward, the hero of the novel, whose diary composes a third of it.

" It can be continued." For heaven's sake no! It is not that the book fails to arouse the keenest interest—a book which Du Bos calls " the subtlest and most powerful counterpoint that we owe to a universe which is the prey of discord." But if it is finished, let there be a full stop at the conclusion like a block of stone placed above the exit from a cavern of charnel ghosts. Dostoievsky's *Demons* is a far wilder hell but a more imposing and more tolerable abode than this coiners' den. *Coiners' den*—there is no need to look for a more appropriate designation than this, given by Gide himself. The title is worth our scrutiny. Or rather its deceptive and insidious character, its ambiguity. By counterfeit money Gide understands practically everything which in the name of a religious or moral ideal has been imposed upon the authentic and original, that is to say, the purely natural life of man. And as genuine coinage the reader is asked to accept this terrible criticism of every Christian creed, indeed of religious faith generally, of morality and the family. It is a demand which even the unbelieving critic Paul Souday refuses with the observation that *The Coiners* is "an immoral and dangerous book." Any one who possesses a modicum of Christianity, even if it be merely latent, detects with an intuitive certainty which no sophistry can explain away, that the first, indeed the sole, coiner in the book is Gide himself. For all the coiners whom we see here at work are not even his mental children, are not creations with an independent life of their own but Gide himself under different masks.

For this reason Du Bos, his friend, can say with perfect truth: " In a novel (*The Coiners*) Gide gives us his life in the most literal and also the most tragic sense. But he has nothing more to give; life he cannot give." The reason why he cannot had been stated long before in his *Essay on Faith* by Jacques Rivière, a writer of acute perceptions whom his master Gide has poisoned to the core of his being. " Even when it is no longer a question of penetrating the secret of things, but merely of inventing characters and events, that is to say even in the novel, Christianity bestows on those whom it inspires a peculiar power, a board so to speak from which to dive into the depths."

Gide's art is burdened with a tragic curse which derives from the very centre of his *personality*.

To discuss Gide without leaving the field of art would be an impossible undertaking. This has been admitted in practice even by a literary critic so accomplished as Du Bos, who in the second half of his dialogue cites Gide with an increasing solemnity before the bar of the supreme moral and aesthetic values. And this had already been done by Mauriac and Rops and above all by the intransigent Massis. Du Bos had indeed attacked the *Jugements* of the latter (Plon, 1924) as dictated by a criticism doomed from the outset to be unjust towards its subject owing to its entire lack of sympathy with him. But he had finally to admit that Massis had understood Gide correctly, for such work and such a personality as his can be understood only *sub specie æternitatis*.

In dealing with Gide we are concerned with matters more important than art. We are concerned with human life in the typical embodiment, questionable in the extreme but contemporary, which it receives in his personality. Most writers stand for particular ideas which they bring into a recognizable if not also systematic connection and to which they subordinate themselves as the ideal which they desire to serve. Gide stands strictly speaking for no idea, declares that he serves no ideal, and binds himself to nothing save the commandment of his nature which rejects all other commandments and bonds. And if there is anything that he wishes to give the world, it is simply the example of a personality emancipated from every restraint.

How difficult to speak with perfect accuracy of a character not known by personal intercourse! The human personality in Gide, Du Bos tells us, is not exactly rich—indeed the Frenchman's nature cannot generally speaking be termed rich— but full (*étoffé*), infinitely fuller than his work. " In Gide's presence," he writes, "you are conscious of an importance, a significance, a power often sublime, above all a third dimension with which his voice invests everything, so that any of his writings when read by him assumes a most compelling significance." This perhaps is a reflection of the spiritual reality which fascinates me in his portrait. Literally fascinates. Chafe against it as I may, my glance as I write returns again and again to his face. It is the clean-shaven face of an elderly man with regular features, not outwardly remarkable. His head is sunk as though by fatigue into his hand which supports it. His expression is overcast by a profound, indeed a tragic gravity. I can understand Du Bos' impression of sublimity. But I cannot understand how this mask of oriental immobility can conceal a spirit as active, impatient, unstable and capricious and always ready for the most extreme mental ventures as Gide's. Possibly it is this which so disturbs and frightens us in his countenance, the enigma of a rigid mobility, the curse of loneliness with which a spirit in flight from itself and God pays for its flight. We should consult Max Picard, the profound and devout revealer of the secrets hidden in "the human face." Yet I cannot but guess the secret of this closed countenance. Recently the true Gide dawned upon my soul, living, expressive and eloquent. As I listened to *The Return of the Prodigal Son* dramatized for the wireless, he arose behind the curtain of his soft and melancholy speech and spoke to me, and uttered his tragic secret. *The Prodigal Son.* The prodigal son who left his father's house "not to seek happiness but to discover who he is," who, overcome by tender memories of home, returned but who on the very morrow of his return looked into the night from the boundary fence, seized once more with nostalgia for those sinister wastes from which he had just fled—is Gide himself. He is always the man who forsakes his home. He is always the prodigal son. This is the tragic secret of his life.

He is fully aware of it himself. In a volume of selections (*Morceaux Choisis*, 1921) he has given us an autobiographical paraphrase of the parable. " I was like the prodigal son who went abroad and squandered his rich inheritance. . . Christ's words blazed out before me, like the pillar of fire which led the chosen people through the night and amid the thick darkness into which I determined to plunge I heard unceasingly the command: ' Sell all that thou hast and give to the poor.' My heart swelled with terror and joy, or rather with terror of the joy. I therefore sought to discover which among the thoughts, opinions and habits of my soul and intellect were most intimate, which I had most certainly inherited from my forefathers. . .

"No doubt if I had pursued this expropriation to the most extreme and absurd lengths I should have reached perfect poverty—for 'what hast thou which thou hast not received?' But this total poverty was the very thing for which I strove as the sole true good. . . I flung away every personal opinion, every habit, all sense of shame, even my virtue, as a man flings off a garment to expose his body naked to the touch of the waves. . . Strengthened by this self-abnegation I was conscious of my soul as simply a force of love (that was how I described it to myself) which stood shivering, exposed to whatever came along, akin to everything, impersonal, a frank chaos of desires, lusts and licentious passions. But whenever I felt alarm at the disorder in which this anarchy involved me I found strength in Christ's " Wherefore art thou troubled?" I therefore abandoned myself to a provisional disorder, confident that a nobler and more natural order would take shape of itself. And finally I was convinced that for my soul even disorder was less dangerous than an arbitrary and artificial order, artificial because I had not discovered it for myself. Thou beam of Divine Light, I exclaimed, is not that which resists Thee most this false wisdom of men, compound of fear, lack of faith and pride? I offer Thee all. I surrender myself. Banish all shadows from me. Inspire me."

This passage provides the key to Gide's life. All the experiences, ideas and sentiments which gradually built up his philosophy of life and gave a definite step to his personality, in short everything which made Gide Gide, is summed up in this central fact of his apostasy. That he regards this infidelity as a higher fidelity, that he appeals to the Gospel in support of it and that he represents this renunciation of a moral formation of character according to the traditional code of Christianity, as precisely the purest form of morality in harmony with the Gospel rightly interpreted, is indeed most bewildering. But the confusion is typical of Gide. He is the most complicated apostate of our age. *The Coiners* should be rewritten not by Gide but by Bernanos. It would make a powerful counterpart to his novel *The Renegade* whose plot is the apostasy of a Catholic priest. Gide's life and personality would provide abundant material.

Gide is a man with a genuine call to religion. We have only to re-read what he tells us on the subject in his memoirs (*Si le Grain ne Meurt,* Paris, 1928, 48th edition, Gallimard) to realize that only exceptional natures, whether among Catholics or Protestants, can experience the bliss of religion with such intensity as it was given to him to experience it. "I carried a New Testament in my pocket and was never without it. Every moment I would be taking it out, not only when I was alone but even in front of people whose ridicule I had to fear." In the tram, at school during the intervals he read it. The gibes of his schoolfellows made him blush, but he offered the humiliation to God. The youth observed a rule of life of monastic strictness. " Getting up very early I read, before beginning work, some verses of the Bible; or rather I re-read the verses which I had marked the previous evening for the day's contemplation. Then I prayed. My prayer was an effort of the soul which may be termed sensible to penetrate more deeply into God. And I renewed this effort from hour to hour. In this way I interrupted my study and I never changed its subject without offering it anew to God. Out of mortification I slept on a plank. In the middle of the night I got up and this not so much from mortification as in the impatience of my joy. At the time I thought that I had reached the highest summit of happiness."

But the day came when he looked down from that summit into the deepest abyss, with a fascinated glance, and a craving ever more hungry and finally irresistible. Is not life on the heights of Christian spirituality cold and abstract? In what seemed a flash of illumination he realized that "subjection to the moral teaching of Christ" had brought him "nothing but a profound disorder of his entire nature." The great " harmony " did not illumine the peak of supernature; it shone from the abyss of nature. When at the age of twenty-four he began his Algerian journey, was it not the new harmony rather than the new land which his soul was seeking? Soul: the word seems very inappropriate when the long and short of it is that this harmony was sought and found in homosexual relations with young Moors. Later on, after his mother's death, in an ecstasy of detachment from the world he will wed the ideal of his youthful reverence and love, his cousin Emanuela: the apostle of the dangerous and uncomfortable life will follow the convenient and truly modern fashion of a division of labour, a separation of powers. He will seek love in marriage and the gratification of the senses outside it. Now in Algiers he experiences a happiness "which he had never believed possible," "an ecstatic and literally dazzling bliss," the fulfilment of what his entire nature had long been unconsciously craving, "the ideal of balance, completeness and health, everything which to-day we call 'classicism'."

That is, what *he* calls by that name. Here we have the living and personal source of *his* classicism, harmony between the demands of the spirit and the flesh—at the cost of the spirit, or his conception of the work of art which "conceals its underlying significance," of his theory of "ethics as an annex of aesthetics," the latter being thus raised to the rank of a deity that pardons everything, understands everything and is served equally by evil and good. For Gide art took the place too late of the confessor, whose aid in the struggle against his abnormal sensuality Calvinistic Puritanism had refused. Now for the first time when he has experienced the fascination of the abyss, he can write *The Immoralist,* and the *Nourritures Terrestres,* the bible of his new immanental and amoral religiosity which can hold communion with God only in a mystical cosmic rapture, or as Victor Poucel appositely puts it, the gospel of the sinner who finds salvation in his sin.

Gide has thus realized half his parable of the prodigal son. He has definitely left his father's house and squandered to the last doit the rich treasure "his most certain inheritance from his forebears" to find in this disappropriation his true soul, that harmonious, impersonal and all-welcoming soul "which is a frank chaos of desire, lust and pleasures." And he even fulfils the second part. He returned to his father's house. Between 1916 and 1918 he went through a religious crisis. Several observers, Schaukel for example, did not take it very seriously. No one, however, who has entered into Gide's utterly illogical and tortuous nature, which seems to have no understanding of consistency, not even of the law of contradiction, can share their opinion. And in fact Du Bos does not share it. Just at this time he was in close touch with Gide and he incorporates in his book large fragments of the spiritual diary in which Gide described the crisis under the title "*Numquid et tu?*" These entries are the entreaties, the tears and the cries of a soul burdened with the consciousness of sin which the glance of Christ has quite unexpectedly frightened out of its false peace. They are a mystery of Christ which Gide experienced in holy fear and hope. Now indeed Christ's words stand out before him like pillars of fire, and cast a glare of appalling revelation upon his African period.

"April 23. Terrible filth, the filth of sin. Ashes left by an impure flame, dross—canst Thou cleanse me from it all, O Lord? That with pure voice I may sing Thy praise?

"June 16. I can no longer pray, can no longer even hear God. Perhaps He is speaking to me, but I do not hear. I have become completely indifferent to His voice. Yet I now despise *my own* wisdom and when I lack the joy He gives me I am deprived of every other. I cannot endure it alone. I cannot. All the reflection of Thy glory of which I was conscious within my soul has faded. It is time that Thou shouldst come; O let not the evil one take Thy place in my heart. Suffer not Thyself to be dethroned. If Thou dost withdraw Thyself wholly from me, he establishes himself in Thy room. For pity's sake confuse me not with him. Believe me, I do not love him so dearly, indeed I do not. Remember that I have been able to love Thee.

" What then. Am I now really as one who had never loved Him?

" September 19, 1916. The storm has raged all night. This morning there is a heavy shower of hail. I get up, with brain and heart empty and heavy, laden with the entire weight of hell. I am a drowning man who loses courage and makes but a feeble struggle for his life. Three calls and all with the same burden. It is time. It is high time. There is no time left. One therefore is indistinguishable from another and the third is already sounding when you think you are still hearing the first.

" If I could at least relate this drama, could depict Satan as he is when he has taken possession of a man, could relate how he makes use of him to influence others! An absurd notion, you may think. But I have lately come to understand it for the first time. You are not merely taken prisoner, but the evil which is an active power demands from you activity in its service. You are compelled to fight in a false and perverse cause. . .

"The great mistake is that we make a romantic picture of the devil. That is why it has taken me so long to get to know him. He is no more and no less romantic or classic than the man with whom he has to do. He is as diverse as man himself, indeed more so. For he increases his variety. With me he has made himself a classicist, because this was necessary in order to catch me and because he knew that I would not easily connect an equilibrium successfully maintained with the evil one. I did not understand that it is possible to keep a certain balance even in the worst evil, for a time at any rate. I regarded as good whatever was in any way subjected to rule. By moderation I thought I could master evil, and precisely through this moderation the evil one has taken possession of me."

Charles Du Bos calls this diary "one of the most heroic victories that introspection has ever achieved." In my opinion it would be absolutely impossible for a Christian to sink the plummet deeper into the human heart than Gide has done into his. For it demands not only a heroic sincerity but the illumination of Christian grace to see so clearly into the Satanic background of the heart. Not the work of art but the heart is the chief battlefield whereon God and the devil fight. Later Gide is once more to forget this truth, though Dostoievsky reminds him of it. But here for once he has experienced it and expressed it with an inimitable prevision and his readers must be grateful to him for that. For he spares them the necessity of passing judgment upon him in the name of an absolute Light, an absolute Truth which perhaps he never knew. He has known it and by its illumination has judged himself, even if afterwards he once more denied it. There is a quality of Gide's work of which his Christian reader is conscious with a tremor—the evil ambiguity of his classicism, the Satanic quality of his aesthetic catharsis which excludes religious and moral purification, the dark secret of his harmony and serenity which, however, one must not utter aloud, for it offends against the good form of a worldly code of behaviour marked by a banal rationalism. All this has been told us by Gide himself. And we are aware of it. For we are Christians. And life, Gide's life, therefore, is far too valuable in our eyes to allow us to regard its meaning as nothing more than an aesthetic game played between God, the devil and the soul.

And this blasphemous game Gide began anew after his spiritual Damascus. It seems almost incredible. But did he not foresee it and foretell it himself? Has not *his* homecoming been of the same kind as the homecoming he described a decade earlier in his *Return of the Prodigal Son?* He too returned with a nostalgia for the desert he had left. He has left the desert, but his old roving heart he has not left. He cannot leave it. That is beyond his strength. And after all *does* God ask it of him? Is not the quality of Christ's Redemption infinitely fine, so omnipresent that it clings to the most secret and intimate folds of a human destiny? The more closely he ponders the sacred texts of the Gospel, the more firmly is he convinced that it is God's will that he should save himself as he actually is, retaining the disposition with which God endowed him. " Who taketh not up his cross and follows me is not worthy of me." Gide therefore makes up his mind to bear the cross of the destiny appointed him by God, though it contains much which before the law is sin—for example his abnormal sexual disposition. What then is sin? " Sin is what a man does not freely choose." And the law? He reads in St John's Gospel: " But this multitude which knoweth not the law is accursed " (*Sed turba haec, quæ non novit legem maledicti sunt*), and is triumphant. " Every word in this sacred text emits a ray of light. . . The multitude which knoweth not the law. . . Grant me, O Lord, to be among their number accursed by the orthodox who know the law."

This exegesis, it is clear, represents in its extreme form the Protestant rejection of a holiness of works. In the Protestant Gide, this would indeed be perfectly consistent. But he who calls himself " the heretic among the heretics" is not satisfied with the liberty of conscience reached by the Reformers. For him, even the orthodox Protestant is a Pharisee who prides himself upon the law and has no understanding of that most sublime evangelical truth on which Gide lives, "Who loveth his soul shall lose it." For he, Gide, does understand it. It means "whoever loves his life, that is to say preserves his personality, whoever cherishes his character in this world, shall lose it."

Thus Gide after his return to his Christian home is at pains to interpret the ancient Gospel in an extremely original fashion and put into currency a new Gospel according to Gide which illuminates the depths of his work and his personality. Above all it explains how, left alone with himself, he is torn away with an irresistible force from the shores of Christianity by the pull of these centrifugal currents of his nature. What was there to hold him back? The Gospel? He has discovered that "it recognizes no commandments or prohibitions." It might perhaps even be possible to convince him that this "discovery" is a pure invention of his own, devised with the sole object of providing a sanction for his inner "disorder." But he would then repeat what he wrote in the *Morceaux Choisis*: "I was convinced that for my soul even disorder was less dangerous than an arbitrary and artificial order, artificial because I had not discovered it for myself." In other words, Gide affirms the primacy of life. Life is the first and supreme value, the sole value of which it is neither necessary or possible to judge, because it is the standard of all valuation. In a conversation about *The Coiners* Gide told Du Bos: "The essential difference between me and you is that you believe in the necessity of an aim, and above all of a model in order to arrive at perfection, I, on the contrary, have sought to portray in my Bernard (a leading character in *The Coiners*) a lofty and noble figure who advances through life without an aim, and for whom the goal is nothing but the act of living itself."

In this indifferent and purely immanental life all objective values are absorbed and dissolved. Good and evil are not values but mere words. And in particular those values which have been regarded as good by traditional morality and religion become increasingly suspect and hateful to Gide. *The Coiners* is full of ridicule. And his latest production, the two novels published together, *The School of Women* and *Robert,* is nothing but a gibe at piety. " In proportion as a soul is absorbed by devotion it loses the understanding, need, taste and love for reality. The glare of its faith blinds it to its environment and itself. I, who have nothing more at heart than to see clearly, am stiff with horror at the sight of the crass lie in which a pious man can feel at ease." For Gide in consequence there is only one virtue, sincerity. And in the latest stage of his life he practises it with a frankness that may almost be called terrifying. He now carries out with an appalling thoroughness the programme of his youth: " We live to reveal ourselves." Homosexuality, like an all-pervasive current, concealed to be sure by the art of allusion of which he is a past master and in which his classicism consists, permeates his entire work. In *Corydon* it is represented with the cold objectivity of the historian of human civilizations as a natural form of sex on an equal footing with the normal type, indeed superior to it. It puts forward its claim to recognition with an astounding shamelessness in his book of reminiscences *Die to Live.* The doctrine that nature even when distorted, perverse and abnormal is above any moral restraints has never been defended so openly in the civilization which derives from Christianity, not even in Rousseau's *Confessions.* "I am well aware of the harm I am doing to myself by relating what follows. I foresee how these confessions will be employed as a weapon against myself. But my narrative has no other justification than this: honesty." Honesty, frankness; it is the sole value to which Gide clings in his moral and religious *débâcle*. Nor is he alone in this. "Frankness" is the literary slogan of our time. A rank growth of autobiographical writings is inspired by this doctrine for which Gide has the dubious merit of constructing a broad and free road. It is an extremely dubious merit. For if this craving for absolute sincerity represents a perfectly laudable need to liberate the soul from a burdensome oppression, we must not forget at what cost this liberation is purchased. Jacques Rivière, seeking to expose Gide's fallacy, has thoroughly investigated the question in his essay *Sincerity towards Oneself.* It proved an anxious and delicate task. In his search for the counter-ideal to Gide's frankness (*sincerité*) he found honour (*honnêteté*). Honour, he concluded, must be opposed to frankness. As he puts it, "To be honourable is to harbour only such ideas as are admissible; to be frank is to harbour all ideas indifferently." We can harbour all ideas, and every conceivable idea is admissible, only when all restraints imposed by a system of ethical and religious doctrine, by preconceived notions of good and evil, duty and conscience, have been rejected. Therefore rejected they must be. The ideal of frankness, as Gide understands it, is purchased by abandoning entirely the demand that life shall be dominated and controlled by any principle whatsoever. Gide calls this 'depersonalization,' or, by a sacrilegious abuse of the Gospel, "*renoncement à soi-même,*" self-renunciation, self-conquest. In reality it is the despiritualization and dehumanization of life and its separation from God. No longer to know what to prefer and to be proud of not knowing, to love everything equally—in this Gide is poles asunder from his masters Dostoievsky and even Nietzsche to whom he believes himself so faithful—is a path that leads not to freedom but to nothingness, to the void and loss of being. If Gide does not see this terrifying prospect it is only because he consoles himself with a pseudo-principle, his "morality of the moment" which he has constructed in the empty space of his negative freedom, and because this morality of the moment, this permanent "adaptability" has enabled him as an artist to indulge in an aesthetic game unrestrained by any law, even the law of contradiction. But with this game, for it is nothing more, he cheats himself out of the real life which is achieved not by refusing to make a decision but by the grim earnest of decision. It is superfluous to observe that faith in any transcendental Being is incompatible with Gide's intellectual attitude. The immanental determination of nature has no more place for an absolute truth than for an absolute morality. Already in *The Coiners* Gide's religious sentiment has withered into a Manichaeism which regards God and Satan as two vital powers immanent in the universe and equally necessary. In his *Journey to the Congo* (1927) even this meagre remnant of religion has gone. To-day Gide is a Communist.

Three years ago the English critic Montgomery Belgion published a book, *Architects of the New Humanism,* which was a study of Shaw, Gide, Freud and Bertrand Russell. I mention the book, which I have not read, for the sake of its instructive title. In the camp of a neo-pagan or at least non-Christian intelligentsia the war-cry is loudly raised of " the new humanism." Gide counts himself and is accounted by others *among the architects of this new humanism*. His conjunction here with the other three names shows us in what sense he is so, if in any sense he can be. We hold that he can no more be the architect of a new humanism than Shaw, the gentlemanly Bolshevik of letters, Freud, the pansexualist, or Russell, the pessimistic philosopher. This so-called new humanism is an illusion which retards the return of the modern world to the truth. Shaw has at least amused the world with his brilliant wit. Freud in the judgment of his biographer Stephen Zweig has indeed "enabled humanity to understand its own nature more clearly, but has not made it any happier." And Russell is the philosopher whose vision of the universe is blank despair. " That man is the product of causes which had no prevision of the end they were achieving. . . that. . . no heroism, no intensity of thought and feeling, can preserve an individual life beyond the grave; that all the labours of the ages, all the devotion, all the inspiration, all the noonday brightness of human genius, are destined to extinction in the vast death of the solar system. . . all these things, if not quite beyond dispute, are yet so nearly certain that no philosophy which rejects them can hope to stand."

Gide, however, is taken seriously because he does not reject them. He is taken seriously because his conception of life—for in the entire world there is not a single important work of literature which is philosophically or religiously neutral—breathes a profound disillusionment with life, a metaphysical pessimism which goes to the very root of things. This is not altered by his refusal to admit it. " How well off I should be if it were not for all the people who scream at me that I am in a bad way." He has in view the critics who found fault with his *Coiners* as a work of art. We readily grant that the book is one of the most remarkable and important novels published during the last twenty-five years. But we maintain nevertheless that a man must be in a bad way, in his life, which is something much more profound than his art, when he can and must write a book so utterly bitter and nihilistic.

Here Gide's "frankness" reveals the inner despair of a heart that with a harsh exaggeration of pitch screams the paean of intoxicating sensations. Nor is there any alternative. That condition of inner balance, that Goethean serenity and calm which Gide affects and which is the ideal of the new humanism can be nothing more than a myth for man as he really is, torn apart by conflicting tendencies and incapable of any living achievement until he has submitted himself to the rule of one supreme and sovereign tendency. And it becomes even more mythical when it scraps as worthless lumber those sublime truths which a religious humanism has made the inspiration of man's ascent to a true humanity. And Gide scraps them relentlessly. For him the immortality of the soul is a stupid imagination which no healthy person takes seriously. The soul is a tangled mass of images and impressions of the outer world without an inner nucleus or a centre, and unable to find peace in what is termed virtue or sin, faith or unbelief. The best course is to let the tangled threads unwind and, when a man has exhausted the possibilities of change, to die in despair. "I want no other rest than the sleep of death. No desire will torment me any more. I would die as one who has hoped to satiety." The usual name for this state of mind is despair. Meanwhile "there remain," St Paul tells us, "faith, hope and charity; but the greatest of these is charity." Gide consoles himself with nature. " If everything else becomes uncertain (and everything is subject to doubt), my spirit would still find rest in contemplating the plants and animals. Henceforward I will know nothing but nature." To become as like nature as possible, to accept nature as the macrocosm by accepting that tiny piece of nature, the microcosm which constitutes oneself, is the true philosophy in comparison with which all metaphysical systems and religious creeds are a more or less thick smoke blown down the wind of nothingness. So Gide sings hosanna to " the nourishing earth." He loses sight of an important fact which Walter Pater and in our own time Ferrero have established beyond the possibility of doubt. Great Pan bestowed upon the heathen world that worshipped him as divine for their " earthly food " a profound melancholy, a food, it would seem, not permanently suited for human consumption. For mankind grasped, as it were with a ravenous hunger, the supernatural food of sacrifice which the Son of Man proffered on the Cross.

In a collection of essays written to celebrate Gide's sixtieth birthday, the majority of which were the work of foreigners, Ernst Robert Curtius wrote: " Like Nietzsche, André Gide has discovered a new man, a new province of the soul." A new man? This surely is an exaggeration. And if Gide is, as he is, the first to believe in this new man, he has nevertheless let slip a remark which reveals this European of the future as an old and very familiar acquaintance, " the genuine article, the *old man* whom the Gospel rejected." Gide's new man is the old unbaptized man, the man who has inherited original sin but refused redemption, who banishes the Holy Ghost from the world and hands it over to the demon who rises from the abyss of man's unredeemed heart; the man who sacrifices to this demon of our lawless passions every higher rule of life, all moral responsibility, all the natural ties of the heart and the family; the man who regards this anarchic eruption of all our impure and unruly instincts from the subconsciousness in which Christianity held them captive into the conscious life as an enlargement and enrichment of his humanity. It may be that in the process of education by which man attains his maturity this peep into his own chaos is unavoidable. But more than ever in this new age humanity needs the support of its good genius if it is not to be made dizzy by the sight, and fall headlong into " the depths of Satan." The phrase is fittingly the coinage of Dostoievsky. He more than Gide, Nietzsche or any modern mind gazed with a clear-seeing eye and a heart shaken with holy dread into the dark, irrational abyss of human nature, man's essential possibility of chaos. But he also spoke of " the restoration of ruined man." And man was ruined by the development of the old humanism which with an increasing momentum of irreligion tore him from the Divine order of being, and with swelling words confronted him, helpless and defenceless, with the chaos it had let loose. This is not the new humanism, but the denial of humanism. The new humanism begins where a new confidence in man begins, and this new confidence begins with the advent of a new and profound knowledge of redemption, of man's essential union with God, of what the Russian philosophy of religion terms the mystery of Divine humanity.

CHESTERTON
THE ADVENTURER OF ORTHODOXY

I am the man who with the utmost daring discovered what had been discovered before. *Orthodoxy, p. 16.*

There never was anything so perilous or so exciting as orthodoxy. *Orthodoxy, p. 183.*

TO write on a sheet of clean white paper the three sonorous names Gilbert Keith Chesterton is an easy task. But to convey in a few pages even an inkling of the brilliant reality, of the countenance prodigiously alive of the man who bears that name, of that personal focus of a most intense humanity which burns in his native England and whose vital flame has long since spread to the continent, to Germany and still more to France, is a feat of appalling difficulty which probably only one man could accomplish, Chesterton himself. We should have to see and describe him as he sees things with the careless spontaneity, unburdened and unconfined, that is divine or at least a special gift of grace.

I put on lately a pair of blue glasses to protect myself against the glare—only to take them off immediately. For the riotous glory of July had faded into the lurid desolation of a ruined world. Most men see the world through glasses which disfigure it. Chesterton sees it with the naked eye. He says somewhere, "I have forgotten that there is only one new thing under the sun, to see the sun." That he sees the sun and what is under the sun and sees them without glasses is, it would seem, his principal achievement and makes him literally unique among all his clever contemporaries, who before they look at the world pour over it the full cask of their personal sentiments and theories, with the natural result that they see it black, grey or red, but never as it really is. What remains of the world in their vision of it is the spectral apparition of some gigantic, monstrous and sphinx-like reality which fills the spectator with horror and a sense of hopeless impotence. If Oswald Spengler had written his *Decline of the West* in England, he would have encountered in Chesterton an opponent who would have wielded the club of his criticism with far greater fury and far more unsparingly than even Theodor Haecker in Germany.

Why is he never weary of thrusting at Shaw and Nietzsche, Wells and Maeterlinck, at the pantheist, the rationalist, the evolutionist and the materialist? Because their vision of the world is warped, because they place the world in a false light, because they are chiefly to blame if our life is literally " disordered." These " heretics " against the healthy human intelligence are the objects of an attack conducted unremittingly from his first to his latest book. This is the mission to which he feels himself called. It is the fundamental motive of his life's work which drives him without rest from his desk to the lecturer's platform and from the platform back to his desk. In an open letter to Chesterton, Comte Begouen, the archaeologist, has complained that in one of his latest books, *The Everlasting Man,* he had poured ridicule and scorn upon the most successful workers in the field of prehistory. The complaint shows a complete misunderstanding of Chesterton. He does not attack those who investigate the past of mankind but those who deny and defame man's *human* past and attempt to substitute for it an imaginaty picture of inhuman monsters. His concern is for the real man, to save his everlasting and spiritual humanity from the cannibalistic maw of a science diabolically proud, which regards itself as its own end. Chesterton maintains that, on the contrary, science is for man, not man for science. But man is for life, the authentic, true and radiant life, still clad, even in suffering and death, with a romantic splendour, the life which has no need to be discovered by scientists because it is always there. But it is this very fact which, it would seem, is hidden from them, " that the world is real and that things are what they are."

" What we know. . . is that the trees and the grass did grow. . . that queer creatures support themselves in the empty air. . . that other queer creatures steer themselves about alive under a load of mighty waters; that other queer creatures walk about on four legs, and that the queerest creature of all walks about on two. These are things and not theories; and compared with them evolution and the atom and even the solar system are merely theories." (*The Everlasting Man,* p. 27)

Chesterton holds fast to the elementary reality which fills all our horizons and presses itself upon all our senses, " man." *His everlasting theme is man.* And he would wholeheartedly agree with the Greek philosopher that man is the measure of all things, if he did not prefer to say with the Gospel, the Son of Man.

Those who do not know Chesterton may well ask with a shrug of the shoulders: why should *this* man in particular be required to preach these pathetically old and obvious truths? Surely a professional philosopher or theologian would do the job just as well as, if not better than, this " outsider." Not so. What is required for the cause which our Englishman champions is not a scholar of greater or lesser erudition but a *man,* and a particular kind of man, just such a man as Chesterton is. I can but affirm my conviction that if Chesterton did not exist the contemporary world would lack not simply a remarkable philosopher, or an indispensable man of letters, but a remarkable and indispensable man.

I have not to prove this assertion. He proves it himself by every page he writes, every word he speaks. And he speaks even when he writes. For to him writing is a substitute, something of secondary importance. Conversation, on the other hand, and discussion are of primary importance, a law of man's nature and a necessity of his being. For the male at any rate. The male loves the public house, the club, the parliament, because he must talk. God wills it so. "No one has even begun to understand comradeship who does not accept with it a certain hearty eagerness in eating, drinking, or smoking, an uproarious materialism which to many women appears only hoggish. You may call the thing an orgy or a sacrament; it is certainly an essential. It is at root a resistance to the superciliousness of the individual. Nay, its very swaggering and howling are humble. In the heart of its rowdiness there is a sort of mad modesty; desire to melt the separate soul into the mass of unpretentious masculinity. It is a clamorous confession of the weakness of all flesh. No man must be superior to the things that are common to men. This sort of equality must be bodily and gross and comic. Not only are we all in the same boat, but we are all seasick." (*What's Wrong with the World,* p. 92)

Do you like, do you understand such language, or do you share the feelings of that meeting of Socialists who roared with laughter when Chesterton told them that "in the whole of poetry there are no nobler words than public house"?

If you do, you are lost to Chesterton, and what is more

serious, you have lost Chesterton. For he always speaks like this. Because he is a literary clown, an incorrigible jester? No, because he is a man and not a pedant, a completely natural and unaffected man with an unrestrained delight in existence, and an unconcealed pleasure in wine, woman and song and all the lovely and loveliest things which God has stored in the homely vessel of our normal and ordinary experience on earth, in everyday life and the average man. There is nothing more stupid, nothing more culpable than to despise the average man. Chesterton loves him, defends him and sings his praises, because the average man is man as such, " the beer-drinking. . . struggling, normal and respectable man," man at every period of his history, the everlasting man who came direct from the hands of God.

Chesterton is the bard and prophet of the common man. In this he resembles Walt Whitman. But his style is less lyrical, and though he has the same democratic temper, his democratic sensibility is far more comprehensive, and in contrast to the American, his enthusiasm is nourished not only by history but by the spirit and dogma of Christianity. Chesterton is a man with a unique vocation. There is a pre-established harmony between the object of which he writes and the way in which he writes of it. We lose sight of the fact that he is a born man of letters of the purest breed in face of the more important fact that he is a prodigiously vital, large-hearted and real (not realist) man. We tend to forget that he possesses the knowledge of a scholar and the subtlety of the subtlest philosopher as he pours out his sparkling wit and brilliant humour. And he is always original. It is not that he does not speak of ordinary things. He speaks of hardly anything else. But when he speaks of them we become aware of something remarkably extraordinary about them which nobody has noticed though it intimately concerns everybody. And if you are not a hopeless lifeless dullard you cannot fail to perceive that a soul is here experiencing the world with the intensity and novelty peculiar to the great poet. To arouse delight in the world and man and love for them is a fine programme. But it needs the right man. Chesterton by his mere presence raises the temperature of life.

"Do you know, Hump," he said, "I think modern people have somehow got their minds all wrong about human life. They seem to expect what Nature has never promised; and then try to ruin all that Nature has really given. At all those atheist chapels of Ivywood's they're always talking of Peace, Perfect Peace, and Utter Trust, and Universal Joy and souls that beat as one. But they don't look any more cheerful than any one else; and the next thing they do is to start smashing a thousand good jokes and good stories and good songs and good friendships. . . I don't know whether God means a man to have happiness in that All in All and Utterly Utter sense of happiness. But God does mean man to have a little fun; and I mean to go on having it." (*The Flying Inn,* p. 59)

The speaker is Captain Patrick Dalroy, a retired sea-captain and a political adventurer, but not only a political but a universal adventurer, a born adventurer, an adventurer of the soul and life. He is an adventurer in the sense in which all the heroes of Chesterton's stories and novels are adventurers, in which *he himself is an adventurer.* For Chesterton life is the most romantic of all adventures and only the adventurer discovers it. The captain and his lifelong friend Humphrey Hump, landlord of the Old Ship, are the heroes of his story *The Flying Inn.* They discover the secret of the true and healthy life at the moment when an attempt is made to deprive them of it. But surely the only thing it is proposed to take from them is alcohol and the unrestricted right to buy it. By order of the Prime Minister Ivywood intoxicants may be sold only at particular places and the sign of an inn will be reserved to denote them. The pair pack up the sign of the inn, a keg of rum and the last large cheese and in perpetual flight from the police carry along with them singing and tippling these last symbols of a free and careless human life, through a world sobered by law. The flying inn becomes the standard of revolt against the suppression of the natural man by the modern social legislation. And Lord Ivywood is the representative of the modern spirit whose quintessence is revealed by the monumental dialogue between Ivywood and Krug, a chemist who has been detected trading in spirits.

" 'Do you think you made the world, that you should make it over again so easily? '

' The world was made badly,' said Philip, with a terrible note in his voice, 'and I *will* make it over again.' " (*The Flying Inn,* p. 253)

In all the mad adventures of *The Flying Inn* healthy human nature is fighting its battle, in its inmost essence ideal and divine, against the unnatural existence of the modern man without boundaries, home or religion, who therefore as typified by Ivywood loses his reason. I have been unable to determine exactly the order of Chesterton's works. But this is not necessary in order to obtain a clear picture of him. Before he left the Anglican Church for the Catholic he had held, so he told the French writer, F. Lefèvre, many Catholic beliefs and when he became a Catholic had almost nothing to alter of his old outlook on the world. I should conjecture he had not even had to alter it, when from his youthful revolt against Christianity he returned to the Anglican Church of his boyhood. What drove him almost irresistibly to the Church, the Anglican and the Catholic, was his innate vision of life. He knew by direct intuition that life is literally a Divine miracle bestowed on man and was determined not to allow himself to be cheated of it, but to do everything in his power to make the full realization and enjoyment of this marvel possible for himself and others. In this perception and appreciation of man and life, at bottom metaphysical, the entire later Chesterton is rooted. He has always been a man possessed by the obvious truth that man is the centre of things. And since modern life has buried this vital truth under a rubbish heap of errors and lies, intellectual, moral, political and economic, it is for him to remove this rubbish heap systematically, or rather quite unsystematically, with his impulsive disposition and a personality which exudes life, and dig out the old immortal truth of man. " God knows I don't set up to be good; " says Captain Dalroy, " but even a rascal sometimes has to fight the world in the same way as a saint." (*The Flying Inn*, p. 59) He is speaking for Chesterton.

Chesterton did not regard himself after his conversion as a father of the Church, any more than Péguy or Léon Bloy. "What then does he talk about in those endless lectures of his? " Lefèvre asked an English lady. " Oh every subject under the sun, but at bottom only a single topic, that humility is a great Catholic virtue and that we are all most lamentably devoid of it." That Chesterton is so noisy is "a clamorous confession of the weakness of our flesh," (*What's Wrong with the World*, p. 92) but that the noise is the noise of *combat,* a ceaseless battle against the world and that from the very beginning he has kept it up is something which Chesterton the sinner, like his delightful swashbuckler Dalroy, claims as a merit. And with good reason. Do not be scandalized if in the ardour of the fray he sometimes delivers his blows in the wrong quarter, as, for example, when in *The Everlasting Man* he is unduly severe upon pacifism. And if moreover precisely from the Christian standpoint we may question whether war is really an indispensable feature of the Divine government of the world, Christianity suggests that, as a manifestation of the struggle between good and evil, war will be man's perpetual destiny. This is Chesterton's view of it. War there must be, not in the service of imperialism of any brand, which he himself attacks fiercely, but war against everything that makes human life narrow, petty and meaningless. Read his great summons to battle, *What's Wrong with the World,* and you will know what he understands by it. What then is so wrong with the world that he leads in charge against it the " thundering gallop of theory " of this tempestuous book? A thousand and one things which cannot be told here—if only because Chesterton alone could tell us—but which always come back to this one complaint, that civilization is destroying culture, that the machine is robbing man of the natural field for the development of his activities, that the professional is everywhere replacing the man, that the predominance of specialism is putting an end to domestic comradeship and equality, and that womanhood is being crushed by the emancipation of women, childhood by the school.

The supreme and primary wrong which underlies all these violations of life is that we do not ask what would be right: "The common sociological method is quite useless; that of first dissecting abject poverty or cataloguing prostitution. . . The only way to discuss the social evil is to get at once to the social idea." (*What's Wrong with the World,* p. 7) This is the path Chesterton takes. There must be no social action without a social ideal, no practice without theory. It is most remarkable how this disconcertingly concrete and practical thinker emphasizes the primacy of the intellectual. The cry for a practical man raised when things go all wrong is the target of his ridicule. "It would be far truer to say, that when things go very far wrong we need an unpractical man. Certainly, at least, we need a theorist. A practical man means a man accustomed to mere daily practice, to the way things commonly work. When things will not work, you must have the thinker, the man who has some doctrine about why they work at all. . . If your aeroplane has a slight indisposition, a handy man may mend it. But, if it is seriously ill, it is all the more likely that some absent-minded old Professor with wild white hair will have to be dragged out of a college or a laboratory to analyse the evil. The more complicated the smash, the whiter-haired and more absent-minded will be the theorist who is needed to deal with it; and in some extreme cases, no one but the man (probably insane) who invented your flying-ship could possibly say what was the matter with it." (*What's Wrong with the World,* p. 11)

This puts it exactly: it is with a regular gallop of theory that Chesterton rides into the huge modern drug store with its thousand medicines for curing our social diseases more dangerous than the disease itself. It is a noisy gallop which leaves plenty of broken glass behind it but makes room for those suppressed truths which are our sole remedy. Amid the concrete and trivial problems of modern life the knowledge comes to us as something disconcertingly obvious that truth is our only salvation. But what is truth? In this book Chesterton deliberately refrains from discussing religion. But he cannot help remarking that we have only the choice between two alternatives, dogma and prejudice. "The Middle Ages were. . . an age of doctrine. Our age is, at its best, a poetical epoch, an age of prejudice. A doctrine is a definite point; a prejudice is a direction. That an ox may be eaten while a man should not be eaten, is a doctrine. That as little as possible of anything should be eaten is a prejudice; which is also sometimes called an ideal." (*What's Wrong with the World,* p. 18).

The modern world is dominated by powerful and uncompromising prejudices, indefinite tendencies, movements with no fixed goal, vague fashions. That is why it is sinking into chaos. The emancipation of women is a tendency which is leading to the surrender of woman and it is only a doctrine of woman's nature which can preserve for the world the wonderful vision of womanhood. Without the dogma of chastity there is no upper limit to the short, the excessively short, skirts. This last remark was made by Chesterton for the first time this year in the above-mentioned conversation with Lefèvre. It is simply the application to contemporary conditions of everything which in 1908, with the profundity of simple truth (women surely must feel some curiosity about the judgment passed upon their fashions by this manliest of all modern men), he said about women and her costume in *What's Wrong with the World*. In other words, even at that date Chesterton judged man not only by the fundamental standards of his human nature but by the standards of religious truth, or rather he had already perceived that religion is an inseparable constituent of man as he really is, of his everlasting humanity. He could not have done otherwise. He is too real a man, too completely human.

This brings us back to the spiritual portrait of the man, which it is our principal concern to draw. Now for the first time we catch sight of him *on the level* at which his personality emerges for the first time into full light and the secret of its inmost being, the abundance and wealth is revealed. Chesterton is an authentic *homo religiosus*. I do not forget that he has countless readers who care nothing for religion. I am aware that the *literary* quality of his work has not been affected by his conversion to Catholicism. That his view of the world has become even deeper, more joyous and more sure, that his heart and mind have been anointed and inflamed by the sacramental mystery of grace which has entered his life is perceptible only to the interior Christian and to those most of all who have made personal contact with the supernatural current of regeneration emitted by the Catholic Chesterton. I repeat: even those readers of Chesterton who on principle refuse to concern themselves with religion must concern themselves with his. For there is no Chesterton without religion. The mere mention of his name brings at once to our minds an ancient and venerable word, *orthodoxy*. It is the word which is the title of his most famous, most pregnant and most original book, one of the best products of contemporary Christianity which is not exhausted when it has been read half a dozen times. It is a word which to modern minds had long become tedious, empty and dead, but which Chesterton made as living as life itself. It was only the modern minds that were empty and dead. For this is the marvellous discovery which Chesterton has made, that orthodoxy and life are the same thing. He has not for example learned from scholarly treatises that Christianity is an ancient and venerable institution, not without its uses even for our modern world. On the contrary he has discovered from actual contact with modern life as a tangible and visible fact of the present time and place that Christianity is the most modern of all things. Searching for a spiritual foundation on which "an active and imaginative life, picturesque and full of a poetical curiosity, a life such as western man at any rate seems to have desired" (*Orthodoxy*, p. 14) could be lived, he found it—in the Apostles' Creed.

This discovery was the decisive spiritual adventure of his life. For to set out one fine day to seek for truth on the boundless ocean of opinion which is the domain of the modern mind or unreason, is a highly improbable, a truly fantastic adventure. So fantastic indeed that we could not believe it if we had not read Chesterton's account. You have only to take a glance at this account, to read such chapter headings as these: The Maniac, The Suicide of Thought, The Ethics of Elfland, The Flag of the World, The Paradoxes of Christianity, The Eternal Revolution, The Romance of Orthodoxy, Authority and the Adventurer, to feel convinced that it must be all rather mad. And yet this adventurer is probably the greatest genius and the most sensitive among contemporary humorists. In any case you must certainly hear some paragraphs at least from the introduction.

"I have often had a fancy for writing a romance about an English yachtsman who slightly miscalculated his course and discovered England under the impression that it was a new island in the South Seas. . . There will probably be a general impression that the man who landed (armed to the teeth and talking by signs) to plant the British flag on that barbaric temple which turned out to be the Pavilion at Brighton, felt rather a fool. I am not here concerned to deny that he looked a fool. But if you imagine that he felt a fool, or at any rate that the sense of folly was his sole or his dominant emotion, then you have not studied with sufficient delicacy the rich romantic nature of the hero of this tale. His mistake was really a most enviable mistake. . .

"I am the man who with the utmost daring discovered what had been discovered before. If there is an element of farce in what follows, the farce is at my own expense; for this book explains how I fancied I was the first to set foot in Brighton and then found I was the last. It recounts my elephantine adventures in pursuit of the obvious. No one can think my case more ludicrous than I think myself; no reader can accuse me here of trying to make a fool of him: I am the fool of this story, and no rebel shall hurl me from my throne. I freely confess all the idiotic ambitions of the end of the nineteenth century. I did, like all other solemn little boys, try to be in advance of the age. Like them I tried to be ten minutes in advance of the truth. And I found that I was eighteen years behind it. I did strain my voice with a painfully juvenile exaggeration in uttering my truths. And I was punished in the fittest and the funniest way, for I have kept my truths: but I have discovered, not that they were not truths, but simply that they were not mine. When I fancied that I stood alone, I was really in the ridiculous position of being backed up by all Christendom. It may be, Heaven forgive me, that I did try to be original; but I only succeeded in inventing all by myself an inferior copy of the existing tradition of civilized religion. The man from the yacht thought he was the first to find England; I thought I was the first to find Europe. I did try to found a heresy of my own; and when I had put the last touches to it, I discovered that it was orthodoxy.

"It may be that somebody will be entertained by the account of this happy fiasco. It might amuse a friend or an enemy to read how I gradually learnt from the truth of some stray legend or from the falsehood of some dominant philosophy, things that I might have learnt from my catechism—if I had ever learnt it. There may or there may not be some entertainment in reading how I found at last in an anarchist club or a Babylonian temple what I might have found in the nearest parish church. If any one is entertained by learning how the flowers of the field or the phrases heard in an omnibus, the accidents of politics or the pains of youth came together in a certain order to produce a certain conviction of Christian orthodoxy, he may possibly read this book." (*Orthodoxy*, pp.12—18)

"Possibly." But why possibly? Did a troublesome doubt that his adventure would not interest the public suddenly cloud the adventurer's delight? By no means. But he knows that his hunt for paradoxes exasperates many people. They cannot endure the way in which when he is treating of the most serious and sacred topics he must be poking fun at something or somebody. It is certainly strange, Chesterton admits, but it is true nevertheless, that the more he jests the more surely does he hit the mark. And it is no stupid caprice or accident. Already in the book which preceded *Orthodoxy, Heretics,* he had recognized clearly that "paradox is nothing other than a certain joy in defiance, which is proper to the faith." The believer is not mealy-mouthed, nor can he be if he takes his faith seriously and believes that Jesus Christ is the Saviour of the world. He did not stand on ceremony but asked men bluntly whether they wished to be saved or damned. He made statements so improbable and socially subversive as that well known saying that the first should be last and the last first. Apparently He turned things upside down. But in reality things were upside down and He set them on their feet, that is to say put them back in their proper position. The law and doctrine of grace must necessarily be paradoxical. Therefore Chesterton too is paradoxical, and if stiff and solemn pedants are infuriated that he pulls their leg, Chesterton is delighted at having made fun of their insincere seriousness. They deserve nothing better. There is a diabolic seriousness and a divine gaiety.

Such is the adventure of orthodoxy. It takes all sorts of Christians to make Christendom, all sorts of parishioners to make a parish. So thought Péguy, and Chesterton would be the last man in the world to disagree. And just because he is so completely different from Christ's other "parishioners," he has his place in this book which seeks to present a small selection of characteristic types from the great spiritual family of Jesus. He too is a man who wrestles with Christ. Not indeed in the tragic sense that he falls into Christ's hands as into the hands of the living God with whom he must wrestle for the salvation of his immortal soul. But in the sense that Christ's hands raise him to a new and splendid vision of the world before undreamed of. And he feels it his duty and vocation to proclaim and praise this world of Jesus Christ, to display it to souls and open men's eyes to see it. In his dealings with

Christ he does not seem to have lost a disproportionate amount of time on his personal concerns. He has probably had no special experiences of a mystical character like Bloy, Gide and Soloviev. But he has perceived that the whole of life is a vast mystical experience and that Christianity alone has preserved the instinctive sense of its mystical and romantic nature. Christianity finds room for "wonder, curiosity, moral and political adventure, righteous indignation" (*Orthodoxy*, p. 248) because it has room for the personal and world-transcendent God. Pantheism is obliged by its very nature to regard everything as of equal worth, since everything is divine. Since everything indifferently is good, everything is indifferent. Man is and must remain debarred from any possibility of developing anything new. Many religions leave men at least the possibility of following the traces of the Divine in the labyrinth of his own ego. "But only we of Christendom have said that we should hunt God like an eagle upon the mountains: and we have killed all monsters in the chase." (*Orthodoxy*, p. 247)

This is the principal reason why Chesterton became a Christian, a Catholic Christian with such a tempestuous joy. He is all for gaiety, struggle and adventure, and Christianity brings him into the arena of the most tense spiritual activity. Christ has in all ages possessed in his family intellectual spirits who serve him principally by fighting as militant confessors. To-day perhaps there are more apologists than people willing to learn from them. They are often too ponderous and too solemn and pack their windows with too large a stock of learning or piety. Bloy was dubbed a muck-raker because he does not avoid even the most unpleasant expression. "If," was his reply, "as a religious writer of uncompromising convictions

I were to allow myself to write mildly, nervelessly and tediously, nobody would read me and the cause of Christ would suffer."

Chesterton has this undoubted advantage over Bloy and all those other Christian spirits depicted in these pages that he is not obliged to do any violence to himself to remain in the most living contact with his public. He is never alone when he writes. For strictly speaking he does not write, he discusses and carries on a polemic, he speaks in his excitement with bated breath, he whispers, he shouts, he laughs unrestrainedly like a born orator to whom the souls of his audience are as visible as their faces. When you read him, you receive the impression of watching a fencing match. There he stands up, a fencer seemingly omnipresent, turning in every direction a sword perpetually in motion which he wields with a tireless and confident skill. He is Christ's fencer or gladiator, and how expert he is! And the spectacle is like a storm blast blowing into many contemporary minds and sweeping a thick layer of dust from a number of ideas which survived only as an empty form of words.

"Soldier of Christ" is one of these dusty relics of the catechism class which, if it suggests anything at all, calls up an early Christian martyr or a medieval monk. Then this Chesterton comes along and by his mere presence proves that the modern mind at its shrewdest and wittiest, the mind of a most accomplished man of the world, is an ideal qualification for this ancient service as the soldier of Christ; and that Christianity, far from being the affair of pious priests, morose and ignorant of the world, is the only door to a cheerful and vigorous life of variety and romance on this earth of ours. It is a peculiar and very unusual type of apologetic, nourished by a powerful and full personal life, which is not satisfied with repelling attacks upon the doctrines of faith, but reveals in the faith a magic wonderland to whose shore man is borne by a daring voyage of discovery undertaken by his sound and uncorrupted reason. It may well be just the apologetic most urgently needed by the average man of to-day whom Chesterton loves and for whom he writes. I am convinced that if the average man could be brought to see life as Chesterton sees it, with his incorruptible and sincere vision and his whole-hearted aim at a complete and fully developed humanity, he would find himself in the long run proudly and passionately "orthodox."

This would not indeed of itself bring him to that purely supernatural position where the truth is revealed self-supported and absolutely indubitable filling our entire horizon, a position in the spiritual world reached only by the believer. But he would perceive with astonishment how the mental atmosphere was gradually cleared of all the chimeras and phantoms, the illusions and hallucinations which had troubled and poisoned it before. He would share Chesterton's experience. The latter tells us that his assent to Christianity is rational but for that very reason not simple but resting upon a vast multitude of facts trifling perhaps in themselves but all pointing in the same direction. " My own case for Christianity. . . is an accumulation of varied facts, like the attitude of the ordinary agnostic. But the ordinary agnostic has got his facts all wrong. He is a non-believer for a multitude of reasons; but they are untrue reasons. He doubts because the Middle Ages were barbaric, but they weren't; because Darwinism is demonstrated, but it isn't; because monks were lazy, but they were very industrious; because nuns are unhappy, but they are particularly cheerful; because Christian art was sad and pale, but it was picked out in peculiarly bright colours and gay with gold; because modern science is moving away from the supernatural, but it isn't, it is moving towards the supernatural with the rapidity of a railway train." (*Orthodoxy*, p. 275) This passage shows me too clearly that when I placed my hopes just now on the average man I was too optimistic. The average man is no Chesterton, nor is Chesterton an average man. To be sure he possesses all the good qualities of the common man, but purified, ennobled and raised to an enormously higher power. He is the common man as he ought to be and might be but unfortunately is not. Where to-day shall we find the average man—be he the man in the street, the scientist or the writer—who approaches the world with the healthy and naturally open mind, the unlimited readiness to see and accept the truth about things and above all their mysteries which are innate in Chesterton?

In one of his lectures Theodor Haecker remarked bitterly that "what our men of learning, even philosophers, desire is not truth but power, pleasure or life." Chesterton too desires the pleasure and the power of life, but in and through the truth. His books are one cry increasing in intensity for joy, or rather a cry of joy. For he possesses joy as one who knows that he is living under the eye of God, bathed in the eternal Light which enlightens all men, even though its source is hidden from them like the flaming sun in an overpowering invisibility. If he loves Christianity it is for the very reason that it reveals the final secret of joy. There is no joy if there is no God. Happy paganism is a myth. The pagan enjoyed little things, but took a dark view of the great things. " Giotto lived in a gloomier town than Euripides, but he lived in a gayer universe. . . Christianity satisfies suddenly and perfectly man's ancestral instinct for being the right way up; satisfies it supremely in this, that by its creed joy becomes something gigantic and sadness something special and small. The vault above us is not deaf because the universe is an idiot; the silence is not the heartless silence of an endless and aimless world. Rather the silence around us is a small and pitiful stillness like the prompt stillness in a sick room. We are perhaps permitted tragedy as a sort of merciful comedy: because the frantic energy of divine things would knock us down like a drunken farce. We can take our own tears more lightly than we could take the tremendous levities of the angels. So we sit perhaps in a starry chamber of silence, while the laughter of the heavens is too loud for us to hear." (*Orthodoxy*, pp. 294-6)

What is this? The magnificently polished prose of a master craftsman, the lyric frenzy of a hidden poet or—? We have not far to search for the answer. It is Chesterton *the mystic* breaking through the crust of that average humanity which he cultivates and professes so ardently. We will complete the picture we have drawn of his personality by calling attention to this mystical factor in his composition. In an essay whose sympathetic insight penetrates deeply Chesterton's spirit (Hoehland, January 1923), Karl Bry wrote " that a man of his disposition and outlook might have been a mystic, but lacked the ultimate indescribable factor." It may be true that he cannot be called a mystic in the strict sense. In his nature and work there is such an intense devotion to the colourful variety of outer life that what strictly constitutes the mystic, the passionate wrestling of the soul with God and the experience of His presence in its depths, falls into the background, or at least is not a predominant feature. He would himself regard it as presumption to take a place beside the mystic Newman—not to mention the most exalted names. But his right place is certainly between Bloy and Soloviev. He may claim an honourable seat among the mystics of a predominantly literary and philosophic type—most certainly an authentic type. Everything in the world dances through his books, but in the harmonious dance, the restored divine balance which implies perfect gravitation around the mystic centre of life. Christian mysticism consists not in denying the material but in affirming the spiritual universe. Like Pascal or Bossuet in his *Discours sur l'Histoire Universelle,* Chesterton has a thoroughly supernatural vision of the world. His world is the world of *Orthodoxy,* the world of St Francis to whom he has devoted a book which displays a profound spiritual affinity with his hero ; and the world of *The Everlasting Man.* If his early writings may be regarded as a victory of sound human reason, these last two are a victory of man's mysterious being in its entirety, conscious that its inmost centre is rooted in the blessed abysses of God.

After all I find in Chesterton the "ineffable" of the mystic. I cannot read anything he has written without finding it. And in his novels and tales above all. He does not, it is true, like Bernanos at present in France, handle directly the most exalted themes of the mystical life. But his stories, which always turn upon religion and irreligion (in particular *The Ball and the Cross* which the *Revue Universelle* translated into French), contain pages glowing with mystic fire. All his novels are prodigiously fantastic. Chesterton's mystical view of the world reveals the truth of Pascal's saying that reality is more fantastic than man's power of imagination. They are often more gruesome than Poe's. But his horror is not Poe's, but Dostoievsky's horror of Antichrist whose visage stares through the smooth mask of humanitarian atheism.

Apart from this mystic vision, Chesterton bears of course not the least resemblance to Dostoievsky. He is no "man from the underworld." He is no prophet who stammers of the metaphysical abyss, like Pascal. Such apotheoses would make him laugh; for he is always merry. The mystical depth he possesses he would presumably regard as the obvious equipment of the average well disposed man. And if the mystic afflatus has raised him unawares to prophetic utterance, he quickly makes himself little once more, bursts into a gigantic laugh and declares that it is most certainly God's will that man should have his joke on His earth. If he has any definite ambition it is, if I read aright between the lines of his St Francis, this: to be like the Poverello God's fool and on his own initiative and in his own way to praise the work of His omnipotence, the permanent miracle of the world.

DOSTOIEVSKY
THE MAN FROM THE UNDERWORLD

> The roots of our thoughts and feelings are not here, but in other worlds. —From the original draft of *The Brothers Karamazov*.

> I have never been able to conceive mankind without Him. —From a sketch for *The Young Man*.

IN January 1931, exactly half a century had passed since Dostoievsky's death. But the life of a great writer cannot be circumscribed by particular biographical dates. In the vast world of Europe his life is only now beginning. In Russia itself he seems condemned to death after having been a source of intellectual life for sixty to seventy years. For a select few abroad he has been living for several decades; for the mass of educated readers since the war. And he lives in the fullest sense. His old bulky volumes seem almost more up to date than our current literary output of contemporaries. Writers who have themselves a message to give us pore over them with the keenest attention to make the discovery that what they are trying to say has already been said by him and in a way not to be surpassed. It would seem that whatever you are looking for in the sphere of literature, sociology or philosophy, you can find in Dostoievsky. Hermann Bahr learned from him how Europe can be saved from chaos, Hermann Hesse how it is sinking into it. Leo Chestov saw in him principally the man from the underworld, the rebel against every authority in science, philosophy and religion; Hans Prager on the other hand has found in his life-work a new Christian philosophy, the product of constructive genius, an absolutely incomparable theodicy. When you have read Eduard Thurneysen's profound study, you are convinced that this Russian is an apologist of the neo-Protestantism of Karl Barth and his followers. But the philosopher Berdaiev corrects our mistake and proves that no theological system of Western Christendom but the neo-Russian religious gnosis with its distinctive doctrine of man breathes the genuine spirit of Dostoievsky.

Who of all these is right? In some respects and partially all Dostoievsky's commentators up to the present have been right; his world is evidently so rich, so teeming with life and so many-sided that all find in him not only their personal problems but the answers and possible solutions. The fact is, by some experience, aspiration, mystic fear, burning passion or peaceful intuition, by a bundle of their heart's fibre they are bound so closely to this Russian giant that they cannot judge him objectively. They are spirit of his spirit, flesh of his flesh. They are not above him, but in him. They are not critics of his work but characters in it. Raskolnikov, Stavrogin and Kirilov, Myschkin and the Karamazovs have escaped from his books and are running about Europe under the names of Nietzsche, Lenin, Chestov, Gide and Joyce. This explains the contradictory pictures of Dostoievsky produced in recent years. For Bolshevik Russia Dostoievsky is nothing more than a figure of literary history, a great reactionary writer ; and the social, religious and metaphysical problems with which he concerns himself have all been rendered meaningless by the new Communist order. The west, on the other hand, is absorbed by the passions and problems of which he is master. His mere name is for us a symbol of burning actuality. For us he stands in the front line of Europe's spiritual battle. And *we ourselves* are convinced that he is fighting with the west that has remained Christian for a new Christian humanism.

This to be sure is an assertion which verges on rashness, since it has to be made good in the scanty space of an essay. Not, however, because it is so very novel. Already in 1925 Berdaiev proved it to the hilt in his book *The Philosophy of Dostoievsky* (English Edition: *Dostoievsky.* Sheed and Ward.). It does not of course follow that we of Western Europe should have grasped his proof straight away. It seemed far too Russian and it attempted to reveal Dostoievsky's secret by taking us with him into the metaphysical backgrounds of the Russian mind. Nevertheless this procedure was the right one. To take us through the labyrinth of Dostoievsky we require a native guide who, like Berdaiev, has been fitted for the task by a spiritual affinity with its power of sympathetic understanding. The remains published since Berdaiev's book appeared with Piper (Munich, 1926 and 1928) under the titles *The Unknown Dostoievsky* (*Der unbekannte Dostojewski*) and *The Original Draft of the Brothers Karamazov* (*Die Urgestalt der Brueder Karamasoff*) present a picture of the great poet which generally speaking agrees with that drawn by Berdaiev and what is without a doubt the definite and indestructible portrait of the man he really was, revealing his deepest purpose and his inmost conviction.

" In every man's mind," Dostoievsky once observed, "something remains behind, which cannot possibly be communicated to any one else though he wrote entire volumes about it and turned it over in his mind for thirty-five years. Something always remains over in you which cannot be extracted from your skull and which remains with you always. You will be buried with it, never having shared with anybody what perhaps were your most important thoughts." With an insight profoundly moving he has expressed in these words his tragic destiny. He lived sixty years, devoted his life exclusively to writing, wrote a stupendous amount and in spite of it all—as Strachov the confidant of his literary intentions informs us—executed only a tenth of the work planned. Into these novels he conveyed such a store of life, intellect and soul, of psychology and metaphysics, of a brimming humanity high as heaven and deep as hell, that Gide, a master of the craft, could find nothing to set beside them in the literature of the entire world—and yet in these monumental works which open up depths hitherto unattained he has not said his last word. Soloviev relates how after his rather severe criticism of *The Youth,* Dostoievsky received him with marked displeasure. Dostoievsky was a silent man, but when he caught fire he was irresistible. After he had held forth for two hours, Soloviev could but declare in amazement: "If what he said to me on this occasion had been given to the reading public, it would have beheld one of the most powerful and poetic visions that an artist has ever conjured up." This can be said of practically all his novels. Fate decreed that he should never realize the characters and execute the ideas of his original creative conception. He was usually compelled by poverty to send his books to press unfinished. And his designs were greater and more significant than the work actually accomplished. For the true, authentic and complete Dostoievsky we must go to the *Remains*. And this Dostoievsky is Christian to the core.

All the psycho-analytic vivisections performed on Dostoievsky by Freud cannot shake the weight of evidence which these documents provide. Freud's essay

Dostoievsky and Parricide is an introduction to the heroic world of *The Original Draft of the Brothers Karamazov,* which fits it as a fist fits the eye it strikes. But from such an eye as this the blow of a fist so sacrilegious recoils. If such an interpretation were not refuted by its inherent absurdity, it would be torn to shreds and tatters by the genuinely scientific examination of *The Brothers Karamazov* carried out by Komarovitch. If Dostoievsky had not, to quote Freud's words, " fallen back, after the most violent struggles to reconcile the instinctive demands of the individual with the demands of society, upon submission to secular and spiritual authority, reverence for the Czar and the Christian God," this revolutionary professor with the cold mask of the pedant would have left in peace the suffering hero crucified by life. For he would have had no reason for concerning himself with him. If Dostoievsky had not restrained by the grace of Christ his inner chaos of disordered instincts, he would have become nothing more than an ordinary criminal or a commonplace philistine. As it was he journeyed like a new Dante, through a spiritual, moral and, I am convinced, also a sexual hell. All the talk, however, about the autobiographical character of Stavrogin's confession is nothing more than unproven and unprovable gossip, as André Levinson, a Russian writer who writes in French, has shown in his study of Dostoievsky. Like most intellectual creators, like Balzac for example and even Zola, Dostoievsky shunned sexual excess not only as an indulgence which devours a man's strength but as a misdeed; his hell, even his sexual hell, was within his soul. These hells he traversed: and in addition the purgatory of religious doubt, of a passionate revolt against the order of the world, against God. He traversed them as one determined to go through with his journey, with hands tightly pressed and curses on his lips, but also as one determined to win his way out of the deceit and illusion of life without God, and burning with desire for light, for the " living life," " the great harmony," the "universal joy."

Strangely enough, it is this last aspect of their hero to which many of his admirers blind themselves. They will see nothing in him but the chaos. For them Dostoievsky remained all his life the demoniac who wrote *Sketches from the Underworld.* They are, I believe, pleading their own cause. Gide who professes himself a homosexualist and an immoralist considers Dostoievsky human, interesting and a man of the future in proportion to his perversity. So he composes a Dostoievsky in his own image. Is Chestov more satisfactory? In his book, which I have read in the French translation, *The Revelations of Death,* he gives us to be sure a uniquely profound view of Dostoievsky's chaos, which is indeed the chaos of the world, of its condition as we experience it. Nor could the literature which treats of Dostoievsky dispense with this view. Like Dostoievsky, Chestov is concerned with the ultimate mysteries of man's existence and these are girt with the storms of chaos. We may not conceal and cover over this chaos as it exists in that minute band whom God has doomed to look upon it. Without the chaos Dostoievsky would not be himself. This Chestov sees. What he does not see, is that Dostoievsky was thrust into the abysmal darkness to fashion from its material the "great harmony," " the universal joy," a profound and unique vision of the cosmic-Christ. Or rather he refuses to see it. He is among those Russians who regard chaos as man's normal and final condition. What of Dostoievsky himself? The question has such an important bearing upon his spiritual development, which is religious through and through, and upon his personal expression of Christianity that it cannot be answered off-hand.

At this point Dostoievsky must speak for himself. The *Sketches from the Underworld* are an extremely short composition written in 1864 and now incorporated into a volume of collected stories. The average reader therefore has no time left for it. He imagines that he knows his Dostoievsky when he has taken a look at one or other of his world-renowned novels—Dostoievsky, forsooth, of all writers the most enigmatic and most unfathomable, the man of whom Melchior de Vogüé who first made him known abroad wrote as follows: "Dostoievsky must be regarded as an apparition from another world, an unfinished and gigantic portent unique in his originality and in the strength of his passion." Now what de Vogüé terms "another world"—this strange psychological realm, this more than strange, this truly Satanic realm of experience, feeling and thought in which Dostoievsky was, it would seem, constrained by his nature to sojourn—bursts from him for the first time in the *Sketches from the Underworld,* and with a fury unexampled in literature. An infernal breath blows on our face. This cry from the "underworld" is anything rather than the moral and social sermon delivered for the improvement of his contemporaries which the author in a footnote tries to make us think it. For such things cannot be invented, they are experienced.

The man from the underworld thus introduces himself: "I am a sick man. . . a bad man. I am a repulsive object. I believe I am suffering from a disease of the liver.

But I have never been able to form a correct idea of my entire disease; indeed strictly speaking I do not know where the seat of my pain really is. I do nothing to regain my health, though I have every respect for doctors and the art of medicine. Moreover I am still incredibly superstitious; as indeed is sufficiently proved by my high regard for the medical profession. (I am sufficiently educated not to be superstitious but, as I have just said, I am superstitious notwithstanding.) No, my friends, if I do nothing for my health, my motive is sheer malice. That I am sure you won't be able to understand in the least. But for myself I understand it perfectly. Obviously, I cannot make it quite clear to you who it is that in this case I want to harm by my malice. I know perfectly well that I don't damage the doctors by refusing to let them cure me—yes, I know better than any one else that I hurt only myself and no one else. But all the same—when I refuse to be cured my motive is sheer malice. So your liver is to give you pain? What of it? Let it give me greater pain still it if can."

"I have been living this life a long time—almost twenty years. I am now forty. Formerly I had a position in a government office—I have it no longer. I was a malicious official. I was brutal—and it gave me pleasure. Since I got no pickings I was obliged to compensate myself by picking quarrels. (Yah! a vile pun but I'm not going to cross it out. When I wrote it down I thought it would sound witty. But now though I see myself that the pun was nothing but a pitiful attempt to show off I am quite determined not to cross it out.)"

It is a peculiarity of the style employed by this man from the underworld that almost every sentence contradicts the preceding. And the style is the man.

" Besides I lied just now when I said I was a malicious official. Out of malice I lied. With suitors and with my chief I merely played mischievous pranks—in reality I could not become malicious. Did I make up my mind to be so at once I was conscious of a countless number of conflicting factors in my composition. I felt them swarming in me, these conflicting elements. I knew that all my life they had swarmed there and implored me to let them out. But I did not let them out, I did *not* let them out, I deliberately refused to let them out. They tormented till I was ashamed, drove me into convulsions and oh, how sick I became of them at last, how utterly sick! Or do you suppose my friends that I repent of anything in this connection—before you? That there is something for which I ask your pardon? I am sure you do suppose it. I assure you however that I don't care in the least what you think."

This is a man whose soul is rent to inconceivable depths. So deeply rent that he is infuriated by the thought of his character assuming any clear and definite stamp.

" It was not only that I could not become malicious—I could not become anything, neither bad nor good, neither honourable nor base, neither hero nor insect. And now I live in my corner in the city and make game of myself by calling myself malicious and soothe myself with the superfluous consolation that a clever man—in all seriousness—cannot become anything whatsoever, but that only a fool becomes anything. A man of the nineteenth century must be, it is in fact his duty to be, in the strictest sense characterless. For a man with a character, a man of action must be—in the fullest acceptation of the term—limited."

The man from the underworld is characterless in a

special fashion, of which he is fully conscious, in accordance, so to speak, with a programme which he has laid down for himself—or another perhaps for him. Accursed questions at the very moment when he is trying to send them to the devil plague him with redoubled persistence.

" How came it, for example that I in the same, the very same moments when I was most capable of recognizing all gracious things, 'everything beautiful and sublime,' could not only perceive but commit such loathsome things, things, I tell you, that. . . But the most important feature of the case was that this was in a sense not in the least accidental but happened as though it could not be otherwise, as though this had been my perfectly normal state and by no means disease and perversion, so that finally I ceased to have any desire to struggle against it. . . It went so far that sometimes when on one of the foulest Petersburg nights I went home to my corner, I was conscious—how shall I put it—of a secret pleasure, abnormal and debased, an enjoyable titillation, in violently forcing myself to recognize that I had that day committed another blackguardism, that I could not possibly undo what I had done in order to delve inwardly and secretly into myself, to gnaw myself, as it were, with my teeth, suck my own blood, pick myself to shreds, torture myself. This continued until the pain and the bitterness gradually changed into a shameful, accursed sweetness, and finally into a decided and real pleasure. Yes, pleasure, pleasure, I will dwell upon it. . . I will explain it to you more in detail. The pleasure consists precisely in the too glaring sight of one's own debasement, in the knowledge that you have already reached the last wall, that this is disgraceful but cannot be otherwise, that there is no possibility left of becoming a different man, that even if you still possessed the faith and the time to change into something different you would most certainly not want to do so, and if you wanted to, you still would not, because at bottom perhaps there is nothing into which you could change."

When the man from the underworld surrenders himself from time to time to vice, he does not do it for the gratification of a frank sensuality. For with a shuddering horror he has tasted to the full "all the loathsomeness comprised in the notion of debauchery." No, he does it from despair. Despair—this is the one thing left him. He finds himself in the position of "the mouse confronted with the last wall." Indeed he so stands or crouches before this wall, so gnaws and bores into it that he "seriously regards himself with his intensified knowledge as a mouse, not a man!" For man, the orderly, normal (for nature intended him so) and direct man, the man of action—"such a man I envy with the utmost bitterness"—stands in an entirely different relation to the wall of which he is conscious. For him "the wall is always something comforting, morally decisive and final, even, I should say, something mystical." Confront a bull with a wall; he stands still with lowered horns, he respects the existence of the wall; the wall is sacred and exercises a calming influence upon him. But the mouse respects no wall, feels injured and humiliated by the wall, is determined to get through it, and gnaws, and gnaws and gnaws at it though it sees the senselessness and uselessness of its gnawing with the clear vision of utter despair.

What then is this wall? "The impossible. What is it? Clearly the laws of nature, the facts of science, and mathematics. If for example it is proved to you that you are descended from monkeys, you are no longer free to hold any other belief, you must take it as it is. Or if it is proved to your satisfaction that a single drop of your own blood must be more precious to you than hundreds of thousands of your brothers', that in consequence all so-called virtues and duties and other such fooleries and prejudices have been finally exploded, take it quietly. There is nothing to be done about it. For as we have said: it is the mathematics of the multiplication table, twice two are four. Refute it if you can. . . Good Lord, what do I care for the laws of nature and mathematics, if for any reason I dislike these laws and your twice two are four? Naturally, I will not run my head into such a wall, if I have not the strength for it. But I will not reconcile myself to it just because it is a wall and I do not possess sufficient strength." Is the man from the underworld a complete nihilist? He appears literally to have lost all ground under his feet; he hangs in the void. It is no consolation to him that the thinkers of the nineteenth century claimed to have discovered the boundaries of human knowledge and experience. This is simply one wall more, would in fact be a new barrier erected for our confinement by an unknown power that we might have no escape from the empty space, from nothingness. "Absurdity of absurdities! What rather we should all do is to understand everything, every impossibility and every stone wall."

But there is no help for it, " he must pine in a lustful lethargy silent, impotent, gnashing his teeth with the thought that there is not even, it has been proved, any ground to be angry with anybody, that no *cause* for it can be discovered and perhaps never will be discovered, that there is some secret deception at work, an artificial arrangement of facts, foul play, in short a muddle, and we don't know what it is or who is the muddler." " If only," groans the man from the underworld, "one had received from providence the grace of indolence, a quiet steady character, highly respectable and proper, dispositions that promoted the common good, a sympathy for everything noble and elevated! One would then grow a pot-belly and a double chin three times over and drink every day the health of everything noble and elevated; and every one who met me would say at the sight of me: 'Good Lord, here is a surplus indeed. This is certainly something positive.'" A mouse that has eaten poison and mad with pain tears around the cellar in which it is confined is the likeness which the man from the underworld (some translations render it cellar) has chosen for himself. No better could be found. In its frenzy it sheds its venom on everything which men regard as a surplus, as something positive. But strange to say at these moments something great becomes visible for the first time in his distorted visage, something which reaches the inmost heart of the man commanding a mysterious assent. It is when he is speaking not of the world and life, of man himself and his life. And what have they made of him? A miserable heap of contemptible rationality. A being with a narrow forehead and erect posture who drives in the carriage of his life, a fine handsome fellow, along the streets rationally laid out for his personal profit and the general interests of humanity and civilization. "You infant to have said this! O, you pure little innocent!" Profit! What then is a gain? Is it "the crystal palace" of civilization, the blissful "ant-heap" of which you dream when "the new economic conditions have been realized, perfectly worked out and calculated, as it were, with mathematical exactness so that all problems will be solved by turning a handle?" What however "if amongst all this rationality of the future a gentleman should suddenly rise up who, setting his arms akimbo, should say to us all with an expression of mockery: 'How now, my good sirs, shall we not trample all this rationality to powder with one powerful tread, and send all these accursed logarithms to the devil, so that we can once more live according to our irrational will?' " That is to say we have at last found something which this uncanny destroyer and curser does not reject and curse, the human will. " How ever did you come to imagine that man needs at all costs a rational purpose profitable to himself? The only thing man needs is an *independent* will, whatever this independence may cost and wherever it may lead." To this he holds fast even when it leads to "real suffering, that is to chaos and destruction." Suffering does not keep man, when he is a genuine and living man, from independent choice. On the contrary he loves the suffering and often seeks it. From many motives. The man from the underworld mentions one of them, which we should never have expected from this spiritual nihilist. " Suffering—to be sure it is the sole source of knowledge. And if at the beginning I said that in my opinion knowledge is man's greatest misfortune, I am well aware all the same that he loves it and would not exchange it for *any* gratification. Knowledge is worth immeasurably more than the multiplication table."

Is then the man from the underworld after all a spiritual nihilist? Could a spiritual nihilist speak as he speaks: " Reason, my friends, is a good thing, no one will deny it. But reason is and remains nothing more than reason and satisfies only the rational part of man. Will, on the contrary, is the revelation of life as a whole, that is to say of the whole of human life with its entire surroundings. And though the revelation often displays our life as a scurvy affair, it is nevertheless life and not a mere extraction of cube roots." It thus comes out in the end that the man from the underworld who scoffs at all ideals secretly cherishes an ideal. He is a wicked, repulsive and ignoble fellow. And he does not confess it in the spirit of Rousseau who, from mere love of showing off, chattered to himself and others of his misdeeds. He confesses it because it is true. The man from the underworld only seems to be writing for readers, because he finds it easier to write in this way. He must in fact shed his poison somewhere, must bawl out his rage in some one's ear. But just when his frenzy is at boiling point, his great hidden craving also begins to cry aloud. "The consequence, my friends; it is best to do absolutely nothing. Contemplation is preferable. Therefore—long live the underworld! I said, to be sure, that I envy the normal man from the core of my being. Nevertheless under the conditions in which I see him I would not change places with him (though I will not therefore cease to envy him). No, no, the underworld is always preferable. There a man can at least. . . Oh here I am lying again, yes, I am lying. I am lying, because I am certain, as certain as I am of the multiplication table that the underworld is not in the least better, merely *something different, totally different, for which I crave, crave beyond measure but which I am nevertheless quite unable to find. To the devil with the underworld!*" What is it for which he craves? Something that he does not yet know, has not yet discovered, but of which in the hell of his underworld he is at least obscurely conscious as a longing. And this consciousness brings to his lips for the first time instead of rancorous abuse, words of noble courage. He challenges those who despise him for his degradation. "So far as I am concerned, I have but carried to its conclusion what you have not even dared to carry half way. And you mistake this cowardice for prudence and thus console and deceive yourselves. It is clear that when all is said I am *more alive* than you, my good friends." And the phrase escapes him, "*living life*." It is a great phrase, the new slogan. It is the lightning flash whose liberating stroke explodes the chaos of the man from the underworld. "But enough, I shall write no more from the underworld."

What a long, slow and torturing process of thought, the reader sighs. No doubt. But how much more painfully must it have tormented Dostoievsky who had not merely to think it out in his mind, but to battle through it as an experience. For the *Letters from the Underworld* represent not a literary fiction but an experience. It is an experience which is here given literary expression, not an autobiography. When his contemporaries looked the author of this extremely unusual story in the face they did not behold the countenance of a fool or a knave. They saw a melancholy man shut up in his own inner world and completely unskilled in the arts of so-called practical life. What they did not see was the kind-hearted man, the victim of the first rogue who chose to exploit him, the extremely sensitive, jealous and passionate man whom his frenzied love of gambling could deprive for hours and even days of the use of his mighty intellect, the man who guarded the purity of his soul as a precious treasure, as his wife Anna Grigorevna knew. He took from her a French novel. "No, not this one. Why will you sully your imagination? Why do you read it? Why befoul your imagination? . . I require many sorts of book as material for my work. . . But I assure you, I cannot endure obscene descriptions. They merely disgust me." And from the experience of fourteen years spent with him she expresses her firm conviction " that he was in the highest degree a chaste man."

The man from the underworld is not Dostoievsky's portrait but his experience. It is the experience of a genius, raised by the stamp of genius to a more than personal, to a universal significance, and thereby has become a portrait, a symbolic portrait of the human heart. Dostoievsky has here laid bare with a cruelty indeed and a brutality which strikes us as barbarous the eternal heart of man. Amid unprecedented torments he has cut it out of the bleeding body. But the operation has resulted in a literal discovery. I do not know when or where before Dostoievsky literature has thrown up the profoundest depth of the human soul with such an unsparing frenzy, such a tempestuous and demonic force. Demonic—no word is more inevitable in speaking of Dostoievsky. Du Bos who has investigated the diabolism in Gide and Nietzsche postulates a direct co-operation of Satan in the *Letters from the Underworld.* If a writer becomes diabolic by depicting the diabolism of the human heart, Dostoievsky was certainly a fiend. But in that case the Saints with the profoundest insight and understanding of human nature were also demons. If we are to believe an Augustine, a Theresa and a John of the Cross, their heart was an abyss of wretchedness, turpitude and depravity. Péguy came to the conclusion that the Saints were not exactly " peaceful folk." And we have not forgotten the horror which Léon Bloy experienced when in the evening of his life he looked into his heart. These great and real men and women see themselves partaking through the murky element of their sinfulness in the dark abyss of nonentity by which man is surrounded. They have felt themselves crushed by their experience of the nothingness of man involved in the contingence of all things finite. Pascal called man a " monster." And since man was and still is capable of crucifying God, he is a monster indeed. So thought Dostoievsky, and was a Christian in thinking so. Though the word Christian does not occur in the *Letters from the Underworld* they are the work of a Christian, even if unconscious of his Christianity. Only a Christian for whom man is a mystery and no mere appendage of nature can bend over the human chaos with the passion of despair. Only a Christian is capable of such anthropological passion. Moreover a Christian such as Dostoievsky then was, who has forgotten Christ, is determined to forget Him, but cannot forget Him entirely. The place that God or rather Christ had taken in his heart—for he could not see God otherwise than through Christ—was empty. This evacuation was considered a great gain by the thought which in Dostoievsky's time called itself modern, as contemporary thought will always boast of its modernity. But Dostoievsky found that the place remained empty, a yawning abyss which all the riot of passions on the surface of the soul can never fill. This man with the abyss in his heart became in the creative symbolism of his thought the man from the underworld or from the cellar. This book seems to us of such deep significance because it is a vision of human nature without Christ, in the solidarity of sin, as it is called in *The Brothers Karamazov*. But even this is an understatement. Human nature is here exposed not only in a state of sin, of wrong-doing and semi-lunacy, not only as emancipated from every moral, religious and metaphysical tie, but in the ultimate formlessness and indetermination, the tragic potentiality of its fundamental being.

Zola denied Dostoievsky's originality. He understood by realism simply the capacity to grub about with a lustful zest in the dunghill. There are those who condemn Dostoievsky without qualification. Thomas Mann cannot endure him, because he cannot endure " the apocalyptists." An apocalyptist is a man who concerns himself with the last things. But for man the last things are not only at the end but also at the beginning, in his origin. If there were no mystery at the beginning there would be none at the end. The primordial and omnipresent mystery spans with a single bow man's origin and end. In the underworld the apocalyptic Dostoievsky dives down into the source of man, into his *inner* and spiritual origin. He leaves the psychological realm built up by civilization and descends into the primitive, the primeval world in the depths of his soul, a region which is not yet a world but a sheer desert and void, the bare possibility of a spiritual world, where personality does not exist but merely a naked ego lashed by a tempest of contradiction. What Hermann Hesse regards as the significance of Dostoievsky's personality and work is true only of the man from the underworld, " the rejection of every definite morality and code of ethics in favour of a novel, dangerous and horrible type of holiness which sympathizes with everything and accepts everything." Hesse confuses Dostoievsky with the man from the underworld. But this genius was far too " alive," and far too human to remain in the underworld. No man can remain there. For the underworld is a beginning, an origin, the lava flow whicn constitutes the core of man's being, the state of pure potentiality, of unlimited possibilities. In this state the man here described by Dostoievsky has long been living. But he feels that he cannot continue to live in it. Otherwise he must become mad, no longer knowing what is true and false, good and evil, whether indeed anything is worth thinking, speaking or doing. One thing however he knows even amid the terrors of despair; that the question is whether he can or cannot be a man.

In other words: this is a tragic vision of the most intimate mystery of human nature, *the mystery of free will.* And perhaps it is not only the vision which is tragic but free will itself. For in reality free will is anything but a cold and calculating choice between different possibilities. It is not just one endowment of the human spirit amongst others. It is that which makes it what it is, its substance, its living destiny created together with it and which it must fulfil. It is an ultimate metaphysical reality, a substantial centre of energy, the irrational and individual ground of man's existence which is filled to bursting with the passionate impulse to choose one of two alternatives, to become light or darkness, man or devil.

This was Dostoievsky's vision of the ultimate realities in the background of human nature. The underworld is nothing but the primordial human mystery of free will and its testing. It is not in itself diabolic. But the devils come forth from it. Man, born to be a free agent, becomes a demon when he makes a bad use of his freedom. For use it he must, for good or for evil. The mere fact of existing confronts him with a decision. It has availed Gide nothing to shirk the choice and take refuge in art as a sphere raised above life. He was compelled to choose in the end nevertheless; and at a particular moment he was aware of this and even admitted that he has chosen the diabolic use of his freedom. Just such men are all the demonic characters in Dostoievsky's work, Raskolnikov,

Svidrigailov, Stavrogin, Kirilov, Verchvensky, Ivan, Dmitri, Smerdyakov, and the father of the brothers Karamazov. That which distinguishes them from one another, the degree and quality of their diabolism, corresponds exactly with the particular individual way in which they abuse their freedom. Every deep view of life proves that Dostoievsky has not painted devils on the wall, that they are no products of his literary imagination, unparalleled though it certainly is. To-day and at all times devils go to and fro on the earth. But not every one recognizes them. For that the gift of discerning spirits is required. Dostoievsky is among those rare geniuses who plunge a glance of almost unique penetration into the dark abyss of the human heart.

Nevertheless we are not justified in speaking with Berdaiev of the new knowledge he has given us. Nor can we agree that Dostoievsky's conception of freedom is irreconcilable with the orthodoxy of Russia or Rome. Obviously the average Christian does not undertake such a profound scrutiny of the mystery of man's being. But we find it in St Paul, for example, and in Pascal. And surely it is exactly the same deep insight which finds expression in Guardini's definition of man: "not a being rounded off and fixed, not a self-sufficient humanity, but something to a very large extent potential which, open to incalculable possibilities, lies in the hand of God." "We remember," he continues, "how He who was the Son of God called Himself the Son of Man. Man's actual situation is so hopeless and God's purpose for him so divinely great that we must conclude that God alone can realize pure humanity. To be truly man is nothing natural, no starting point which we can take for granted. The real man must be the work of God." Possibly the man from the underworld does not yet know this. But he has an inkling of it. He desires to ecsape from the underworld. He desires to become a man. But he can achieve his desire only when he no longer surrenders his free will to the anarchy of aimless whim and submits it to "something different, totally different, for which I long, long beyond measure yet which I am quite unable to find." The man from the underworld longs for God. For the underworld, the marvel of human freedom, this absolute centre of man's personality, though it is open to the devil as well as to God, has been created by God and for God. *The abyss of human freedom calls to the abyss of Divine grace.*

In the same year 1864, in which the *Letters from the Underworld* were published, Dostoievsky stood beside the coffin of his first wife. The experience of death drives a deep man into the presence of life's ultimate mystery. Dostoievsky was a man with a boundless capacity for love, and love demands eternity. The love of a spiritual human being is, however, but a gleam which shines from the holy grail of the " living life." Can the lover perish? " I will not drown in the passing moment," said Goethe. Living life, living life, this was the only note which the funeral bell tolled in Dostoievsky's heart. Nature is iron, many tell us, guarded by everlasting laws. Is man alone unprotected, man with his foolish but unfathomable heart? He sits all night long in the presence of the dead and broods and broods. This is his great hour. Now he must prove whether he is emerging from the underworld, whether he can break through to the " living life," for himself, for her.

"April 16. Mascha lies on her bier. Shall I see Mascha

again?" He has hope. But he craves certainty, indubitable certainty. Who will answer his question? Where these deep problems are debated a Man presents Himself in whom the profoundest self-knowledge of humanity took shape as a concrete event, so that He could say that in His own person He is the way, the truth and the life. And Dostoievsky plunges into deep reflection about *Christ.* It is a hard struggle, as indeed was every experience of his intellectual and spiritual life. The numerous, in part gigantic, designs for novels, charged with highest speculative tensions which surround his completed works with a vast field of fragments, are sufficient proof of this. The man who is emerging from the underworld drags with him too heavy a load of problems to be able to fling himself into the arms of Christ with the élan of a faith untroubled or at most anxious only about personal salvation. He meditates not only for himself and Mascha, but for the life of mankind as a whole. Like Péguy's, his thought is solitary, but far deeper, more universal and world-embracing.

How, then, does he conceive of this living life? Obviously it includes personal immortality. Of this he is convinced. Man survives death. But how, in what form? The earthly ego is not the final self. It belongs to the order of generation which is merely a process of development in time. What then when time is no more? The ego in its earthly and temporal form has no place in eternity. And it is good that this should be so. That self is not yet the true man, the ideal man. The ideal man, the final and complete man, is the self " that is merged in undivided and unlimited surrender to each and all." Only such an enlarged self open to the entire world can be the true human personality, the realization of the genuine humanism. When and how shall we realize this eternal and essential humanity? Not here and now. Dostoievsky quotes the Gospel text: " They neither marry nor are given in marriage but are as the angels in heaven," and adds: "a profoundly significant hint." For the saying confirms his view that man's earthly and temporal imprisonment in the order of sexual generation is " the supreme denial of humanism." And it is a saying of Christ. Christ, Christ! He alone can help us in this problem. He brings light into darkness, life into death. Not only do we live after death but we live as true and complete men, universal men. That "man is merely a creature in process of development, therefore incomplete and in a state of transition" Dostoievsky had already guessed in the underworld. Now he is clear what this transition is to which he perceives himself subject. It is the passage to Christ. There are many "great improvers of humanity." But " the great and final ideal of man's development, the development of the entire human race, which has appeared to us in accordance with the laws of our history in the flesh " is Christ. And most important of all, not only does He develop us farther in the upward direction, He develops us in Himself. " The comprehensiveness of Christ's nature is amazing. Fot it is the nature of God. And Christ is therefore God's likeness on earth. . . Christ has fully entered into humanity and man strives to transform himself into the Person of Christ as his ideal." Christ is man's ideal because He represents " the final condition of human nature."

Here in these few pages of his " Meditations by the Bier " (in *The Unknown Dostoievsky*) is the clue to all Dostoievsky's later creations. The mighty realm of his creation is like an ellipse with two foci: one is the underworld, the other Christ. Our task here is not to make an analysis of his works, a task which has already been sufficiently performed by the voluminous literature dealing with him, but to present a clear outline of his spiritual personality. This, however, can be understood only if we take hold of it and study it in its vital centre, in its intimate, wholly original and unique relationship to the two fundamental mysteries of humanity, the tragic underworld of free will, the mystery in man, and Christ, the mystery of salvation and grace above man.

It is no exaggeration to say that there is not a single modern writer of his rank who has clung to Christ with such burning of heart and mind *alike* as Dostoievsky. Clung—this is undoubtedly the right word. He cannot mention Christ without an outburst of love. Because of this we gladly pardon him his misconception, so easy to understand, of the Catholic Church. At that time the misunderstanding between eastern and western Christianity was mutual. In his diary for 1873 Dostoievsky relates how the critic Bielinsky tried to convert him to atheism. It had happened long before; but the mere recollection of the attempt is enough to provoke his fury. "This fellow in a conversation with me abused Christ." In *Pages from the Journal of an Author* he writes: "To offer the other cheek, to love your neighbour better than yourself—not because it pays to do so but because it is a joy, to love him with fiery emotion, with passion. That Christ was mistaken—let it be granted. But this fiery passion exclaims: I would rather remain in my error with Christ than be with you." These words must not be misinterpreted as in any way supporting the heresy of an emotional faith incapable of rational proof. For Dostoievsky knows only too well himself that "atheism never found such a powerful expression" as in *The*

Brothers Karamazov, and that he therefore did not believe in Christ "as a little child." "My hosanna has passed through the great purgatory of doubt" (*Pages from the Journal of an Author*). Dostoievsky's spiritual relationship to Christ is based upon an extremely profound meditation upon His life and teaching. "I have never been able to conceive mankind without *Him.*" A single sentence is often enough to classify a writer. This short sentence with the pronoun in capital letters taken from the draft of his *Raw Youth* betrays the unbounded veneration, the adoration which Dostoievsky the thinker and philosopher of man's destiny felt for Christ. We receive indeed the impression that the part played by Christ in his published works is not so plain and so dominant as their drafts or in *The Plan of Life of a Great Sinner,* which is a mere sketch. But Komarovitch is right when he calls the completed novels "accidents" in comparison with what they were intended to be.

Nevertheless even in the case of the finished novels, if we study them thoroughly, we can hardly recover from our astonishment at their profound Christianity. However extensive the field they cover, their deepest meaning is revealed to the reader who will dwell upon them in profound contemplation. And the work of Dostoievsky's interpreters will be of further assistance. Dostoievsky is an intellectual giant with whom it is practically impossible to cope unaided and without preparation. Though I have been steeped in him for a lifetime, it was through Guardini's commentary that I first perceived in its fullness the wonderful mystical Christology of *The Idiot.* If Guardini is not mistaken—which to me is unthinkable—this book must be regarded as a unique jewel in the literature of Christ for which no parallel can be found.

There is obviously no question of the " Russian Christ " whom a superficial criticism is so prone to find in it. Dostoievsky knows only the one unique Christ. But because he cannot " conceive mankind without Him " he attempts to depict a man who is the most faithful likeness of Christ possible. A Saint, therefore, a character who imitates Christ by love of God and his neighbour, in action and contemplation? That would be nothing in the least new. Dostoievsky, on the contrary, gives us what is new and unique. He depicts a man who seen from the outside is a complete man of the world, but when seen from within proves to be a man not of *this* world but of another. He is a man for whom the counsel " to offer the other cheek " signifies no self-abasement but the affirmation and fulfilment of his own being. Prince Myschkin—the soubriquet of idiot was given him on account of his epilepsy—replied to a box on the ear received before a large company with "a strange smile which was not at all what the situation demanded." The smile is incomprehensible to all who live only in that particular situation. Prince Myschkin is a man who is at home on a higher plane of life. By everything that occupies his consciousness and subconsciousness, his intellectual and spiritual being, and impregnates them, as the form of its potentiality, he belongs to another world. He is in this world but not of it. Therefore he understands all men, but they do not understand him. *Just such a man was Christ.* And in this precisely the unique character of the book consists: on the psychological foundation of this appurtenance to two worlds Dostoievsky has created in *The Idiot* a human likeness and symbol of Christ. He has not portrayed the mystery of Christ as it is, divine and human, nor yet in the mirror of an imitation of Christ, like the hagiographer. He has portrayed it in a purely human form, but through the symbol of a man whose life is other-worldly. Since for Dostoievsky man is a transitional being, it is clear that he must have been powerfully attracted by the notion of depicting a Christ-like man amid the disorder of this world. For he saw in Christ the ideal form of humanity. But the astounding thing is this. His attempt was so successful that eminent theologians have learnt from it to understand better St John's picture of Christ. The latter, Guardini informs us, was first seen by Dostoievsky himself while he was engaged upon *The Idiot*. " In his attitude I found, I believed, something akin to the Johannine Christ."

Yet even this great achievement was not enough for the passionate love of Christ which consumed Dostoievsky's soul. A project took shape in his mind, which he called " the highest goal," " the entire hope of his life." He would display the mysterious power of Christ in its direct, visible and tangible influence upon the spiritual world of humanity. *The Plan of Life of a Great Sinner* was to bring the entire social, intellectual and religious life of Russia into the realm of Christ. " The sinner " would descend into the uttermost darkness of sin and desolation that by vanquishing it the all-transfiguring power of Christ should break forth in its ultimate and supreme triumph like a new revelation. It was to be an overwhelming victory of the " living life," " the universal harmony," over all the diabolisms of the underworld. But the Christocentric *thinker* in Dostoievsky was stronger than the Christocentric *poet*. In the end, it was better so. That he never carried out his sketch is an artistic loss. That he *could* not carry it out was his religious gain. His religious realism, which is also the realism of the Church, triumphed over the conception of a universal harmony which, as no doubt it presented itself to his mind, completely swallowed up the existence of evil. We must accept the fact of a sin from which there is no conversion.

Dostoievsky was too great a metaphysical realist not to bow, though with a holy awe, before this mystery which indeed constitutes the tragic centre of spiritual reality. He has stated it with all the force of his gigantic creative genius in the great novels *The Brothers Karamazov* and *The Possessed,* which are but broken fragments of the above mentioned design. These men make their choice between God and the devil with the full responsibility of their free will. The following words from the draft of *The Possessed* are of particular significance in this connection: " It has never struck you who deny God and Christ that without Christ everything in the world becomes filth and sin." And even more clearly: " I believe that man will become either angel or devil. We are told that eternal punishment is unjust and this French philosophy which assists the digestion teaches that we shall all find grace in the end. But life on earth is a process of change. Whose fault is it if you transform yourself into a devil? "

Thus does the man who has emerged from the underworld and has experienced the mystery of human freedom in its tragic depth grapple with Christ's mystery of grace. And he never wearies of it. Never does he come to an end, never is he satisfied with the insight he has achieved. On the twenty-fourth of December 1877, that is to say a few years before his death, he wrote on a sheet of paper: " Memento. For the whole of my life." Four projects follow. Among them: " To write a book about Jesus Christ."

After all this, is there any need to insist that the man, accompanied at every step by the figure of Christ, was a Christian in the full sense, a believer in the Christian revelation? Unfortunately it is necessary. For Dostoievsky's Christianity has been too often obscured by those who approach him from the philosophical standpoint. Prager was indeed right when he found the meaning of Dostoievsky's work in a gradual victory over a many-sided individualism and his incorporation into a universal humanity. But he failed to see that for this great seeker after God this redemption of all by all is guaranteed only by faith in the individual God-man, Jesus Christ, in personal immortality and a personal resurrection. It is a matter of the first importance for the contemporary Christian world that all the distorted and ambiguous presentations of Dostoievsky should be replaced by his authentic portrait. He claimed Christianity for himself—and with what unparalleled force! We therefore claim him for Christianity and will not stand by without protest when this spiritual giant is pressed into the service of an order of ideas which he of all men fought most vehemently. Every attempt to transform Dostoievsky into an apostle of a new and pure humanism superior to Christianity is false, and must be seen as false by one who carefully examines his work. No man has ever exposed the diabolic character of a naked humanism more convincingly than he. With an imagination of unequalled creative power and an organic process of thought translated into red-hot experience he has shown us a most extraordinary spectacle, how this ideal of a pure humanity left to its own resources produces in practice its opposite, the cult of the individual or collective superman.

Again and again Dostoievsky's demonic characters proclaim the fearful truth that modern anti-Christian humanism violates the inmost nature of man. By wresting him from the transcendent world of spirit and making him a passing phenomenon of the empirical world, it robs him of that depth which is of his very essence. By denying the existence of good and evil it emancipates man from his tragic abyss with its responsible acts of choice, but at the same time makes it impossible for him to climb the highest summits of morality and holds him captive on the material and utilitarian surface of existence. And it is on the surface of a purely secular and rational civilization that all these diabolisms, utopias, follies and inhumanities bear sway which contemporary history sums up as the crisis of western culture. Here man becomes the "man-god," dreams of "the will to power" and that "everything is permissible." And life sinks to the Karamazovian bestiality. He dreams of universal happiness for mankind and there comes into being the iron dictatorship of a small group over the universal ant-heap. So the dream remains a dream and even becomes a nightmare because man was not made for power or the happiness of the herd. But he is made primarily, before anything else and at all times, to become man, that is to say the being who, though entangled in space and time, in virtue of his inmost freedom seeks union with his eternal divine Source. Dostoievsky was not a Christian because he was childlike (to put it in his own way), but because he was a realist. It is the demons whose thought is unreal. In Dostoievsky's pages they are all confessed visionaries who, confined by the discursive reason or the lusts of the flesh, have lost the capacity to apprehend "living life." Up to a point they seem strong and weighty. But their powers are in the service of destruction. Whatever they do proves destructive because it comes from men whose inmost soul is already perverted.

What strikes the reader of Dostoievsky at first sight as a pathological study of inexhaustible significance is in reality an inexhaustibly profound debate with a godless humanism. And more than this, it is the attempt, which indeed is the only possible attempt, to vanquish it by starting from the metaphysical centre of human nature, which for him is Christ-like and Christological. Tertullian's concept of the *anima naturaliter Christiana*—which the average man regards as a rhetorical commonplace on which only a simple piety cares to dwell, has become for Dostoievsky an overwhelming experience which dominates his thought and artistic creation. He is therefore in our age, when the culture of the old godless humanism is in process of suicide, the father of a new and deeper Christian humanism. For it is he, the seer of the underworld, who beheld the soul of man poised above a grim abyss of freedom and peril, who discerned in that soul the eternal Christian. In this vision which in our day at least has an entirely novel air, Russia's great religious thinkers have seen Dostoievsky's deepest significance and the secret of his influence, still far from exhausted, upon the intellectual world. The philosophic lifework of Soloviev and Berdaiev is at bottom nothing else, nor does it seek to be anything else, than the employment of the inspiration received from Dostoievsky to construct an anthropology in harmony with the hidden currents and aspirations of Oriental Christianity, with its apocalyptic orientation.

Dostoievsky is an amazingly typical representative of that Russian religious sentiment for which the above mentioned thinkers have attempted to provide a philosophical formulation. He does not speak only for himself but in the name of " holy " Russia. This is a new and essential aspect of Dostoievsky which indeed has been brought fully into the light only by the material for *The Brothers Karamazov* which he left behind him and the truly New Studies of it carried out by Komarovitch. These sources prove the powerful hold which towards the end of the sixties the line of thought distinctive of that Oriental Christian wisdom which Berdaiev terms orthodox gnosis took upon Dostoievsky's mind. Under the influence of a vital exchange of ideas with Soloviev and Fyodorov, the religious and philosophic intuitions which he had moulded hitherto into artistic form suddenly arranged themselves into an almost systematic whole. But whereas Soloviev had been made known to the general public by Radlov as the systematizer of Dostoievsky's ideas, it is only recently that the chief source from which the poet of the Karamazovs drew his inspiration, the eccentric apocalyptic thinker Fyodorov has emerged from the anonymous obscurity which he jealously preserved all his life.

At the time when Dostoievsky was working out the conception of his Karamazovs, he received an unsigned manuscript which filled him with delight. " I have seldom read anything more logical. . . I have so thoroughly absorbed these ideas that they seem my own. . . The writer's thesis undoubtedly contains the most essential truth, our duty to resuscitate the ancestors who have lived before us, our performance of which will bring childbearing to an end. Then will ensue what the Gospels and the Apocalypse call the first resurrection. . . I tell you at once that we, Soloviev and myself at least, believe in real, literal and individual resurrection and that it will take place upon this earth." Ever more abundantly and more perfectly does Dostoievsky find that "wholly other" for which he had craved in the underworld.

At this juncture he met with a man who not only dared to dream but hoped at a not too distant future to realize the abiding dream of the Russian soul — and Dostoievsky's personal dream — of the transfiguration and restoration of all things in Christ, and the new holy life of all with all on a new holy earth in the Holy Spirit of universal brotherhood. The world is no chaos but a divine-human, theandric, organism; and upon man the microcosm in Christ also the microcosm of God, is laid the task of revealing the hidden potentialities of the world and hastening the resurrection by the conjoint will of mankind to rise from the dead. This is what Fyodorov means by the duty of resuscitation (incidentally there can be no doubt that it was from him that Berdaiev has derived his religious and apocalyptic conception of human "creatorship"). And Dostoievsky was captivated by this ideal. He had dreamed of it in the underworld. He had meditated upon it by the bier of his dead wife. Child-bearing and the mere succession of generations can never bring mankind to its goal. The transformation of the world must begin at the point where man is bound most closely to the world as it is, namely sex. When sexual passion, the pledge of man's cosmic relationship with nature, has been transformed into the spiritual Eros, mankind will be on its way to the new earthly paradise. In *The Idiot* Dostoievsky attempted to symbolize in an individual figure this ascent of blind instinct to the supernatural Eros. And what did he mean by his *Dream of a Queer Fellow*? It was written in 1877 after he had become acquainted with Fyodorov. Now we know. It is Fyodorov's dream—and his own: the dream which gave birth to his last creation, the vast world of the Karamazovs.

In its inner purpose this novel is purely religious. It becomes intelligible only when it is understood as the novel of Russian religious gnosis. To be sure it did not become what its creator had desired it to be. Such was the relentless and unremitting tragedy of his fate. It remained a fragment. Whoever would get to know the true Dostoievsky must study *The First Draft of the Brothers Karamazov*. As Komarovitch rightly insists, "in proportion as the original synthesis of the draft coincides with the final synthesis of the completed novel, the symbolical significance of the finished whole emerges from the symbolic tasks which the poet set himself in his draft or rather is seen to be the sole meaning possible."

And conversely in view of this incontestable meaning, Freud's psychoanalytic lucubrations about *Dostoievsky and Parricide* are shown to be sheer nonsense. If in this novel Dostoievsky assigns a central position to an act of a parricide, it is not the result of an Oedipus complex, but because he wished to represent by it the most extreme contrast possible to the apocalyptic ideal of the resuscitation of the fathers, the universalist ideal of the new community embracing the whole of mankind, whose annunciation and painful advent was the subject of the work as he designed it. "The parricide from a motive of lust was the negative symbol of this new world in which the spiritual transfiguration of fleshly love would restore the forefathers to life."

Nothing would be more perverse than to conclude from Dostoievsky's choice of dark material to an incurable demonism in himself. After the fashion of Rembrandt he produced his light from fathomless darkness. A dynamic and tragic art laden with suffering was his allotted portion. For art is a fate over which a man has no control but which controls him. Dostoievsky's conceptions descend to life's utmost depths, and his characters do not preach but live them. They must therefore often present an "underworldly" appearance. Dostoievsky knew how deadly and parricidal a force is the isolated and selfish love of the sexual instinct. To embody it he required the "unbridled licence" of the Karamazov father and his son Dmitri, just as he required the furious atheist Ivan who denies the meaning of creation, the resurrection and the great harmony, to provide a theoretical justification for the extreme of anarchy, parricide. But he needs all this chaos and conjures it up only to vanquish it—not by rational argument but by those characters of his who "are surrounded by the great mystery of God, the mystery of harmony and order" and " have experienced the cosmic joy of the living life," Zozima, Alyosha and Gruschenka. In like manner he made his own chaotic humanity, which he neither concealed nor spared, his own poor, great, dark soul clear and bright by that primal Figure, the abundant source of grace, whom he had long loved without knowing it and who became the avowed and passionate love of his heart, Jesus Christ.

SOLOVIEV

THE PROPHET OF DIVINE HUMANITY

> Men of action live a false life. They do not kindle life. Those alone kindle life who are strong in faith, those whom men call enthusiasts, dreamers, fools—they are the true prophets, the genuinely good men, the leaders of mankind.

WHEN Soloviev penned these words he had in mind the great Dostoievsky. But when we have learnt to know Soloviev himself and have long searched in vain for a description which shall convey the total impression of his personality these words strike us with the force of a sudden revelation. When in 1882 he uttered them in his second panegyric of Dostoievsky the thought that they might depict himself could have presented itself at most as a vague suspicion, an unavowed desire hidden in his inmost heart. To-day when a quarter of a century has passed since his death, we see that he had in fact drawn a true portrait of his own character and work. He was an enthusiast. He will be and is already a leader.

An enthusiast, a dreamer of Utopian dreams—this is an aspect of his character to which we may not close our eyes. Miliukov shook his head: "A brilliant philosopher this Vladimir Soloviev, but into what boundless dreams is he seeking to entice us?" Michel d'Herbigny reverences him as the Russian Newman and has devoted to him the first and so far the only biography written by a foreigner, a work inspired by the highest regard for him (*Vladimir Soloviev Un Newman Russe,* Paris, 1911). And as a Catholic, d'Herbigny cannot, like Miliukov the unbelieving Liberal, reject as folly his boldest dream of a free theocracy. But even d'Herbigny knits his brows at many of his hero's flights of thought. The reason we shall discover later. Those who do not know him but wish to make his acquaintance must be quite clear from the outset that Soloviev most emphatically does not belong to the category of men labelled as positivist: he understood absolutely nothing of "practical life." He had the air of an Old Testament prophet but was as absent-minded as the typical professor. On one occasion he spent the entire night on the landing because he had returned too late from a solitary walk of philosophic meditation, and meanwhile the long row of bedroom doors had mischievously withdrawn into impenetrable darkness. He was quite unable to keep the money which he earned by all-night vigils, for he was besieged all day by visitors of every description, like the writer in his last book *Three Conversations* who felt it his duty to receive every caller, answer every letter, read every book sent him, write every review he was asked to write, and lost his reason in consequence. The days on which he received payment were red letter days for the beggars. What need has he of filthy lucre, when he can live on tea and vegetables, is a vegetarian on philosophical grounds and at times even treats his daily lunch as a luxury in which he will indulge only on alternate days that the meal he has saved may feed the hungry? His entire life was marked by a lofty indifference towards possessions, honours and everything that the world regards as important, profitable or necessary. He on the contrary believed that by occupying himself with that which lies behind and above the world, with useless metaphysics, he was treading the highest summits of existence. And what did he regard as important and essential in his personal life? That at the age of twenty-one he qualified with brilliant success for the post of lecturer on philosophy in the university of Moscow? Or that he was very shortly dismissed from the post for political reasons? His journeys abroad to England, Germany, France and Egypt? " The most important event that so far has befallen me," he assures us in accents verging on solemnity, "is a dream, a vision or rather three visions." *Three Encounters* is the title which he gave to the poem in which he has recorded these fundamental experiences of his life, which were as unforgettable for him as was for Pascal that night of vision which he immortalized in his memorial. But whereas Pascal's experience seems obviously credible to the Western Christian, since it is one of those supernatural invasions of the soul by God with which the lives of the Saints have already made him well acquainted, he is taken aback and perplexed in the extreme by the experience of the Russian mystic. What can it mean? Who is this mysterious " she," this "eternal friend of female sex " who makes him deaf to earthly love, " blind to this life "? Is she a poetic personification, an innocent and non-committal loan borrowed from the vocabulary of pantheism to express a profound feeling for nature in the dignified language of philosophy? So it might seem from such a passage of the poem as the following:

> To thee I bow my forehead, Lady Earth,
> To feel a kindred heart that beats and burns
> As mine, beneath thine odorous veil and hear
> Once more the universe quicken with thy life.

But the small selection from his poems available in a translation is by itself a sufficient proof that Soloviev is not merely expressing a feeling for nature, a poetical personification of nature, but his own most serious conviction that a soul of nature, a world-soul, is an objective reality. Obviously such a belief can and normally will be based on philosophical speculation. But Soloviev explicitly denies that it originated in this way.

> Thrice hast thou shown thee to me face to face
> No pallid thought fashioned thy living form.

And it is indeed a remarkable fact that he experienced the first "encounter" at the age of nine, when in spite of his precocity the conception of a world-soul must have been unknown to him and the religious conception of the Divine Sophia as held by the Orthodox Church can hardly have taken such a passionate hold of his childish mind as to give birth to an actual vision. But whatever may be the explanation, he beheld " her " whom he cannot and will not "name" at the solemn Mass on the feast of the Ascension standing where the priest stood at the altar until she disappeared in the sea of light from which she shone forth with smiling countenance and in her hands " flowers from the meadows of Paradise."

From that moment he became the mystic of " the eternal friend." To be sure it seemed as though in the intellectual growing pains of the years which followed the experience she had vanished from his life without leaving a trace. The mind of the young student was occupied completely first by physics and mathematics then by history and philosophy. Moreover, and this was of far greater importance, at this period the intellectual life of Russia was dominated by German materialism. He caught the infection of unbelief (which does not come upon the normal man until the crisis which attends the attainment of maturity in his twenties) at the age of thirteen from the materialistic swamps of Vogt and Buechner. From this he was freed by the pantheism of Spinoza. But who would free him from Spinoza? Certainly not Schopenhauer, nor Eduard von Hartmann whom he so greedily devoured. Though they enriched and fertilized his thought and left behind them traces that would never be obliterated, they could not liberate him from chaos. Soloviev, to employ a classification made by the philosopher of religion Florensky, was far too much a mystic of the heart to remain the permanent captive of this mysticism of the head, which with an intellectual fanaticism bores its way undeviatingly into one aspect of the universe; and the longer and deeper it bores, the farther it penetrates into a desert of one-sided views, exaggerations and absurdities. In Pascal's phrase, "*Le cœur a ses raisons que la raison ne connaît pas*" (the heart has its reasons of which the reason knows nothing). This is the experience of all men with a universal outlook to whom it is given to see things not dissected by the merely discursive reason but in the all-embracing whole which is co-extensive with being.

In this sense Soloviev was a mystic of the heart. It was on the road of love that he experienced, guessed and felt the secret of the universe. To put it plainly, on the road and by the mediation of the mystic Eros. We shall not, however, obtain an adequate insight into these aspects of his inner life until the autobiographical pieces and the letters have been translated. In his *W. Solovjeff, Eine Seelenschilderung* (*V. Soloviev, The Portrait of a Soul*), Matthias Gruenewald, 1923, Lange gives us one such document. In it Soloviev relates how love between the sexes was the source from which there came to him at the age of nineteen the great mystical certitudes, revelations of the bond uniting all creatures with God. Any one who is disposed to see in this experience nothing but a metaphysical efflux of the enthusiasm of a young man's love should recollect that in the following year he made a vow of lifelong celibacy which he kept with the strict fidelity of a priest. No, it was an authentic mystical experience of which sexual love was simply the psychological starting-point and the exciting stimulus and which stands side by side with the " three encounters." The first of the three, that of which we spoke above, happened at a time when the nine-year-old boy was in love with a girl of the same age. The second and the third lacked this emotional background. But on the other hand, he was then—1875 in London, 1876 in Cairo—engaged almost exclusively in studying the doctrine of " Sophia " and "was dreaming, God be my witness, only of her."

Who is she, the " eternal friend "? Kobilinsky-Ellis warns us against reading an erotic and romantic meaning into Soloviev's mystical poetry. In this he is in agreement with Soloviev himself who in the preface to the third edition of his poems calls " the transference of fleshly relations common to men and beasts into the sphere of the superhuman the extreme degradation, and reverence for the female sex as such the utmost folly." But he hastens to add that this folly and degradation have no connection whatever with that worship of the eternal femininity that he serves, "reverence for eternal womanhood as conceiving in truth and from the beginning the Divine Power and bearing within herself the fullness of goodness and truth and through these the immortal light of beauty." In these words he indicates pretty plainly whom he means by the eternal friend, the eternal womanhood which for him is no abstract ideal or metaphysical concept but a concrete and living being, "possessing the fullness of power and action," God's holiest and dearest creature, the primordial creature at once individual and social created from all eternity, the living personal synthesis which is the all-embracing unity of God and the world. But with this accumulation of definitions we are already going too far and are in danger of reading into Soloviev's poetry things which he has not put into it, at least not with this precision. We are attempting a philosophic interpretation of his visionary experience, based upon his doctrine of Sophia, decidedly an unprofitable undertaking.

But the experience itself is important, and not only because it reveals Soloviev as a fundamentally mystical nature, but because, as he tells us himself, it was the hour when he became conscious of his personal destiny. It was the hour when the enormous overwhelming certainties, God, immortality, resurrection flashed upon his soul with such evidence that years of disappointment could not rob him of them; the hour in which he beheld that secret of humanity as a whole which he calls divine humanity and moreover the secret of his own life, namely his vocation to be a prophet and apostle of divine humanity and the union between God, man and the world. In so far as his philosophy is theoretical it is a search for this union and when he directs his thought to practical and immediate tasks it is in an ardent endeavour to realize the eternal harmonies in temporal existence. In these experiences Vladimir Soloviev found the colour, form, purpose and significance of his life and work. If we would understand him who simply as a Russian often presents a strange aspect to the Western European, in his relation to God, the world and civilization and follow his processes of thought, many of which strike us as extremely peculiar, we must not pass over these experiences with a shrug of the shoulders. It was for this reason that they have been discussed at such length here. We are usually inclined to form a too " occidental " picture of Soloviev. The fact that no Russian has seen so clearly the distinctive weaknesses and defects of the Russian mentality that he strove to overcome them in himself, and in the end even passed from Orthodoxy to Catholicism, is apt to blind us to the fact equally true that he remained notwithstanding typically Russian in his character and thought. Berdaiev his disciple, and himself a thinker of European repute calls him "our national philosopher." We have only to penetrate to the bottom of his ideas, instead of merely reading a few selected pieces, such as he collected himself in his *Spiritual Foundations of Life,* to see this most western of all Russians in his wholly Russian and oriental character. And we are astonished that he found his way to Rome. For he came from far, from a mental world remote and foreign. It is precisely this great and noble Russian thinker ready for the most heroic self-sacrifice who reveals most clearly the difficulty of reunion between the east and west.

As a student of eighteen, Soloviev abandoned the study of science for philosophy on the ground that it would better enable him to serve his fellows. This impulse to give practical help was thoroughly Russian. But the idea that philosophic truth would make him of use to others was completely un-Russian. Once in the past, Tchadaiev had entertained the same belief but not only was he not understood, he was shut up as a lunatic. The Russian, in fact, knew only of political truth, and was interested in philosophy only in so far as it provided political and social movements with an intellectual basis and justification. To study philosophy for the pure love of truth was regarded as practically treason against the people. Soloviev who loved the enthusiasts, the Utopians, the dreamers of strong faith, was convinced of the contrary, and flung himself ardently into the study of Plato, Origen, Seneca, Augustine, Bacon, John Stuart Mill, Descartes, de Bonald, Kant, Schopenhauer, Hegel and Schelling in their original language; and when only one and twenty delivered his inaugural lecture at Moscow University. His theme was "The Crisis of Western Philosophy." He stated his conviction that western philosophy was at the end of its course and was confronted by intellectual chaos, a plunge into nothingness. He was, no doubt, simply formulating in terms of philosophy a belief to which Tolstoy and Dostoievsky had given artistic expression. But it was not only by his sure intuitive vision of what was diseased in the development of life in Western Europe that Soloviev proved that he was rooted in the Russian soul. His next great work was a philosophic exposition of its most profound religious aspirations. It was not for nothing that he knew, loved and admired Dostoievsky. The ideal which he recognized as central in Dostoievsky, "the ideal of a Christian community of mankind, a world-wide brotherhood in Christ's name" took an increasingly powerful hold upon him. Like Dostoievsky, he saw in this ideal, the Russian ideal, Russia's historic vocation, the new watchword which Russia had to proclaim to the world. In his mind it became intimately linked with that mystical experience of his boyhood of which we spoke at the beginning of this essay. The experience was repeated during his travels abroad where he was sent to study after his first lectures. He steeped himself almost exclusively in the mysticism of Sophia which had long fascinated him. Already in a letter of 1872, quoted by the contemporary mystic of Sophia, Florensky, in a collection of writings published under the title *Christi Reich im Osten* (*The Kingdom of Christ in the East*, Matthias Gruenewald), he wrote: "I have found in the mystics many confirmations of my own ideas but no new light. I have come across three who concern themselves specially with Sophia, Georg Gichtel, Gottfried Arnold and John Pordage. All three had a personal experience almost identical with my own which is the most interesting thing about them. But all three are unsatisfactory, disappointing in their theosophy. They follow Jacob Boehme but do not reach his stature. . . On the whole only Paracelsus, Boehme and Swedenborg prove true men. A very wide field is therefore left for me." The results of his work in this wide field up to that date he published in 1880 in his Petersburg lectures on Theocracy and Theandrism. In the German edition they compose the third volume with the title *Zwölf Vorlesungen über das Gottmenschentum* (*Twelve Lectures on Divine-humanity*).

Theandrism, Divine-humanity: this is a conception so important for Soloviev's philosophy and life-work, and occupies such a central position in the Russian metaphysics of the Spirit which derives its inspiration from him, that we must dwell upon it. He admits himself that his views of the significance for human life of the fundamental Christian truths, especially those concerned with the Trinity and the Divine-humanity, are " too unusual to be intelligible in a brief statement." We are moreover of the opinion that only those who have previously read the *Twelve Lectures on Divine-humanity* can really appreciate even the synthesis of his religious and philosophical ideas to be found in his *Spiritual Foundations of Life.* The same is true of his great book on moral philosophy *The Justification of the Good,* and generally of all his important insights and essential ideas. For the concept of Divine-humanity is for him the first and most essential of the spiritual foundations of life. Upon it he built not only his theories, but his life, and thenceforward his entire work down to the *Three Conversations* (whose central figure is Antichrist), completed on the very eve of his death in 1900, pursue with unswerving consistency the one object of driving the notion of Divine-humanity into the heads of the public. His writings are a symphonic development of this *leit motiv* of ever increasing power and intensity. What content and meaning then did the idea of Divine-humanity possess for Soloviev?

Divine-humanity is not simply a Christological but also an anthropological conception. Man must be shown his true position in the universe, and his civilization must be based upon the sole, true and eternal foundation, the Divine truth of Christianity. The misfortune and sin of the civilization of modern Europe consists in its lack of this positive basis and absolute spiritual centre. " In place of an absolute centre we have as many relative and temporary centres of life and consciousness as we have different needs and interests, tastes, preferences, opinions and points of view." In consequence, man has lost both in his outer and inner life the last remnant of unity, integrity and concord. Nor has he been saved from this fate by the most strenuous efforts which have latterly been made to provide mankind with a unifying and organizing principle. Socialism is precisely such an attempt at organization in the domain of man's practical interests, as positivism is in the theoretical sphere of scientific knowledge. They are plainly doomed to fail because they exclude just this absolute and all-embracing religious principle which alone, by its very nature, possesses the vocation and capacity to unite all the living forces in man and his world. Western civilization as a whole "represents a complete and consistent revolt of man's natural powers against the Divine Principle, their exclusive self-affirmation and the attempt to construct with these unaided forces the edifice of a world-wide civilization of humanity." But its very failure, Soloviev foretells, will save human civilization from the final doom of annihilation by enabling it to see and accept the sole and universal salvation of the world, the truth of Divine-humanity.

This truth comes from the east. And like the east, the west received it from Christianity but has lost it by the development of a culture which came by degrees to lay an exclusive emphasis upon the *human* factor. The east preserved it, but undeveloped and buried beneath the débris of an uncultured millennium. Because it produced no culture, the east lacked the historical and social soil in which the Divine element of Christianity, which it had faithfully preserved, could have developed. Therefore the east needs the west and its faith in man, and the west needs the east and its faith in God. The west has made man absolute outside and against God. The east jointly with the west must make man absolute with and in God. This is the perfect and comprehensive truth of Divine-humanity which is the principle which must unite not only the eastern and the western Christendom, but mankind as a whole. So Soloviev thought; and it was the conception of Divine-humanity that inspired his work of union for the whole of mankind.

We have already said that the spirit which includes the doctrine of Divine-humanity is anthropological. At least it is this aspect of it which strikes us most powerfully, indeed amazes us. We are confronted with a bold, an almost disturbingly bold, form of absolute anthropocentrism. There was once a scientific anthropocentrism which made assertions regarded by the science of to-day as no better than childish dreams. Astronomically, the earth is as far from being the centre of the universe with its boundless spaces as any minute particle of dust, and from the standpoint of biology the existence of man on earth is merely the enrichment of the animal kingdom by one more species and a biologically retrograde and degenerate species at that. But the cosmic infinity in which man and his world vanish into nothingness is merely the " Evil infinity " as Soloviev terms it with Hegel. The true infinity bears man in its bosom; and as a spiritual being he breaks through the revolving circle of nature (to which as a natural being he is bound) in the conscious strength of his appurtenance to another and an absolute world. The secret of man which no science can explain away consists in the fact that he represents a reality which lies beyond the world and beyond nature.

The highest, purest and absolutely adequate expression of the mystery of man is Christ the God-man. He alone really and finally places human nature in the right light. His appearance in history entitles man to regard himself as more than a mere creature. If there is really a God-man there is also a Man-god, that is "man" who has received the Godhead into himself. For Soloviev the Man-god is collective and universal, that is to say, mankind as a whole or a world-church. For it is only in communion with all his fellows that man can receive God. This is a deduction from the principle of all-embracing unity which dominates Soloviev's entire philosophy: even as an individual and of his very nature, man is something other and higher than Western Christianity conceives him. No doubt in this statement of his faith Soloviev is far more cautious and reserved than his successors in the doctrine of Divine-humanity. He does not define the latter like Karasavin as the duality in unity of man and God. He does not indulge in the radical antithesis (too sharply pointed and brilliant as polished steel) which Berdaiev employs in speaking of these great mystical realities. "There is a human desire for God; but there is also a Divine desire for man. God is the supreme idea, the supreme concern and the supreme desire of man. Man is the supreme idea, the supreme concern and the supreme desire of God. The problem of God is a human problem. The problem of man is a Divine problem. . . Man is the counterpart of God and His beloved from whom he expects the return of love. Man is the other person of the Divine mystery. God needs man. It is God's will not only that He should Himself exist, but man also, the Lover and the beloved."

The formulation is Berdaiev's (*Oestliches Christentum* [*Eastern Christianity*], Vol. 2), but the ideas are derived from Soloviev. They are indeed to be found in the very book in which he advocated the reunion of the Orthodox Church with Rome (*La Russie et l'Église Universelle,* First edition, 1889; Third edition, 1922, Paris, Librairie Stock). But he does not thrust it into the foreground. To be sure even in this gospel of reunion as Soloviev preached it, there is quite enough to startle minds trained in western ways of thought. But the western reader is conscious of the consideration which he shows for him and his unremitting pains to render his mystical philosophy as acceptable as possible to the western mentality. This consideration is entirely lacking in those modern philosophers of religion whose work is published in Ehrenherg's collection. They plead, it is true, for closer relations between the Churches, but with Berdaiev reject the ideal of reunion "as essentially dishonest, a false idea." This explains the fact that their expositions of Divine-humanity and its philosophic presuppositions are more precise, pointed and strange, but also more contestable than those of Soloviev. He was in search of an irenicon, and was increasingly captivated by the idea of reunion: but he begins with the same root-principles which his successors have developed to their utmost extreme and often distorted in the process. It is as interesting as it is important to compare the ideas of "the spiritual father of Russian Catholicism," as a Russian Catholic magazine has termed Soloviev, with the form they assume when reflected in the minds of his successors. Divine-humanity does not purport to be a philosophical speculation, but a purely religious doctrine, Christianity in its ultimate anthropological aspect, the complete revelation of the anthropological significance of the Incarnation. For Soloviev however, there is not and there cannot be any opposition between the truth of Christ—which is the spiritual foundation of perfect religion—and in general of complete and universal life and philosophy. On the contrary he regards Divine-humanity as the fulfilment of all the highest aspirations of philosophy in as much as the doctrine of the Trinity is not only a revealed truth, but the crown of all speculative thought. In this sense Soloviev describes Divine-humanity as grounded in the fundamental nature of man, so that in the depths of his spirit a mysterious instinct points to it with the unswerving constancy with which the magnet points to the pole. This fundamental human mystery is the absolute nature of man. Man is not absolute in his actual and empirical condition but in his potentiality, capacity and compelling need to appropriate the Divine Absolute. The atheistic civilization of the modern world is fain to content itself with recognizing in man an absoluteness which is purely negative. For his incapacity to be satisfied with what is merely relative, and to remain permanently within the boundaries of finite and empirical reality never transcending every limited object, cannot be seriously denied. Man cannot however be satisfied with this negative absoluteness unless, indeed, he could be satisfied by sheer irrationality. " Without the positive absolute, and all-embracing reality and fullness of life, or at very least without the possibility of its existence the negative absolute is deprived of all significance or rather has the significance of an insoluble inner contradiction. Nothing is left of the mechanist philosophy but the conclusion that man is a fact that refuses to be a fact, a phenomenon that refuses to be a phenomenon. This is the deliverance of lunacy. If we would state correctly the truth immanent in human life, we must conclude that the human self is absolute in potentiality, nothing in actuality."

Thus man stands before the shrine of his own mystery. And he enters it the moment he becomes certain of his own *eternity*. To Soloviev this is obvious. Apart from eternity there is nothing that can strictly speaking be called man, for without it there is no humanity, that is to say no freedom and no immortality. Reduced to the phenomenon of his visible nature, his outer being, man exists only between bodily birth and death, like all other phenomena which emerge for a moment from the womb of space and time. If his sole origin is in time, in time he must also perish. He can be immortal in spite of and after death only if he already existed before birth—as an eternal essence. Moreover without eternity there is no freedom. How, demands Soloviev, can a being such as the empirical man, created in time out of nothing, wholly determined by God's arbitrary fiat and therefore in relation to Him completely passive and accidental, be free?

"Only when we acknowledge that the profoundest depth of every man in existence is grounded in an eternal and Divine world, and that he is not only an external phenomenon, that is to say a series of events and a collection of facts, but an eternal and unique essence, *a necessary and irreplaceable member of the absolute whole,* can we reasonably accept two great truths absolutely indispensable not only for theology, the science of religion, but for human life in general, the truth of freedom and the truth of human immortality."

We see how vehemently Soloviev insists upon man's eternal essence. And we shrink instinctively from this stupendous conception which seems to lead directly to pantheism. But the Russian mystics are obliged to take this path and they follow it with an ecstatic confidence and abandonment, because no other leads to what Berdaiev terms "the dizzy truth" of Divine-humanity.

It is becoming increasingly clear that this ascent to Divine-humanity is guided by a distinctive conception of God and the universe, or to put it more correctly by a type of feeling which apprehends life in a particular way. Hans Prager aptly terms it universalism or more plainly panentheism. Soloviev and his disciples speak of a philosophy of total-unity. All these are different names for the same thing. This panentheism rejects alike the pantheistic confusion between God and the universe, and the sharp dualistic cleavage between them which the Russian mystics of the total-unity attribute to Western Christianity, though it is in fact characteristic only of certain schools of Protestant theology. It teaches that the union between the universe and God is as intimate as is consistent with the completely independent subsistence of the former as other than God. It recognizes that the independent subsistence of the universe and man, the reality of sin and redemption presupposes dualism. But it also holds that the deification of the creature is possible only in the Divine world order of total-unity. And deification, theosis, is the ancient and most profound aspiration of the east.

Does not this aspiration receive a far more passionate and unrestrained expression in the new doctrine of Divine-humanity than the Greek fathers gave it? Berdaiev holds that the anthropology of the latter was unduly dominated by the sense of sin. They were content to teach that man must prepare himself to receive God by purifying himself from sin and earthly passions. According to them it is only by this negative way of asceticism that man can be deified. That in the very nature of man there has been implanted from the beginning a positive principle of deification is a topic on which they are silent, though here and there, in Gregory of Nyssa, St Macarius of Egypt and Simeon the New Theologian, we find a trace of this "Consciousness of the kingdom of man." The doctrine of the heavenly Adam has indeed been revealed in the doctrine of Christ; but its anthropological implications have never been worked out. Man, however, must be understood in the light of Christ, if he is to be understood at all, and not placed in the category of lower and unspiritual nature. Soloviev's conception of man as potentially absolute, as potentially all things and in his essence eternal has become for contemporary philosophers of Divine-humanity the conception of the Christological man who has a higher vocation to fulfil than atoning for sin and making himself and the world partakers of redemption. " The meaning of the cosmic process cannot be exhausted by redemption. Man must share the work of God's continuous creation of the world. Nor is the cosmic process a juridical process between man and God. And man's vocation cannot be fulfilled by his justification before the Divine tribunal " (Berdaiev).

These conceptions also have been derived from Soloviev, though he does not embody them in the formula of the Christological man. For him also the significance of the cosmic process is not a purely negative redemption from sin, but the deification of the world, "a transformation, a transmutation of matter into spirit, of fleshly life into Divine, the return of the universe to the total-unity with God which it lost in the pre-temporal fall. Without man this return is impossible and inconceivable. " Man was predestined to be the universal Messiah whose task it is to redeem the world from chaos by uniting it with God and embodying the eternal wisdom in created forms. This mission comprises a threefold human ministry. Man must be the priest of God, King of the lower world and Prophet of the absolute union of both. He is a priest when he sacrifices his own will, his human selfishness; King of the sub-human world when he subjects it to the Divine

Law; and Prophet of their union when he aims at the absolute unity of existence and progressively realizes it by the joint work of grace and free will, thereby gradually transforming nature separated from God into the universal and complete integration in Him which it originally possessed." (*La Russie et l'Église Universelle*) The entire cosmic process in all its vast extent culminated in man, the historical process in the spiritual and absolute man, Jesus Christ. The heavenly Adam includes the earthly in Himself. He comes not only from heaven but also from earth. He is, to be sure, more than the natural man who was only God's image, for He is " truly God Himself. For in Him a creature of God's containing in itself the true significance of all that exists appeared in the world for the first time as a creature and thus displayed to the world what the creature is in its absoluteness." Christ therefore is the absolute man, and man himself a phenomenon to which Soloviev also gives a purely Christological interpretation. He brings man in Christ closer to God than Catholic theology does. So close in fact that for him the absolute even of the Divine Incarnation begins not with Christ but the first Adam. The Incarnation of God in Christ is but a greater and more perfect theophany in a series of other more imperfect theophanies, which prepared the way for it by moulding the human nature which received them. " Even the natural man is a theophany." Hence according to Soloviev the Incarnation is not a miracle in the strict and crude sense of the term, any more than the Resurrection, which is the inner union of matter with spirit, is foreign to the universal order of existence. On the contrary, both are essentially bound up with the history of the world and mankind and constitute from the very beginning an integral part of the cosmic scheme whose goal is universal deification and the restoration of " the evil infinity " of the outer world to the inner total-unity of God.

If the deification of the creature is the goal to which the mystical thought of religious Russia aspires with such a powerful craving, *the principle of total-unity* is the conception by which the aspiration is philosophically justified. Karasavin explicitly maintains that in Orthodoxy total-unity is the fundamental category in terms of which the universe is explained in contrast to the culture of western Christianity which is based upon separation, multiplicity and a system of abstractions. Without this principle of total-unity the Russian mystical conception of Divine-humanity is unintelligible. It proves everything else but is itself incapable of proof. It is a supreme and ultimate concept, an axiom of thought and being, the foundation of all human knowledge and life to which all attempts to understand the nature of knowledge and existence necessarily lead. This is the presupposition underlying Soloviev's Lectures on Divine-humanity.

These lectures are a religious and philosophical synthesis. The doctrine of Divine-humanity is displayed as the ripe fruit of a long development of the religious consciousness. This development is "a positive and objective process, a real interaction between God and man, therefore a Divine-human process." It is based upon three factors, nature as the material of all life and consciousness, the Divine principle as the content of life gradually revealing itself, and man as the mediator, enabled by the combination in his personality of the spiritual and the physical, to introduce into the separated multiplicity of nature the unifying Divine principle and thus unite nature with God. This process, which must necessarily be a long development, since it is only by degrees that the Divine principle can enter the human consciousness, Soloviev terms revelation. Its initial stage is constituted by the nature religions in which the religious consciousness apprehends the Divinity in the form of the forces of nature. In the phase of negative revelation, of which Buddhism is the purest expression, the Divine is revealed in opposition to nature as freedom from all natural existence. Only in the third stage of the religious consciousness is the absolute positively revealed in its distinctive content, as that which It is in and for itself. This is the epoch of the Platonic idealism, of the Hellenistic philosophy of the Logos, the Jewish religion of the personal God and finally their consummation, God's self-revelation in Christ the God-man. Berdaiev maintains that revelation has not been concluded by the Gospel. Soloviev, who carefully avoids rash statements, is content with saying that the complete and comprehensive truth of Christianity is made manifest for the first time in Divine-humanity. Only in Divine-humanity, as Orthodox mysticism conceives it, is the logical end and goal of man's religious development attained and the meaning of the world revealed as its transfiguration and deification by the union of God and man.

Since this goal is true and divinely ordained, the way that leads to it, the principle of total-unity, is also true and ordained by God. If Soloviev offers any proof of it, other than its intuitive self-evidence which he obviously regards as decisive, it is that religious development has actually taken this path. It was for this reason that in his philosophy of Divine-humanity he makes such a thorough employment of the copious material provided by the history of religion to justify by its witness the conception of total-unity.

He finds it enunciated and proved for the first time in Plato's doctrine of ideas. After the philosophy of India had denied nature and conceived the absolute principle negatively as the non-existence of all being, Nirvana, Greek philosophy took with Plato the next step towards a positive apprehension of the nature of the Divine Principle by the doctrine of ideas. This philosophy beheld the true content of the Divine Principle which is not to be found in the world of appearances in the supernatural sphere, the realm of the ideas. Soloviev regarded it as possessing an imperishable truth and in his fourth lecture shows its compatibility with the view of the universe taught by modern science. He does this by starting from the necessity of postulating as the basis of phenomena an independent substantial nucleus which alone guarantees a certain relative reality, and defining this substantial nucleus with the aid of the theory of monads and atoms as the world of fundamental, living and metaphysically immutable ideas. This world of ideas constitutes the positive content of the Divine Principle. It must not be understood as a plurality of *absolute* individual beings. For if it were such a plurality its units would not be, as they are, necessarily connected intrinsically; there would be no basis for interaction of any kind and the real world which could not otherwise come into being would be impossible. It must on the contrary be regarded as a plurality of elements composing an organic system determined by the essential unity of its common Divine Principle, that is to say, an *ideal organism*. "All the ideas are inwardly related to one another, because they equally participate in the one all-embracing idea, the absolute love which of its very nature includes everything else in itself and is the epitomized expression of all, that is of *all as a unity*. That this unity or sum may be a reality, that is an actual unification *of anything,* the separate existence of that which is to be united, its *existence for itself* in real distinction from the unity is obviously necessary." In other words, the unity requires the plurality, as the plurality postulates the unity. Thus we reach the conclusion that *the absolute Divine Principle is the idea which comprises all and unites all.* This perception marked Greek idealism as the first positive phase of religious revelation.

The combination of this apprehension of God as the idea which is the unity of all, and the aboriginal ideal world, with the Judaeo-Christian revelation is the foundation of Soloviev's entire religious philosophy. Starting from this synthesis he reaches by the logical route *his* distinctive doctrine of Divine-humanity. Against this last statement he would indeed have protested. For him, Divine-humanity is no purely personal subjective belief but an objective truth. For it is the inevitable goal of the entire process of religious development, which as a Divine-human process possesses an objective character. This conviction he cannot sufficiently emphasize. No factor in the process taken in and by itself can be error or falsehood. The perception reached by Buddhism is not erroneous. It is simply a partial truth. Similarly the Platonic conception of the absolute idea as the aboriginal ideal world is a truth, indeed a positive and imperishable truth. Platonism is error and falsehood, only when it is held in isolation, as rejecting the higher stages of development attained in Judaism, Alexandrine Hellenism and Christianity. The idea of total-unity is in fact but *one* constituent of the process of revelation. Its full truth is, as we should have expected, revealed only in combination with all the other essential constituents to which it is teleologically related. Taken alone the absolute all-uniting idea is a wholly inadequate embodiment of the Divine Principle. It is no basis for religion. The Greek philosopher did not in fact possess a religious attitude to God, that is an attitude which determined his practical conduct. His attitude to God should rather be called aesthetic. The absolute idea without a corresponding subject, a person to realize it in the concrete, is completely passive and impotent, a mere object, a pure object of thought which has no real existence. The partial truth of the absolute idea had to be completed by the revelation made to the Jews, that God is the absolute Self, the absolute Personality. Taken by itself, even this conception of God is incomplete. Therefore with the prophets this aspect of God as a personal and purely subjective reality began to be combined with His objective aspect as the universal Divine essence. But the philosophic synthesis of the personal and the ideal-essential factor in the conception of God was the mighty task which Alexandrian Hellenism was the first to undertake. Philo developed the doctrine of the Logos, reason as the expression of the Divine essence and the mediator between God and everything that exists, a development which Neoplatonism (Plotinus) carried further with its doctrine of the three partakers of Divine Being who together realize the absolute content of Deity.

Arrived at this point Soloviev surveyed the entire development of the religious consciousness outside Christianity—though Plotinus lived in the third century after Christ he knew very little of Christianity and developed his philosophy independently of it—as an organically developed synthesis which wanted only the crown which should complete the revelation of Divine truth, namely Christ. As Clement of Alexandria, Origen and Augustine regarded the Platonic vision of the ideas, Soloviev regarded the entire course of religious development as the laborious but glorious ascent of humanity to Christ. In its essential content Christianity existed before Christ. Its fundamental truths were known to man before His advent. In what then did the novelty of the Christian revelation, that which had never existed before, consist? The sole answer possible to Soloviev from the standpoint of his religious philosophy was the following: " Christianity possesses a distinctive content which is independent of all these elements which are contained in it. This content is simply and solely Christ. In Christianity as such we find Christ and Christ alone. This is a truth which has indeed been repeatedly stated, but very little assimilated." What is novel, original and unique in Christianity does not consist in general doctrines but concrete facts, is not the speculative content of its ideas but their embodiment in the living historical person of Him who could call Himself the way, the truth and the life. Christ is the personal living synthesis of all the religious truth revealed in the course of the centuries. And He can be appreciated and understood only in the light of a religious and philosophical synthesis which "embraces the entire content of religious evolution without excluding a single positive element."

In this last thought we have surely found the true key to Soloviev's Christology, Sophiology and doctrine of Divine-humanity. They are all most intimately bound up with each other. And the bond which unites them is precisely the concept of total-unity, whose justification lies in the fact that it is a positive factor of the religious development. Soloviev places the figure of Christ under the mystic illumination of the concept of total-unity. Only thus does the mystery of Christ shine upon him in its full brightness, and become visible to him as the common mystery of all men, the cosmic mystery, " the meaning of the universe." Only thus does he hear the Name which in St Paul's words "is above every name" and in "whose name every knee must bow in heaven, on earth and in hell " resound in the harmonious thunder of a cosmic hymn through the abysses of creation. This thinker has in fact fashioned a completely Christocentric representation of the universe on a colossal scale. We are transported by the vastness of conception and the daring with which he philosophically and systematically bases the central supremacy, the absolute kindgom of Christ upon the inmost constitutions of the universe. We are not only transported but staggered. For it is all well-nigh too daring, fantastic, audacious. The paths which lead to the ultimate truth of Divine-humanity are, as Berdaiev admits, " dizzy."

According to Soloviev, God is the living, personal and all-unifying idea. He is not only one but all. He is not only the absolute Person, as He was regarded by the monotheism of the Jews, not only the absolute Subject, but the absolute Substance. He is more than a personal form of existence: He is also the absolute all-unifying idea which gives content to this form of existence. God is all. If the Godhead is not recognized as the entire fullness of reality and therefore also of its essential plurality it is reduced to an empty abstraction. God then becomes nothing, the universe all. In Soloviev's view it is the failure to recognize this truth which has led to the atheism so wide-spread in the modern world. The Godhead having been stripped of its positive significance, that significance is transferred to the universe. God is rejected as an empty concept and we have frank atheism; or the universe is identified with God and we have a naturalistic pantheism. Hence, according to Soloviev, the true concept of God is contained in the following definition: "God who exists from eternity, realizes Himself from eternity by realizing all. This all (in contrast to God in his essential existence as absolute Unity) is plurality, but a plurality as the content of absolute Unity, a plurality mastered by the Unity and reduced to it. A plurality reduced to Unity is a whole. The real whole is a living organism. God. . . is a living organism." Moreover He is an organism at once individual and universal. For the more diverse and unique the components and beings which the unifying principle of an organism embraces, the more powerful and the more original its Unity must be and the more individual the organism itself. An absolutely universal Being is also an absolutely individual Being.

Do we ask who Christ is, what is the reality which bears His Name? Christ is precisely this individual being who expresses in His Person the absolute content of the Divine Principle, the universal organism of the Divine total-unity.

This then is the point at which Soloviev's Christology passes into the Sophiology which seems so fantastic to the Western Christian; and must inevitably do so, given the fundamental determination of his entire thought by the idea of total-unity.

For Soloviev, as for the contemporary religious philosophers of Orthodoxy, there is no Christ apart from Sophia. Their correlation is axiomatic. As in the case of every organism we must distinguish in the Divine organism of Christ between the unifying principle and the unity which it effects. The principle in virtue of which Christ represents in Himself the total-unity is the Word, the Logos. The total-unity in so far as it is created and embodied by the Logos is Sophia. " Sophia is the body of Deity, the materiality of the Godhead permeated by the divine principle of unity." Soloviev is, of course, aware that he is employing the language of symbols and applying to the Godhead purely relative categories. He speaks of the Divine materiality or corporeality only in the sense that the universe within is, as it were, the organic body to which the Logos is related as its creative soul. Sophia therefore is simply the mystical expression already employed by the Sapiential books and the Greek fathers for that universe within God, that aboriginal cosmos of ideas which God has created from eternity, as the necessary presupposition and object of His self-revelation as the Logos.

For the Russian mystics, however, Sophia is more than an object, more than the Divine Wisdom conceived as a pure object of thought, an intelligible world. It is a living, even a personal Being. In support of this view they appeal to Scripture and the Fathers—with what justification we cannot now enquire. But they appeal primarily to intuition. In the doctrine of Sophia intuition has evidently the last word. If there is to be the least hope of reaching an agreement with the Sophiologists we must not approach them with the concepts of a purely discursive reasoning, to quote Bulgakov's gibe: so long as we are obsessed by concepts, victims of Hegelomania, *mania*

Hegelomania, we cannot penetrate the mystery of Sophia. And he frankly declares, " From our point of view the sole use of concepts is to describe and expound as accurately as possible the content of those mystical intuitions in which the Sophianic nature of the universe is immediately revealed to every man according to the intellectual capacity." This moreover is the general opinion of all those Russian religious philosophers to whom we are introduced by Ehrenberg's *Oestliches Christentum.* Are we to regard these genuinely impressive and original thinkers who have evidently been strongly influenced by German idealism, particularly by Schelling, as genuine representatives of orthodox Russian theology? Possibly the *Theologia Dogmatica Christianorum Orientalium ab Ecclesia Catholica Dissidentium,* whose first volume has just been published by Martin Jugie, will throw more light on the entire problem of Sophia and in particular will perhaps answer the fundamental question whether Sophiology in any form plays the predominant part in the system of orthodox theology attributed to it by Soloviev and the modern Sophianic mystics.

To return from this digression; even for Soloviev, who of all Sophiologists is the greatest and most constructive systematizer and who, as none of his successors, struggled to achieve a conceptual and rationally demonstrative expression of the Sophia mysticism, the latter remained in the last resort an object of intuition. The poems of which we spoke at the beginning of this essay leave no doubt that his Sophianic mysticism was rooted in a visionary experience. And in *Twelve Lectures on Divine-humanity* he expressly condemns the mechanistic mode of thought on the ground that while it analyses reality as immediately experienced, that is to say breaks it up and dissolves it into a series of abstractions, it is unable to display its higher unity, its source in the metaphysical depths of being. This can be accomplished only by the living organic thought—on this point Chesterton would most heartily agree with this Russian whose mentality is in other respects so different from his own—"which finds expression in the religious and artistic creation of a people, in the living growth of its language, in its myths and legends, in the forms of the people's life, in fairy tales and songs." Soloviev claims to rehabilitate this organic thought which philosophy has neglected and return to a mode of knowledge which is "no subjective process but expresses a real relationship to a world of ideal beings or a correlation between them." He is deeply convinced that the results attained by this type of thought are not arbitrary imaginations but "genuine revelations of a supernatural reality." This conviction is common to all the Sophiologists. Florensky speaks of a living experience, a religious datum which is attained not by proud construction but by humble reception and to which the terminology of metaphysics is applicable not in a strictly scientific but only in a symbolic sense. According to Bulgakov rational thought is not the Logos but merely logic. The Logos is the organic and absolute thought, as it is employed in apprehending the dogmas of faith, logic a relative and temporary mode of thought in correspondence with the present disintegrated and sinful state of the world which in spite of its formal universality only gives the illusion of absolute validity. In other words, the mysticism of Sophia, like all the great truths of Christianity, tears asunder by its antinomies the net of mere reason and can be apprehended only by the higher intuitive thought of faith.

This Sophianic mysticism is in my opinion extraordinarily profound, at once in the closest possible contact with the world and the most remote from it. But can it be made convincing to the Western Christian? The ultimate proof and the sole resource is the appeal made by the Russian mystics to intuition. Let us consider the conclusion thus reached : Sophia is an individual living being and at the same time a universal being, the unity of a plurality comprehending as subordinate factors in its higher self other living beings subsisting in themselves. This "plurality," this "all," which is ideally united with the Godhead as its content, this organism of ideas is raised by the creative fiat of the Divine Logos from the ideal sphere of the Divine mind to a real, living and independent existence. " The object of the Divine action becomes a genuine and active agent and the Divine activity a genuine interaction." This is Sophia.

Sophia is thus a being of double aspect of which it is not easy to give a rational definition. It eludes the ordinary metaphysical categories of absolute and relative, eternal and temporal, divine and created. It occupies a position intermediate between time and eternity. It is temporal in as much as of its nature it does not transcend time but on the contrary is the foundation of time. It is ideal time. It is divine in so far as it expresses the divine principle of total-unity—in so far as it is the eternal body of Christ, His pre-existent Divine-humanity; in as much as it is determined by the Logos and received its content from the Logos. And it is created since it comprises all beings, souls and ideas, the primordial universe which is the indispensable ground of the created universe in time and space. It is not the world, but the ground of the world, the first created, undivided and entire being of creation, the ideal personality of the universe and in particular of mankind which represents the most perfect and comprehensive quintessence of the cosmic manifold. It is that "eternal man" who pre-existed his physical creation and without whom God could not exist, the primordial ideal man, at once individual and universal or—what is the same—the individual-universal organism of humanity as a whole, which comprises really all individual men and in which every man as a natural being is metaphysically grounded. " Sophia is ideal and perfect humanity eternally contained in a perfect Divine Being, in Christ."

We have had to traverse a long route to reach the metaphysical foundation of the truth which Soloviev regarded as the peculiar and supreme revelation made by Christianity and the sole key to the mystery of the life of the universe and man. Sophia is the primordial mystery in which the truth of Divine-humanity is grounded. Only in the light of Sophia are its entire scope and significance disclosed. There is an eternal Christ, a God-man united with humanity not only from a particular date in time, but before all time. And there is an eternal man, a man who not only as a result of the historical fact of the Incarnation but in virtue of an aboriginal and pre-cosmic reality partakes essentially in the Godhead. There is a Divine-humanity, therefore also a human-divinity. Mankind is not only the temporal but the eternal mystical body of Christ and this not in an allegorical, but in an absolutely real and literal sense.

The metaphysical truth of Divine-humanity is of course also a historical truth. It is indeed the ultimate and final truth of all life. It is the most powerful motive force behind all the energies of the universe and all the events of human history. It impels them along paths wholly determined to a goal equally fixed, the historic realization of Divine-humanity. This is the sole meaning of the cosmic process. What pre-cosmic humanity lost in eternity, its unity with God, it must win back in time. The history of the universe is a progressive reunion. Man who in his Sophianic pre-existence destroyed the union with God, must become in his temporal existence its agent prophet and messiah. He must transform the chaos of temporal existence discordant, anarchic and alienated from God into the cosmos of the Divine total-unity. This is the task on whose fulfilment the salvation of mankind depends.

Truly a drama of well-nigh inconceivable magnitude in which man finds himself an actor. Our planet is the stage, and the great historical epochs the acts in which he confronts as his sole opponent the anarchic principle, the power of darkness, Antichrist. Yet he is neither solitary nor forsaken. The Divine Logos possesses His mystic bride " the friend "; and He has not abandoned Sophia though by her own fault she fell from the unity of God. Left to herself she would be unable to conquer the chaos which she herself called into existence and into which she has sunk. By her sin she changed the primordial cosmos which reposed in the total-unity of God "into a mechanical conjunction of atoms," the true infinity of ideal being into the evil infinity of external being in time and space. Sophia the self-conscious, all-ruling world-soul has become the unconscious and blind world-soul which no longer has any knowledge of the total-unity and in which the total-unity is still present only as a hidden potentiality. But the Logos, the active principle of total-unity, watches over the blind world-soul and unites with her in ever new and more complex combinations of the cosmic elements. And when the material chaos has been externally vanquished by the cosmogonic process its inner conquest begins in the perfect form of the human organism which has now at last been made possible. Man now comes upon the scene as representative of the idea of total-unity and the champion ordained by providence of the reunion between God and humanity. His spiritual personality is in itself nothing but a living expression of the first "inner union of the world-soul with the Divine Logos." Through him history will be liberated from the insignificance of a process determined in every respect mechanically and elevated into a universal order determined by God and spirit. It becomes a Divine-human process marked by progressively more perfect revelations in its religious depths of the mystery of God and man and finally leading to the living individual synthesis of all truth, the Incarnation of the Logos, the advent of the God-man. Is this the conclusion of human history? Strictly speaking it is its starting-point. For Soloviev, history is in its inmost essence religious, all culture a divine order, man's entire being Christocentric. Divine-humanity having achieved its absolutely perfect individual realization in the Person of Christ, must be realized socially by the historical process which He inaugurated. In Christ the Divine Principle became a physical reality, and this reality constitutes the new vital substance from which humanity united with God derives its nourishment. Or rather, as it assimilates the essence of Christ, it is gradually raised into the sphere of Divine-humanity. Sophia which before time was, is in eternity the mystical body of the Logos, is now in the historical development of Christianity by free co-operation with grace growing into the social incarnation of the Incarnate Logos, the universal Church. The universal Church is humanity united to God, Sophia restored to the original Divine total-unity.

The philosophy of Divine-humanity becomes of itself a *philosophy of the universal Church.* This is the case not only with Soloviev, but also with the contemporary representatives of Russian Orthodox religious philosophy. But the universal Church as understood by these philosophers is not the universal Church as understood by Catholic Christianity. This is a fact which must not be overlooked. In so far as the universal Church is conceived simply as a deduction from the idea of Divine-humanity, it is mankind united to God in Christ. For Catholics this conception of the Church is inadequate; it lacks what belongs to the very essence of the Church, the entire external aspect, the organization, the external unity of a hierarchy culminating in the supremacy of the Pope and a dogmatic creed as the necessary expression of the inner unity of faith which otherwise could scarcely maintain itself in face of the world. The historical character of the Church as Catholicism understands it, whereby it is in contact with the world, is explicitly denied by the Russian philosophy of the universal Church which denounces it "as an attempt to achieve a quantitative universality based upon compulsion," and in Berdaiev's view "represents the same universalist Utopia as Communism." The true universal Church, in the opinion of these philosophers, is the universe gradually transformed into the kingdom of God, the glorified world and the new humanity, and must decidedly not be identified with the numerical unity of any historical Christian Church. Its relationship to these Churches is on the contrary that of a symphony "in which the specialized spiritual types of

Eastern and Western Christianity find the justification of their existence and will continue to find it to the end of the world." For Berdaiev therefore and orthodox religious philosophy in general, a reunion of the Churches in the Catholic sense of their submission to a single Church "is essentially an insincere, a false ideal." The sole reunion of Christians possible and absolutely necessary is simply a union of mutual charity and understanding. (See Berdaiev's essay in *Christi Reich im Osten* [*Christ's Kingdom in the East*].)

It may be objected that Soloviev is not Berdaiev and that we are here concerned with the question how far Soloviev's philosophy of Divine-humanity is a philosophy, an ideology of reunion. But in fact from the beginning we have had nothing else in view than this extremely delicate and, it would seem, important question. In the opinion of some who have thoroughly studied the problem of Russian religion the existence or non-existence of a Russian Catholicism depends upon its answer. Richard Knies, the editor of *Christi Reich im Osten,* categorically states this view which the two Catholic contributors Ernst Michel and Bertram Schmitt defend at length, the former on historical, the latter on theological grounds. The recognition of Soloviev's intellectual significance is pronounced, as, even in the very sub-title of the book, by the Catholic contributors, an indispensable inner presupposition of reunion. To signify his importance an ardent champion of Soloviev's theological ideas, Professor Grivec of the University of Laibach, terms him the "spiritual father of Russian Catholicism." "On the question," he writes, "of the universal character of Christianity and the doctrine of the Church as the body of Christ I have found in Soloviev's works so profound and original conceptions, that the most eminent Catholic theologians could learn from him. From the universal nature of Christianity he deduces the profound metaphysical necessity of a united Church. The ideas of universal Christianity and of ecclesiastical unity are closely bound up with his entire philosophy and theology." And with these words as his text Bertram Schmitt seeks to prove that the doctrine of Sophia in which he sees the fundamental conception of Soloviev's entire philosophy "is acceptable at least in its general trend." Soloviev's philosophy and theology culminate, as our account has surely proved, in his philosophy of Divine-humanity, not in the doctrine of Sophia which is to be regarded rather as the final argument for the conception, the central conception of Divine-humanity. Is then this philosophy of Divine-humanity really bound up so closely with the principle of ecclesiastical unity that without it Soloviev would never have come to recognize the authority of the Catholic Church and in turn unless she recognizes the doctrine of Divine-humanity the Catholic Church will never be able to effect a reunion with the Orthodox Russian Church?

We should be deterred from returning too hastily an affirmative answer by the mere fact that the contemporary Russian religious philosophy, which on the whole agrees with Soloviev in his doctrine of Divine-humanity, is by no means favourable to the ideal of reunion. Is the reason simply that the psychological factor of national prejudice, whose importance must certainly not be minimized, makes it difficult to carry into practice the logical conclusion from the doctrine of Divine-humanity, namely reunion? Perhaps the reason is rather that the reunion of the Churches is not the inevitable corollary of this doctrine. The correlate of the religious doctrine of Divine-humanity is the universal Church in the general sense of a free union of mankind on the Divine basis of Christianity. This is its sole immediate corollary as Soloviev himself states it at the conclusion of his Lectures. How then did Soloviev actually reach Rome? By what route? For it is obviously a long journey from the universal Church as he envisaged it in his Lectures to that other universal Church which he discovered for himself and his compatriots in his profession of faith, *La Russie et l'Église Universelle*. It took him almost a decade. When in 1880 he taught his philosophy of Divine-humanity he had begun his search for the universal Church. But when in 1889 he published *Russia and the Universal Church* he had found it—and its centre was Rome. And the conclusion was anything but a discovery made in the calm field of philosophy; it was a truth for which he had to fight step by step in the grim reality of stern conflicts on the battle-field of Russian life. He lost all his friends in the process, sacrificed all the comfort of a secure life. An atmosphere of mistrust and hostility gathered around " the fool, the Utopian, the enthusiast." And when at last he possessed the complete truth which alone, he was convinced, can save Russia and the world he became a voice in the wilderness, was silenced in his native country and constrained to publish the supreme and the most precious truth by which he lived abroad and in the French tongue.

Thus for Soloviev the true and genuine conception of union ripened in the soul not of philosophy but of life. His philosophy of Divine-humanity had led him no further than a universalist view of life and history. Dostoievsky's ideal of universal brotherhood assumed the more definite shape of union between east and west. The initiative must come from the east because the Eastern Church had preserved at least in germ the all-uniting truth of Divine-humanity, whereas Western Catholicism had lost its religious power. The Russian idea, and the spiritual vocation of Russia was to effect in union with all the other nations the perfect and world-embracing unity of the human race. So Soloviev forsook his chair of philosophy to preach to the general public in the pulpit of the newspaper and magazine the ideal of union in the widest sense. He attacked the anti-universalist philosophy of civilization professed by Danilevsky, who in anticipation of Spengler taught in his *Russia and Europe* that human history was the history of distinct types of historical cultures, mutually independent and pursuing a parallel course. Danilevsky's philosophy was inspired by the nationalist desire to justify the existence of a native Slavonic culture permanently separate from that of Western Europe and closed to its influence. Soloviev combated national selfishness wherever he found it. And he found it in every sphere of Russian life. Politics, art, science, even religion were poisoned by it. And these struggles opened his eyes. How could Russia give the world the universalism which would save it? It did not itself possess that universalism and its official Church, the Orthodox Church, least of all. It was a purely national Church without any self-government, completely in the power of the state. And it was a dead Church which, if religious liberty were conceded, would lose half the peasants to the schismatic Raskol, and a considerable section of the educated class to Catholicism. The ideal of religious universalism found no support either in the national Church or in the people of Russia (see *La Russie et l'Église Universelle*), and Russia's part can therefore consist only in giving by her submission the true universal Church, already in principle realized in the Church of Rome, that powerful position which is required for the regeneration of Europe and the world.

It is no accident that in *La Russie et l'Église Universelle* in which Soloviev states his fundamental convictions his theological theory of the universal Church is confined to the concluding section, whereas a critical review of the religious situation in Russia occupies the first, and a historical study of the foundation of the Church the second. For the result of this double enquiry, the recognition of the facts it reveals is the reason why he found the embodiment of the universal Church in the Roman Church—not the theory of the universal Church developed in the third section of his book. This is the ground of our convictions that this theory cannot be regarded as primary, but merely as subordinate and that the ideal of union in the strict sense is not an organic growth from the philosophy which moulded Soloviev's inmost nature. Of this he is himself fully aware. He admits it publicly when he bases his new theory of the universal Church no longer on Divine-humanity but on " the Trinitarian principle." In the God-man he sees the individual, in the Church the social embodiment of this principle (the threefold office of priest, king and prophet). To the ontological primacy of the Father in the Blessed Trinity the primacy of the chief priest, the Pope, corresponds in the Church. Soloviev most certainly does not abandon his philosophy of Divine-humanity, but finds himself compelled to adapt it with the aid of the Trinitarian principle to the theory of a universal Church, whose actual existence he had come to recognize in the Catholic Church by following other paths than those of his philosophic theory. And who can tell whether the theory would not have undergone far more fundamental modifications, if he had been granted a longer life after joining the Church—he died in 1900—and he had come into closer contact with Catholic philosophy?

For us, at all events, it is a most consoling reflection that Soloviev did not become a Catholic as the direct result of his doctrine of Divine-humanity. For had the latter really been for him the indispensable route to Catholicism, it would be the same for many others and "the Trinitarian and Sophiological question" would "actually be at the centre of the problem of reunion between the Eastern and Western Churches." (Schmitt) And a careful survey of Soloviev's theology is sufficient to show what a mountain of difficulties this question of Sophia raises. Can these difficulties be solved, as Schmitt attempts to solve them? Are they indeed capable of solution? Schmitt proposes to restate Soloviev's doctrine of Sophia in terms of St Augustine's doctrine of wisdom. But even if Catholic theology could accept the notion of indirect creation which the doctrine involves, it is not likely that the modern Russian religious philosophy for whose sake it is propounded would be satisfied with the doctrine of Sophia in this form. For like Soloviev it completely subsumes God and Sophia, the mystery of the universe and the Church, under the category of total-unity; and it is impossible to eliminate from the doctrine of Sophia, as understood by it the concept of the universal man and of the Church as a single metaphysical entity which has existed from the beginning, at once individual and collective. However attractive, profound and original the Russian metaphysics of the Spirit may seem, and however valuable an ally in defeating the purely humanist view of man, the Catholic will hesitate to put forward as the theoretical basis of reunion this rather dubious philosophy.

Soloviev who forced his way so courageously through the barbed wire entanglement of every possible obstacle which barred his way to the Church of Peter, were he living to-day would assuredly be the very last to mistake even the most profound philosophical formula for the vital secret of reality itself, of the peaceful and blessed reality of a human race truly united in Christ. For proof let us hear the moving words with which he concludes the introduction to *La Russie et l'Église Universelle.*

"I have come to utter this Amen on behalf of the eastern Slavs. I have come to utter this Amen in the name of a hundred million Russian Christians in the firm and full conviction that they will not disown me. Your watchword, O people of the Word, is free and universal theocracy, the true solidarity of all nations and classes, a Christianity realized in social life and politics made Christian. This watchword is liberty for all who are oppressed, protection for all the weak, it is social justice and the true Christian peace. Keybearer of Christ, open to them; and may the gate of the world's history prove to them and the entire world the gate of the kingdom of God."

Surely it is this heroism of faith and unquestioning self-sacrifice, this absolute sincerity which recognizes and confesses not, like Berdaiev, the "inadequacy of every Church," but the inadequacy of the Orthodox Church, this sublime renunciation of all personal, national and racial prejudices which has made Soloviev in the strict and highest human sense the Russian Christopher, and the true leader and father of Russian Catholicism.

BERDAIEV
THE ORTHODOX GNOSTIC

Perhaps the mystery of God is better revealed by the mystery of man than by a direct search for God to the exclusion of man. —Berdaiev, *The Philosophy of Dostoievsky.*

IT requires a special mentality still rare in the west to read the religious philosophy of Russian Christians with understanding or even with the serious purpose of understanding it. And even the reader whose attitude is sympathetic is confronted from the outset by difficulties and surprises. When Peter Wust read Berdaiev's *The Meaning of History* he was filled with enthusiastic admiration for it as one of the most profound contemporary philosophies of history. But shortly afterwards when he came to read *The Meaning of Creative Work* he regretfully admitted that Christian philosophy in its struggle for the objectivity of being could not count upon Berdaiev who in this work showed himself the apostle of "a glorification of man's creative genius in the spirit of Lucifer" rather than a representative of Christian thought. We must allow that this particular book is liable to produce this misconception. But generally speaking it is very easy to misinterpret this brilliant philosopher. What then should be our judgment of Berdaiev's fundamental position?

Not a very favourable one, in the opinion of Bishop Michel d'Herbigny, who as a leading apostle of reunion would surely be disposed to take as favourable a view of him as possible. In a collection published under the title *L'Ame Russe* (Bloud, Paris, 1927) Berdaiev contributed an essay on The Russian Religious Ideal. D'Herbigny writes of it as follows: "A reader who is unacquainted with the Russian way of stating a religious idea will find here an unshakable trust in and a passionate enthusiasm for a confused and vague but highly dramatic conception of a Christianity which professes itself apocalyptic." What is here "confused and vague"? Is it Orthodoxy? Berdaiev himself in the essay terms the latter "passive, inert and static," a judgment which other Orthodox Russians vigorously contest, at least so far as the passivity is concerned. Or is it the conception of Christianity which certain religious philosophers, among them Berdaiev and Bulgakov, have constructed with the spiritual materials and tendencies of Orthodoxy, which is "confused and vague"? The question cannot be answered off-hand. The periodical *Les Documents de la Vie Intellectuelle* quotes excerpts from Berdaiev's latest work, *Freedom and the Spirit,* published in France in Russian, or rather from a particular chapter " The Church and the World," with a commentary which is the reverse of approving. But it regards Berdaiev's view as extremely important because so much of the book expresses the unformulated thoughts and aspirations of a large number of Russian religious souls, and not Russian souls alone, but the aspirations "of an entire family of spirits which chafe against the intellectual and moral discipline of the Catholic Church." From which it follows that even Berdaiev's "confused and vague" conception of Christianity merits our closest attention. And we would add a sympathetic and benevolent attention. At a meeting in Paris arranged by Catholics to promote reunion, such offensive remarks were made about Orthodoxy that Berdaiev, who lectures at the University of Paris on Orthodox philosophy and theology, left the room in protest accompanied by the

Orthodox clergy present (*Westoestlicher Weg,* Nr. 9-10, 1930). If we are to understand each other we must in the literal sense meet each other. In what follows it is our purpose to make as sincere an effort to understand the character and fundamental conceptions of Berdaiev's work, as he makes to be fair to western, and in particular Catholic thought.

For this is the first and the most lasting impression which the student receives from this latest work of Berdaiev's, *Freedom and the Spirit,* the impression of an astonishing effort to understand and be understood. What a difference in this respect between *The Meaning of Creative Work* and the present book! In the case of the former the reader must read most carefully between the lines to detect the Christian believer beneath the language of religious revolution and a thought which parades its independence, and to perceive in the "Creativity" it proclaims a gospel not of secular culture but religious transfiguration. The new book speaks the language of a genuine Christian who, although in many respects he experiences Christianity otherwise than we, is conscious of his brotherhood with us in the profound experience of faith in Christ and in His mystical body. He knows and prizes our great modern theologians, Newman, Moehler, Scheeben; he is delighted when he can appeal to Lippert or Guardini; and Catholic mystics such as Angelus Silesius, St John of the Cross or Léon Bloy, a mystic who has strayed into profane literature, are friends with whom he shares his experience of God and the world. *Freedom and the Spirit* is certainly not the philosophy of a spirit that is free because it is not tied to any creed. For Berdaiev on the contrary there is no philosophy without faith, without the Christian faith. This, however, is not a faith in authority, but a faith won independently of any external authority " through an experience of the inner life of a most painful character, through freedom." Is this the rejection of ecclesiastical authority by a subjectivism of Protestant type? Protestantism is in its fundamental principles as alien to Berdaiev as is modernism in the Catholic sense. He has a frankly ecclesiastical temper. A purely invisible Church is inconceivable to him. Since the Church has her sphere of action in the world she must be anchored to empirical reality by her physical, psychological and social nature. But the Church is a thousandfold more than her visible aspect; more than a community of believers subject to the hierarchy; more than one object of this world amongst others. In her integral, mystical and ontological nature the Church plunges into the depths of the spiritual world. To this Church Berdaiev belongs and is conscious of solidarity with her in the fullest sense. On his communion with her his spiritual life depends; for without her he must face all the problems of life as an individual condemned to solitary impotence. The world of spirit transcends individuality and can be revealed only by a guide that is more than individual, namely the Church. " In this experience of the Church I am not alone, for I am one with all my brethren in the spirit in whatever place or time they may have lived. I am myself limited as regards the extent of my knowledge; my experience is restricted and cannot pretend to cover the whole of existence in all its variety and fullness; I have not myself known a great number of spiritual contacts of a determining character. . . In the religious experience of the Church, and in his contact with Christ man is not alone and confined within his own limitations, for he is drawn near to all others who have known this experience, to the whole Christian world, to apostles, Saints and to all who are in Christ whether living or departed. . . We all form part of one Christian race, the spiritual seed of the New Adam. This new race possesses the mind of Christ, by which we apprehend that which is beyond our own intelligence." (*E.T.*, pp. 329-30)

Berdaiev is a thinker whose boldness often verges on a fantastic audacity, who handles mysteries and proclaims mystical experiences, or rather "truths," which he himself terms "dizzy." But the basis of his speculation is absolute and complete faith in Christ, the God-man. He thinks as a Christian. We must never forget this. *And he thinks as an Eastern Christian.* It is sheer waste of time to study Berdaiev if we lose sight of this essential fact. And it is among the great merits of this latest work that it brings home to us so clearly that his thought is rooted in the ideas and tendencies of oriental Christianity. If this is recognized, the amazingly profound philosophy of human destiny which he sketched in his *Meaning of History* loses much of the queerness which makes that book so difficult to understand. This is not to say that his conception of Orthodoxy and Orthodoxy as it actually is are the same thing. It is very difficult for the outsider to form an objective picture of Orthodoxy. *Westoestlicher Weg*, the periodical devoted to the cause of reunion which has now ceased publication, has published during the last few years a number of valuable Russian expositions of Orthodoxy. These, however, entirely fail to give us a consistent account of it. This is obviously due to the fact that the vast material of Christian life and truth which in the West has been moulded by an almost uninterrupted process of theological and philosophical speculation and practical organization has remained in the East so to speak unworked and unfashioned. But that the distinctive nature of Orthodoxy consists simply in the fact that its development has been slower and more backward as compared with the West, so that it is simply an undeveloped and more primitive Catholicism, and the peculiarity of Russian religion is therefore the absence of any positive character peculiar to itself, is a conclusion which, though accepted by the Orthodox Russian Vilinsky, is denied even by Russian Catholics and sympathizers with Catholicism and by the vast majority of Orthodox Russians, Berdaiev among them.

The question need not be discussed here. It is, however, important to discover whether Berdaiev's view of Orthodoxy agrees in the main with that of other Orthodox writers, that we may determine how far his thought is inspired by the ideas prevalent among Russian religious thinkers and his philosophy may be regarded as the Russian philosophy of religion. For Berdaiev, Orthodoxy represents a unique positive type of Christianity. It is not so much a lack of history, as an undeveloped theology and ecclesiastical organization which distinguishes Oriental from Western Christianity as a positive spiritual experience of a divergent type from that of the West, a different experience of God and the universe, time and eternity. In a series of essays dealing with the heroic epic of old Russia (published we believe in *Westoestlicher Weg,* 1930) Kobilinsky-Ellis maintains that the Russian people display a different sense of time from that of the Western European, and that its object is not strictly speaking time but its content. If this is true it provides a most natural explanation of Berdaiev's remarkable theory of the relation between time and eternity in *The Meaning of History*. The tendency to a cosmic outlook, the cosmic wisdom whose progress from the nature-worship inherited from Asia to the worship of the heavenly and Christian Sophia can be observed according to Kobilinsky in the old Russian epic, which is " the entrance of Deity into man, the universe and history and the consequent transfiguration of the creature," is also represented by Arseniev as the quintessence of Eastern Christianity (*Die Kirche des Morgenlandes* [*The Eastern Church*], Sammlung Goeschen). Berdaiev's interpretation of Orthodoxy is the same. Its cosmic interest, its passionate pre-occupation with the thought of Resurrection and the second Coming of Christ, its longing for the glorification of nature as a whole and the salvation of the world by its transfiguration and deification had already found expression in the Eastern fathers. An Origen, a St Gregory of Nyssa, were typical of the East. And the doctrine of a salvation exclusively personal, of heaven for the saved and hell for the lost were equally products of the West. As a result of his psychological constitution the Oriental Christian has placed in the foreground of his religion the question of the Apocatastasis, the restitution of all things, the Western Christian, whether Catholic or Protestant, the question of justification by faith and good works.

We are therefore confronted with the inevitable fact, a fact moreover not in the least astonishing, of a well-marked Oriental and an equally well-marked Western type of Christianity. Nor is the distinction the result of the external separation or vice versa. Berdaiev expressly remarks: " Vital experimental spiritual differences were manifested well before the division of the Churches and need not necessarily have provoked it." (E.T., p. 349) It is a consoling thought! But why then is he so anxious to deduce from the distinctive character of Oriental Christianity a conception of the Church which in practice makes reunion impossible or rather superfluous? For it is a conception of the Church which renders the question of authority meaningless. Why meaningless? Because the airy Christianity of the East has no interest in such "a juridical question of social organization." And this does indeed appear to be the case. Arseniev writes (in the above-mentioned essay): " The true unity of the Church is not to be conceived as constituted by a formal authority, a sovereignty legally binding which can be expressed by juridical formulae. The Eastern Church knows no other head than the one Head of the mystical body, Christ... Nor does she recognize any formal and juridical authority. For her Christ, the Apostles and the Councils are not authorities of this kind. We have to do not with an authority but with an inexhaustible stream of the life of grace of which Christ is the source and in which each one of us is born along as a drop, a wave, in company with the rest."

In our view, the problem of authority is not settled by the fact that Orthodoxy has no understanding for it, no interest in it, no need of it. And is it after all true that Orthodoxy finds no need, is conscious of no necessity for a doctrinal and pastoral authority, because unlike the turbulent West it has not been exposed to the powerful temptation of a pagan humanism; because its deeper ontological roots in the Divine world enable it to be satisfied with a smaller measure of the external juridical and organizing function of the human factor in the Church; and because, to mention the ultimate mystical reason, external authority is necessary only for nature regarded as separated from God and subject to a purely outward discipline, not inwardly Christianized, but is not required by a cosmic experience which is conscious of nature rather as aspiring towards God than separated from Him and which already enjoys a foretaste of its final transfiguration and deification? Would not a formal authority binding the conscience of its subjects have proved the salvation of Orthodoxy in this present persecution and calamitous internal dissension? This at any rate is the belief of those Russians who seek reunion with Rome without in the least rejecting Orthodoxy. Berdaiev says of Soloviev that he was never really at home in the world of Western thought. This is true. Berdaiev is better acquainted with it. But although Soloviev's thought was nourished entirely by the doctrinal content of Eastern Christianity, he developed into the champion of Papal supremacy over the Eastern and Western Churches alike.

Nothing could be more instructive in this connection than the selection from his writings published by Kobilinsky-Ellis under the title *Monarchia Sancti Petri* (Matthias Gruenewald-Verlag, Mains, 1929). And Kobilinsky regards his recognition of the Papal supremacy as simply the logical consequence of the integral Orthodoxy which in his opinion has received its most perfect expression up to the present in Soloviev's religious philosophy. We do not altogether share his opinion. But we are only concerned here to point out that Berdaiev is attempting to solve the problem of external authority in the Church too easily. It is impossible to decide a question of such capital importance on the basis of a mere difference in the emotional apprehension of the universe. It can be decided only by the facts of the Gospel history. Berdaiev subscribes the orthodox profession of faith in the " holy, Catholic and

Apostolic Church." What did this belief mean for the age of the Apostles? Though Newman most certainly did not find the question easy to answer it drove him from the Anglican Church. For he could not escape the recognition that for the apostolic Church faith plainly consisted "in submission to an external authority." Then as now this submission constituted what to-day we term the external criterion of faith. If we profess the Christian faith, we must receive it as the Apostles understood it. This was equally the decisive consideration for Soloviev.

We must, however, also take Berdaiev as he is and as he will have us understand him. And he is evidently a typical representative of Russian Orthodoxy which, though not hostile to Rome, has no desire for reunion. *This Russian Christianity is a fundamental presupposition of his thought*. His thought is not strictly speaking philosophy as philosophy is understood in Western Europe. Nor is it theology of the systematic Western type. On the admission of Berdaiev himself it has deliberately broken through the boundaries which in the West divide philosophic, theological and mystical knowledge. His thought—and Russian religious thought in general—is philosophy, theology and mysticism in one, a philosophy whose speculation is fed by the living religious sources of being, and which is the creative revelation of the soul enlightened. If we would understand the Russian religious thinkers we must accept the fact once for all that their philosophy is, as Berdaiev puts it, "illumination;" or, to employ Kobilinsky's description of Soloviev's philosophy, "a mystical and intuitive doctrine of wisdom." Or we may adopt Soloviev's own description, " free theosophy," by which he means an organic combination of Christian mysticism, rational philosophy and positive science. In any case, however widely their views may diverge, all these Russian religious philosophers build on a common foundation. This foundation, as Bulgakov shows in a profound criticism of modern Western philosophy, is "an empiricism which proceeds from the uttermost depth of a mystical experience pregnant in life." But the simplest, briefest and most appropriate expression for the distinctive quality of Russian religious thought—if we must have a formula, a label—is gnosis. It is among the merits of Berdaiev's latest book that it brings out so clearly the gnostic character of his religious philosophy and of Russian religious thought in general.

Berdaiev's philosophy is Orthodox gnosis. We cannot say Christian gnosis. For it has been and still is confined to Eastern Christianity. There is an elaborately developed and extremely specialized Western theology. But there is no Western gnosis. For the West lacks the intellectual and emotional subconscious background which in the East provides a favourable soil for gnosis. When Berdaiev defends the rights of gnosis, he does not mean by it—and this must be made clear—that ancient gnosis so justly condemned by the Church, which was a pagan doctrine of wisdom mingled with Christian elements and would have made of Christianity an aristocratic sect instead of a world religion. He means that genuinely Christian gnosis represented by such men as Clement of Alexandria, Origen, Gregory of Nyssa and Maximus the Confessor. But they were all Eastern Christians. Western theology, Berdaiev urges, has had no point of contact either in its character or methods with the authentic gnosis, which is not only fully compatible with the Christian revelation but is actually demanded by it. For Western theology is not the acquisition of knowledge but the explanation and defence of truths laid down *a priori*. Does not the gnosis as understood by Berdaiev also presuppose unconditional acceptance of the Faith? Most certainly it does. But it proceeds to subject the content of faith to a process of speculation in order to derive from it further truths. To take an example: it cannot be maintained that the whole truth about man and the universe has been revealed in the Gospel or by the subsequent development of Christianity. The Christian revelation contains implicitly the most complete anthropology conceivable. But it has not yet been discovered and brought into the light of the Christian consciousness. The Greek fathers by their doctrine of deification (*theosis*) did no more than begin to reveal the true anthropology. For their excessive preoccupation with the experience of sin, with the negative aspect of the process of redemption, prevented them from attaining a sufficiently clear vision of its positive aspect, the glorification and deification of human nature. To display strictly Christological, that is Divine-human nature, is the great task to which the new Orthodox gnosis is called.

This new Orthodox gnosis must not be confused with the traditional systematic theology of Orthodoxy. The latter is in ill repute with the representatives of gnosis. In the opinion of Professor Ilijin of the Orthodox theological institute in Paris it has long since succumbed to "sterility and decadence" (*Westoestlicher Weg*, Nr. 7 & 8, 1929). It is laymen who have re-awakened the native but slumbering spirit of Orthodoxy to a living search for truth. Soloviev was the first among the *pioneers* of the new Orthodox gnosis. For in spite of its strongly gnostical temper even Orthodox theology was strictly speaking no more gnosis than western. And cosmology throws further light on the meaning and aim of Orthodox gnosis. Russian gnosis regards the cosmology of official Christianity as completely unsatisfactory. There might just as well be no cosmology at all. For the Church continues to display the suspicion of cosmological speculation which the heretical gnostics impressed upon her with their cosmic processes which nullified the central mystery of Redemption and in general were fatal to the Christian conception of God and man. Ever since cosmology has been suspect. Fear of ascribing Godhead to the world has suffered it to become ungodly. By refusing to speculate upon the cosmic mysteries the Church has treated the universe as the province of positive science, the natural sciences, and technical invention. The cosmic consciousness which was still alive in the men of the middle ages has vanished from the modern world.

This was the subject of a powerful complaint which Theodor Haecker published within the last few years in an essay in *Hochland*. Haecker also laments that our contemporaries are seeking to repair this sin against their great and mysterious mother nature by an orgiastic cult of life as such, a brutal and irrational cosmic mysticism. Berdaiev, however, holds the agnosticism of the Church directly responsible for the fact that the cosmic sphere which it has surrendered is at present a happy hunting ground for the adepts of occultism, the cosmosophists and the anthroposophists of Steiner's following. To check these pagan growths and fill this fatal gap in the cosmological speculation of Christianity is precisely the scope and the passionately desired goal of the Russian Sophiology.

On first acquaintance with it the Western Christian experiences an uncomfortable feeling that it hangs in the void. This is not the case. Without convincing and intrinsically compelling grounds, thinkers of such exceptional ability as Soloviev, Bulgakov and Florensky would not have devoted this persistent and determined effort of speculation to the doctrine of Sophia. Nor must we overlook the fact that besides its iconographic and Scriptural basis the doctrine has its psychological source in the distinctive and scarcely definable sense of God and the universe which characterizes the spirit of Oriental Christianity. It is quite impossible to dispute Ilyrin's contention that " the problem of Sophia is bound up with the theological and philosophical explanation of an experience peculiar to Russian Orthodoxy, an experience of God's relation to the essence of creatures as it ontologically transcends and precedes the world." But his own interpretation of Sophia is by no means so incontestable. Indeed the doctrine of Sophia as such—and this must not be forgotten by its few but enthusiastic western adherents—is essentially a problem, not the solution of a problem.

Why should we be more Russian than the Russians themselves? Berdaiev is not content to prize Sophiology in the abstract; he is himself a Sophiologist. The mysticism of Sophia is a strain audible in the background of his thought like the music of the spheres, but soft, hushed and held in check. Were it permitted to become an *allegro con brio* and dominate the entire composition, the divinely ordained harmony of the true Christian philosophy would be in imminent danger. For Berdaiev the doctrine of Sophia is for the present no more than an attempt undertaken by the spirit of Russian religion to restore to cosmology a place in the Christian scheme, an attempt to safeguard Christians from the rationalist attitude which regards the function of the Sacraments as almost exclusively psychological and social, dogma as predominantly the basis and justification of ethics, and the Church as little more than the embodiment of social religion, the organized community of believers, and re-awaken the Christian mind to the literally world-embracing and truly cosmic nature of all the mysteries of faith. The doctrine of Sophia is one of the expressions of Christian Platonism. "Its aim therefore is to bring back to the mind of the Church the Platonic doctrines" of the world of ideas and the world-soul and the Platonic realism "in opposition to the nominalistic decadence of Christianity." This is the aim which Berdaiev pursues. But the route taken by this Russian champion of Sophia leads him close to the rocks of pantheism. We are delighted that since he wrote *The Meaning of Creative Work*, in which he made full sail for this dangerous reef, he has learned caution. "The characteristics of Sophiology are such that the problem of the cosmos threatens finally to overshadow completely the problem of man. Human freedom and creative activity disappear. Nevertheless, to-day the main religious problem is that of man, not of Sophia or the cosmos. Sophiology must be linked to the problem of anthropology." (*Freedom and the Spirit*. E.T., p.300)

And it is precisely *the anthropological problem* which constitutes the special sphere of Berdaiev's gnosis. Whereas Bulgakov and Florensky make Sophia the central point of their speculation, and Soloviev with a great expenditure of thought attempted to attach his doctrine of Sophia firmly to his anthropology, Berdaiev has concentrated on anthropology. But his anthropology is not scientific but metaphysical. Any one who is at all acquainted with the nature of gnosis will not be surprised when we say that

Berdaiev has surpassed all attempts hitherto made in the West to develop a metaphysical and religious anthropology. He maintains the bold thesis of absolute anthropocentrism. Man's infinite spirit claims for itself an absolute supernatural anthropocentrism. "He knows himself to be the absolute centre not merely of our limited solar system but of being as a whole, of all planes of reality, of all worlds." (*The Meaning of Creative Activity*) What does he mean by this? Though the statement seems pantheistic it is not pantheism but panentheism. Man is not absolute in the creaturely and human but in the Christological aspect of his nature. For he also possesses a Christological nature, has something Christly in his nature. And this Christly element, this likeness of Christ is not something first impressed upon his nature in the act of creation, as it were on second thoughts and by God's arbitrary choice, nor has it been bestowed upon him as a special gift of Redeeming grace. No, it belongs to his essential nature and for the reason that as man he belongs essentially to Christ. Christ is the eternal God-man. We Christians of the West are wont to regard the term God-man as standing only for a historical conception. In our view Christ the God-man first began to exist at the time of the Incarnation. For Russian gnosis the Logos, the Second Person of the Trinity, is also from all eternity the God-man Christ. Christ therefore is the absolute Man. There is an absolute man, and Christ is he. Human nature has existed from eternity in the eternal God-man. It is precisely this fact which constitutes the Christological aspect of created human nature. In virtue of this eternal and absolute centre of the universe, Russian gnosis proclaims an absolute anthropocentrism. This concept is simply the philosophic expression of the fundamental religious idea of Divine-humanity.

It is perfectly plain from these explanations that this conception of Divine-humanity is not the same as the conception of Divine-humanity held by the official theology of the Church. Divine-humanity as understood by Russian gnosis has two aspects. The humanity of Christ has its strict counterpart in the Divinity of man, and without the latter the historic Incarnation of Christ would be inconceivable. The conception of man's Divinity held by Western Christendom is expressed by the well-known patristic dictum: Christ became man that man might become God. But this Divinity is not proper to man but a free gift of grace, foreign to human nature which it transcends. For Russian gnosis on the other hand man's Divinity has an ontological foundation in human nature, and is not simply the result of an historical event. And for the Platonizing thought of Russia this ontological Divinity of man is the primary presupposition on which alone the historic process of Christification, that is the redemption, glorification and deification of human nature, is possible. What does not already exist from eternity cannot come into existence in time. In this Platonic spirit Soloviev postulated the pre-existent "eternal man." Not to complicate his gnosis unnecessarily, Berdaiev has never gone beyond the mystery of Divine-humanity as understood by the universal consent of Christendom. He has not like Soloviev elaborated a logical and systematic doctrine of Divine-humanity as understood in the gnostic sense. He seeks rather to display it as the ultimate and primary truth of life, the sole and most intimate centre of all reality, by presenting all the important phenomena of life in the light of this mystery. If this orientation of speculative enquiry does in fact throw a maximum of light on the world, the hypothesis employed, namely Divine-humanity, needs for him no further proof.

This was the conviction which inspired his book on the philosophy of history, *The Meaning of History*. And before this, in *The Meaning of Creative Work* as a critical historian of civilization he sought to show that the primary religious fact of Divine-humanity is the great ideal force which determines the course of history. In this book he depicted all departments of human culture in the throes of a profound crisis which, in the spheres of philosophy, science and art and under the stress of these painful problems still unsolved by official Christianity of sex, marriage and the family, had kindled a flame of longing for spiritual freedom, release from the necessities of " this world." There was, he concluded, a vast hunger for a genuine and deep life of the spirit, a realization that this true life cannot be achieved by the principles of mere humanism and the positive perception that this new being—for the issue is nothing less, not culture but " the religious transformation of life"—is attainable not by a human nature enslaved to the natural causes of the physical universe but only by a human nature of infinite scope and endowed with power to create. In short, the ultimate goal of creative action is a profound creativity which can transform life and this in turn presupposes as its ontological source the Divinity of man. Divine-humanity, the message of Berdaiev's *Meaning of Creative Action*, is at bottom to ring in with full peal the new age of Divine-humanity and its religious transfiguration of life. He was premature. The tempest which since his book appeared has not ceased to shake the edifice of human life to its foundations has shown no sign of being the mighty wind of a new Pentecost announcing a second invasion of the world by the Holy Spirit, the Creator. But in all probability it is not only this disappointment which has convinced the more mature Berdaiev of the insecurity of a method which attempts to prove so sharply defined a conception as that of his Divine-humanity primarily by postulating inevitable demands of a particular epoch. In his new book he pours the old wine into new bottles. Though he still maintains his old convictions he defends them in a new fashion, conciliatory and understanding, and shows that he is fully aware of the difficulties which those trained in the different intellectual tradition of the Aristotelian West must find in his line of thought. His object is no longer by well aimed blows of proof and affirmation to beat this alien thought to its knees before his own convictions but simply to make his beliefs more intelligible to it.

At bottom indeed he is not making any assertions but stating "problems in the form of assertions." Christianity, he points out in his introduction, contains a problematical element and since his struggle with these problems has been his passion, his personal passion, it is his vocation to penetrate as profoundly as possible the vital questions raised by Christianity and bring them to the attention of the faithful. This does not mean that he wishes to originate any heresy or schism or even utter "a single word against the sanctity of the Church." The German translation of *Freedom and the Spirit* bears the sub-title *Problematik und Apologie des Christentums* (The Problem and Defence of Christianity). Spirit and nature, symbol, myth and dogma, revelation, faith and degrees of perception, the freedom of the spirit, evil and redemption, God man and the God-man, mysticism and the way of the spirit, theosophy and gnosis, spiritual development and the eschatological problem, the Church and the world—all these are problems which though they are primarily growths ripened in the spiritual climate of the Christian East are of no less importance for Western Christianity. Berdaiev seeks to solve them as an Orthodox gnostic. And his treatment is such that this superabundance of problems becomes of itself an extremely original profoundly experienced and intellectually powerful defence of Christianity which, in spite or rather because of all the problems which it involves, reveals itself to him irrefutably and irresistibly as the great mystery of Divine-humanity.

What is new in this book is not its leading ideas which he had already stated but the seductive charm and subtlety with which Berdaiev here presents them. *He makes mysticism the starting-point of the road by which he reaches the concept of Divine-humanity*. As Max Scheler in his Catholicizing period found, the fundamental Christian experience of love is expressed not by the theologians and philosophers but only by the mystics. Berdaiev is convinced that it is the mystics alone who can throw light on the primary phenomenon of religion, the mystery of love which constitutes the relation between God and humanity. All systems of Christian theology have inherited too much of Greek philosophy to be able to perceive and express this basic religious fact in its living concreteness. Neither Aristotle nor even Plato with his vision of the ideas attained the vision of the mystic, his profound experience of the Divine Life. The Hellenic type of thought has persistently involved Christian theology as a whole in the danger of rationalizing the original Christian experience of the primordial Life. Not only were the heretical departures from orthodoxy one-sided rationalizations; so also was "the theism of theology which is tied to the concept and absolutizes the externality and the non-divinity of creation." Berdaiev therefore holds fast to the mystics. Their language is bold and paradoxical, the language of dogmatic theology a Procrustes' bed; for when forced into the mould of its rigid concepts the sacred experience of the mystics is easily transformed into an unhallowed heresy. If, however, mysticism is treated as mysticism, not theology, it reveals the primary truth of religion, the fact that the relation between God and man is a drama of love. "In the Bible we see the relations between the loving subject and the loved object, in which not only man, but God Himself is subject to passions, and experiences anger, sorrow and joy. The God of Abraham, Isaac and Jacob is not to be confused with the absolute of philosophy nor with the God of theology. He is rather a God who resembles man, a God who is not inert but who is capable of movement. The *Song of Songs,* which was a source of inspiration to the mystics, is indeed a picture of the emotional life of the Divine. This inner life of God was revealed to the Christian mystics and they found words to express the emotions experienced by God."

For them the primary religious phenomenon was twofold, embracing God and man. The Catholic mystic Angelus Silesius does not shrink from the declaration "I know that without me God cannot live an instant." For Pascal Christ is the God who suffers lonely and misunderstood till the end of the world. For Léon Bloy God is the eternal suppliant for man's love. On this point Berdaiev appeals to the Catholic Saints. In particular, Eucharistic mysticism presupposes as an obvious truth an affective and emotional life in God, is concerned, as Berdaiev says with Pascal, not with the God of philosophers but with the God of Abraham and the God of Jesus Christ, with the God-man Himself who from Bethlehem to Golgotha suffered the great tragedy of love. But for Berdaiev this drama of love is not simply enacted in time and space but is eternal and has its source in the bosom of the Trinity. If this is a stumbling-block to the metaphysician, no matter. "All the great Christian mystics, whatever confession they belonged to, have taught that in eternity, in the depths of the spiritual world, a Divine process takes place in which is revealed the relationship between God and man, and the birth of God in man and of man in God, where lover and beloved meet." If the theologians jib at the statement that there is motion in God—for such indeed is His eternal love and desire for man—they must logically abandon their juridical theory of Redemption. For God's wrath which on this theory determined the sacrifices of Christ is just as much a motion as love. And God's sense of injury which Christ satisfied by His Death presupposes an affirmative life in God of a human type, that is so to speak a psychology of God. And it is in fact with this concrete Divine psychology, not with an abstract metaphysic of God, that we are concerned. That the purely rational thought of philosophy and theology can give us no genuine knowledge of God Berdaiev attempts to show in his discussion of *Symbolism, Myth and Dogma*. The infinite life of God, the ultimate truth of Deity is the subject not of "philosophical statement but mythological representation," and is partially apprehended only by the spiritual experience of mystical union with God. Rational thought serves only to guide man in his relations with this world; it is and must always be relative, even when it reflects upon the absolute mystical facts of Christianity. The obviously inexhaustible Divine Reality is attainable only by symbolic knowledge, by mystic experience, in short by that gnosis which is possible to the man who is enlightened by the mind of Christ.

We cannot discuss the detailed doctrines of this gnosis. Though at first sight they may appear disconnected, on a closer scrutiny they are seen to be closely and organically bound up with the central idea of Divine-humanity and with the genius of the Platonic tradition and Oriental Christianity. In his treatment of these questions Berdaiev's object is not so much to propose definite solutions as to prove that these solutions can and must be sought along the lines indicated in his *Freedom and the Spirit. He is primarily concerned to champion the claim of his Orthodox gnosis to be recognized as a genuinely Christian philosophy*. For this he fights with the passionate force of a mind that is not only convinced of the truth of its thesis but understands it thoroughly. He is among those Russians who desire not a juridical union with Rome but simply a moral union in the spirit of Christian charity. But even this becomes impossible if we refuse to admit their right as Christians to develop their own Oriental Christianity in the oriental spirit. Maritain, Massis and Moenius are correct and speaking in the interests of union when they observe that Europe is not the Faith, nor Western culture the Roman Church, nor Thomism Catholicism.

But is this truth (which is of fundamental importance for Catholic missionary work of every description) fully kept in mind when Thomism as " the most fully developed and most perfect form of Christian thought" is declared to be alone capable of "saving the heritage of the East and reconciling once more the two halves of the world"? And is it really true that Thomism will play this decisive part in saving the Christian and Christianizing the heathen East? There are Catholics well acquainted with the East who think otherwise. Aufhauser, who has made a thorough study "of missionary methods in their practical application to the separated Eastern Churches" (*Westoestlicher Weg,* Nr. 3-4, 1930) and whose attitude to Oriental Christianity is very critical and sober, maintains that it is the special vocation of the mystical theology of the Christian East to bring Christianity to the mystical and intuitive Near East. And finally we must not forget that Russian mysticism is not only oriental but also Christian.

The position is not so desperate as Massis points it. If there is an Asiatic quality in Russian mysticism—we are speaking here only of Christian mysticism—it is certainly not such as to undermine the principles of Christian humanism. A more important constituent is Hellenism, of which it contains as much as Thomism, though it derives from Plato instead of Aristotle. And so far as Christian humanism is concerned we cannot deny that very few living writers have so fully realized the gravity of this issue and its enormous importance for our age, and laid bare its profoundest depths, as Berdaiev has done. We have only to read his *Meaning of History* and *New Middle Ages.* The radical Christianity with which Berdaiev exposes contemporary humanism as "the modern heresy" is not exceeded by the thorough-going Thomist Maritain in his *Antimoderne.* The difference between them lies, as we might have expected, in the fact that Berdaiev is convinced that the crisis can be surmounted only by the forces latent in the religion of the Christian East. And it is the aim of the Russian to make these forces active in the Christian mind. According to Berdaiev it is the process of secularizing the violent religious energy of the West which has produced a civilization which is merely humanist, anti-christian and already inhuman and destructive of the human ideal. What is needed to-day therefore is not so much to preserve and rescue what is still left of religion but a creative religious reaction against paganism. In short, a religious creation! All men's creative forces must be Christianized by the rediscovery of the Christ-like nature of man which has too long been lost sight of. We must tell man who has been stripped of his Divinity and has fallen a victim to a purely natural humanism the full truth about himself and introduce him to the Divine-human mystery of his origin, history and vocation. Men will then at last understand that they are nothing at all, have no true being, if they are not Christian and do not receive being in Christ Himself; that where Christ leaves off hell begins, for save in His eternal Divine-humanity human life has no meaning or justification; moreover that heaven already begins in this world when they have once apprehended with the inmost core of their being that they themselves—together with the innumerable host of human beings who pack our planet as it revolves amid the silence of infinite space—are for the first time at home in the eternal Divine-human heart. Already in their metaphysical depths man and the world are the mystical body of Christ. On the circumference of time and space they must become the mystical body of Christ. This is humanity's historic vocation and it has no other.

To meditate on many of Berdaiev's ideas may

well stir us to enthusiasm. And we may ask ourselves whether what he has written has not been written by the dispensation of Providence as a profound commentary of the Christian East upon the kingship of Christ as it has been proclaimed by the Pope to the Christian West. Indeed a comment upon Catholic, that is to say universally Christian, action in general. We do not forget that the action for which Berdaiev calls and which he conceives primarily as a reaction against the quietism of Orthodoxy follows an entirely different line to Catholic action as we understand it. Its method is not the organization and works of practical charity which we of the West believe to be the most suitable method of vanquishing the chaos of Antichrist, but the truly Eastern method of contemplative absorption in the cosmic mystery of Christ, an expansion and a deepening of the Christian consciousness, which we may term the method of mystical revolution. In our opinion Berdaiev mistakes the spiritual exercises preparatory to action for Christian action itself. But his great objectives are also our own, through Christ to behold man and the world with the eternal, primordial and final vision and in the light of this vision to harmonize the spiritual, intellectual, social and economic orders.

Is this a defence of Berdaiev the stubborn schismatic? By no means. But perhaps a modest and woefully inadequate defence of Berdaiev, the Christian gnostic. For the fact that his gnosis is in many details unacceptable to the Catholic mind is no condemnation of his struggle for a Christian and specifically oriental gnosis. The Church has not condemned Soloviev's philosophy of Sophia, though the simple fact that he recognized the primacy of the Pope did not in the least detract from its distinctive orientalism. For the zealots of that philosophy of Western Christendom which has achieved supremacy in Thomism this gnosis is a reversion to an intellectual obscurity and formlessness which has been laboriously conquered. But clarity is not the sole nor even the principal criterion of truth. For its adherents on the other hand it is the daring sketch of an incomplete philosophy of the Christian East which is in process of discovering itself. For many others, who are Western Christians and Roman Catholics to the core, this oriental wisdom brings a profound spiritual enrichment. It renders audible those mysterious, mystical and cosmic notes more rarely heard in the Christianity of the rationalistic West. We have much to say of the immortality of the soul, but little of the Resurrection of the body. Where and when do we hear sermons in which sin and redemption are placed in that cosmic setting in which the Pauline groaning of the entire creation is no mere figure of speech but the consequence of a primordial spiritual disaster which befell the world and which is repaired only by the Resurrection of Christ as a cosmic event involving the transfiguration and cure of the entire body of the universe?

But this question is perhaps somewhat too rhetorical. Attempts to attach not only the destiny of mankind but the entire universe to Christ the salvation of the world, to base them on Him and to understand them from this standpoint, are becoming increasingly common. To-day in our novel intellectual situation the sharp distinction between nature and supernature worked out by the theology of the Counter-Reformation does not appear nearly so necessary as a profound ontological penetration of every sphere of human life by the supernatural. The "supernaturalization of the natural" is to-day, according to the theologian Alois Mager "a fundamental principle of work for a Catholic civilization." It is no accident that the mysticism of St Bonaventure which has but lately been rediscovered and which Gilson in particular has made accessible to the general public, produces on many readers the effect of a revelation. A Saint here combats another Saint, because the latter, he considers, unduly restricts the sphere within which the supernatural is operative. Thomas sharply divides the two spheres—and in doing so was in Gilson's opinion modern from the very outset. Bonaventure regards them as interpenetrating. For Thomas the supernatural is that which of its nature cannot enter the domain of experience. According to Bonaventure there is no sphere in which the supernatural can be left out of account. For without supernature nature is incomplete and its ultimate significance is revealed only when it is understood as symbolic of the supernatural.

This is substantially what Berdaiev holds. According to Gilson Bonaventure's philosophy proceeded wholly " from those spiritual experiences which are the eternal sources of mysticism." Berdaiev became acquainted with it in Gilson's book and points out with gratification that at bottom Russian gnosis does not differ from the mysticism of this Catholic Saint. Both alike are "illuminism." When an expert of such eminence on the history of medieval thought as Gilson proves that Bonaventure's philosophy is a truly compact system of thought on the same level as Thomism, that in it Augustinian philosophical tradition reached its highest point and Christian mysticism found the most magnificent intellectual expression it has yet received, we can at last understand the claim made by Russian gnosis to a place in the philosophy of the Christian religion side by side with other Christian systems of philosophy as the oriental interpretation of life.

Reality which at every point overflows all fixed intellectual boundaries is so infinitely rich, the material of Christian experience so incalculably vast and comprehensive, that its fullness can be discovered by mankind only by a gradual process and through many different pictures of the universe and many different types of thought.

THE END